OF PRISMS
& ESTUARIES

IF WE DARE TO TREAD
1957–2007

SHARON RICHARDSON

Trafford
PUBLISHING™

Order this book online at www.trafford.com/07-0997
or email orders@trafford.com

Most Trafford titles are also available at major online book retailers.

Note for Librarians: A cataloguing record for this book is available from Library
and Archives Canada at www.collectionscanada.ca/amicus/index-e.html

ISBN: 978-1-4251-2852-4

*We at Trafford believe that it is the responsibility of us all, as both individuals
and corporations, to make choices that are environmentally and socially sound.
You, in turn, are supporting this responsible conduct each time you purchase a
Trafford book, or make use of our publishing services. To find out how you are
helping, please visit www.trafford.com/responsiblepublishing.html*

*Our mission is to efficiently provide the world's finest, most comprehensive
book publishing service, enabling every author to experience success.
To find out how to publish your book, your way, and have it available
worldwide, visit us online at www.trafford.com/10510*

 www.trafford.com

North America & international
toll-free: 1 888 232 4444 (USA & Canada)
phone: 250 383 6864 ♦ fax: 250 383 6804 ♦ email: info@trafford.com

The United Kingdom & Europe
phone: +44 (0)1865 722 113 ♦ local rate: 0845 230 9601
facsimile: +44 (0)1865 722 868 ♦ email: info.uk@trafford.com

10 9 8 7 6 5 4 3 2

In the End
will we conserve
only what we love
will we love only
what we understand
And will we understand
Only what we are
Taught...

Author Unknown,
W.W. 99
Native American Artist

Contents

Prologue

I T WAS SOMETIME AFTER 9/11. My daughter and I were browsing through *The Hudson News* in Toronto Airport on a stop over to Atlanta. We had cleared customs with easy time to pass prior to boarding.

Time stood still for me as I scanned the back cover of a book, one of several biographies of Osama Bin Laden on the shelf. At the time, there were a lot of books coming out on Bin Laden. I don't even remember the author's name or the specific title of the book. I never bought it. I did not want to tempt fate as I waited to board a passenger jet with my child in tow. I thought to myself that I would buy the book at another time, preferably not in an airport.

I still remember the feeling of my organs contracting and tightening deep inside of me. My mind froze as I read his birth date, and reread it several times, like a broken record, replaying the same tune, but not really listening. **Nov 1, 1957**! I know "All Saint's Day", 1957, very well. It is my date of birth. I showed the bio to my daughter. She gave the usual adolescent reaction, not much of one.

Somehow, it was unbelievable to me that Osama Bin Laden and I were born on the same day and in the same year. Despite the obvious, I don't think of myself as looking that old. But the place in our soul where we connect who we are with time and place seemed shaken for me, haunting me ever since. I had grown up outside of the United States. The first place that I actually worked with Americans was in Khamis Mushayt, Saudi Arabia, the ancestral home region of Bin Laden. I have read that twelve of the 9/11 terrorists were from the very same area of Saudi Arabia, the Asir Region.

I am not an intelligence expert or an expert on anything for that matter. I am just an ordinary person trying to find some semblance of hope for our children. I believe that the writing of this book will help me make sense of the intersection of my life journey—how I came to know America and Americans, how I know Saudi Arabia, and how it all has shaped the thinking of a simple girl from Newfoundland.

NOTE:

I have not been able to find confirmation of Bin Laden's birth date on anything that I have read on him since that day. Every article does confirm that he was born in 1957. Sometimes I wonder if I dreamt the whole thing up. It really does not matter. The historical context of my tale spans the half-century from 1957-2007. The date is actually insignificant, other than stirring me to articulate and document the quagmire of my thoughts in the first place. I feel compelled to voice my heart and my hope through the words of my quest.

Chapter 1

NEWFOUNDLAND & AMERICA

ST. JOHN'S IS A BLIP on the radar screen for jumbo jets as they cross the Atlantic Ocean. Many American GIs know St. John's. The airport has served as a standard refueling stop on trans-Atlantic military flights for years. The relationship between the United States and Newfoundland has been very warm, mutually respectful, and friendly from the perspective of my parents' generation and their baby boomer children. The Yanks had several bases in Newfoundland during and after World War II. We called all Americans "Yanks". I did not know that our affectionate slang was not appreciated by citizens south of the Mason-Dixie line until I moved to North West Florida in 1984. When I was a child, all Americans were Yanks, and they appeared powerful, rich, cocky but friendly, and more complicated with political issues such as Vietnam, Civil Rights, and Watergate than we experienced in our lives.

We grew up watching American TV from college football (Notre Dame was reverent in my home) to the Mickey Mouse Club. We had more TV from America than from Canada in Newfoundland during the 60's and 70's. On Saturday nights, the American shows provided standard family entertainment. The kids took one of their bi-weekly baths before the Beverly Hillbillies and the Ed Sullivan Show. Bonanza was a big part of our lives also. I remember many blustery, lazy, winter days with large flakes swirling outside of our double paned windows. The escapades of Little Joe and Hoss helped us to wait out the weather in a happy and warm, trance-like state. I don't even remember a popular Canadian show that Newfoundland kids watched back then, other than Saturday night hockey. My parents watched Canadian news in addition to US news, but it was pretty stale against Walter Cronkite, Howard Kossel, and characters such as Jackie Gleason, Red Skeleton, Dean Martin, and yes, the Gold Diggers!

Newfoundlanders have always lived relatively simple but rich lives, steeped in Irish culture and humor. They have been on the receiving end of "dumb Newfie jokes" in Canada since 1949, when Newfoundland officially became a part of Canada. Just replace Cajun or Polish with Newfie, and it's the same joke—insulting, degrading, arrogant, and mean spirited. Of course, Newfoundlanders have the last laugh. The charming character of the delivering party always shines through whenever a Newfie joke is thrown one's way. Newfoundlanders have the ability to take mainland arrogance with a grain of salt. I think the average Newfoundlander is secure in who they are and where they come from at a core level. They like themselves and they like their fellow Newfoundlanders.

He who knows the least knows it the loudest. That is the unspoken truth in the culture of our humble island home. Honor is seen in modesty and quiet dignity. Silent eye contact speaks volumes across the room. Newfoundlanders tend to let the self-righteous parties hang themselves with the haughtiness of their own words. Usually, the nonsense is not even dignified with a response. It all comes out in the wash. Newfoundlanders are particularly adept at silent communication. Entitlement and selfishness are received as a fool's message; nothing more threatening than the roots of a prickly weed; defiantly clinging to the layered slabs of polished, granite rock, rising majestically from the freezing depth of the North Atlantic. The annoying weeds can be pulled out by their roots at any time, but they are tolerated to a point. It sort of breaks the monotony, mixes it up, and brings a little off-color spice to the orderliness of our isolated, homogenous culture.

"Who does she think she is? Her nibs up there wants to know..." The commentary usually ends with laughter and a sarcastic rolling of the eyes to highlight the shallowness of the lady's need or weakness of character. The sarcasm is not necessarily mean—more of a shaking of the head, putting it in perspective, and then moving on. People will say things like, "Poor thing, she doesn't know any better. She was born with more money than brains you know. What can you expect?" Class and dignity are judged against modesty and strength of character. Wealth is not honored if it is flaunted. I am not saying that Newfoundlanders don't like nice things and to get ahead. It's just that material wealth is put in perspective. So, if you're ever in a room full of Newfoundlanders, and your comments are met with silence or a weak nod, you have probably just made a fool of yourself. They are usually too polite to tell you to your face.

The land of my birth was and continues to be a very peaceful and safe place to be from. When I go back to visit, I see that many Newfoundlanders view others from the context of either "from here" or "come from away". I wasn't as aware of that framing of others when I was a child. We were curious and excited to meet anyone from somewhere else, and especially Americans. During the course of my childhood and in the experience of my family, mainland Canadians were viewed as looking down on "dumb Newfies". We did not feel a deep sense of nationalism. We were proud Newfoundlanders, but not fervent Canadians. As children, we did not give Canada much thought one way or the other.

I have seen a change in the generation of my nieces and nephews in Newfoundland, and in people of my age. They now have a strong sense of identity with Canada. They make it a point of having a Maple Leaf logo on their shirt, hat, or bag when they travel. The young people do not want to be viewed as Americans when they travel abroad, and they make a conscious effort to outwardly demonstrate that they are Canadians. In the 60's, we also did not want to be viewed as Americans growing up anymore than we needed to demonstrate that we were Canadians. We were just plain folk from a poor province in Canada, eager to meet people from mainland Canada or America.

We certainly did not harbor any bad feelings for Americans, and we loved the thought of visiting the States, or of spotting American license plates traveling along our single-lane, dirt highway. I remember crossing the province many times as a child, along the 470 miles of unpaved Trans Canada Highway that connected St. John's to Corner Brook. The slogan was "Finish the drive in '65", as in a paved road. It was eventually paved, but potholes and moose crossings are another story. My father always drove an old car. We had a myriad of break downs, but we somehow made it across the province despite ourselves. Five kids, my parents, sometime my aunt, and our dog—all piled in, no seat belts and definitely no mini-vans in those days. Just elbows, and more elbows! We sang "Row-Row-Row Your Boat" in harmony, led by my mother, a thousand times over during those trips. We were always on the lookout for American or mainland license plates.

The story of Newfoundland's journey with Canada, in the shadow of America, is the background of my understanding of Americans, as a people and as a nation. I have lived in the States since 1983. My worldview has evolved from that of my generation of Newfoundlanders gradually and in degrees. Whenever I have been in Canada in the last decade, I have been somewhat surprised at the level of frustration and even a sense of condescending contempt exhibited against American policies in papers such as *The Toronto Sun* and *The Daily News*. Some stories defend America, but for the most part, the articles express a cynical and critical view of American policy.

To me, it's as if many people in Canada have begun to perceive themselves as having higher morals than Americans, and view themselves as better educated. I don't think that there is a conscious awareness of this evolution of thinking. Nor am I sure of how deep the threads go. The grandparents of many young Newfoundlanders had a unique experience and relationship with Americans between the mid 40's and the late 50's. The memories of that time are very positive and cherished by many. I wonder if today's young people are cognizant of the distancing of themselves from an ideal of American values that many of their parents and grandparents had. What I see most from these young Newfoundlanders is a struggle to make sense of what they read and see on a daily basis against the backdrop of their understanding of the birth of America's democracy. The inherent principles supporting the soul of America's moral compass and the relatively recent historical relationship between America and Newfoundland are being questioned and framed within a global context that oscillates from unconditional support of America to distrust of America. Most Americans have no idea of the impact of the American Constitution to the common folk of small and distant lands who hail from ordinary places such as the rocky shores of Newfoundland.

I will try and tell the story of my personal journey with America which begins with my father and a remote island in the North Atlantic. My father was born on Dec 31, 1923, in Calvert, named after Sir George Calvert, who was later given the title Lord Baltimore. Calvert first brought settlers to Newfoundland in 1620. Calvert brought his wife and family, and a couple of Roman Catholic priests to the barren island around 1627-1629 to settle there. Apparently, a single winter on the south-east coast of Newfoundland proved to be too harsh for the Englishman and his family. The Titanic sank 20 miles off of the same coast 300 years later, so one can begin to appreciate the effect of a good nor'easter blowing in off of the big pond; carrying the bight of the frigid Arctic across the huge bergs that migrate down Ice Berg Alley from Greenland, dotting the shores of the Avalon Peninsula. Sir Calvert moved on to purchase land in a warmer climate. His son, Cecil, settled this warmer land in Maryland around 1632 after his father drowned crossing the North Atlantic on a return voyage to his beloved England.

Perhaps, my link with America goes back to the place and history of my father's birth. Calvert was a very small community of cod fishermen, isolated and poor, even by Newfoundland standards. The community was entirely Irish and Catholic. That is how Newfoundland was settled. Poor Irish immigrants landed there as early as the 16th century, and eked out a life in a land that was too harsh for the English explorers to stay in over the winter. Over the next couple of centuries, Newfoundland was settled in small communities that lined the coast of the island. The population became evenly split between Catholics and Protestants (a combination of all other religions of European descent). The communities were settled by religion, so that a small community was entirely Catholic, and five miles down the way, another small community might be entirely Anglican. Religion was and still is a very big part of the culture and personal story of Newfoundland. Even when I grew up, there continued to be two separate public school systems.

There was a Catholic Public School System and a Protestant Public School System. The two public school systems became a single system in Newfoundland as recent as the mid-90's. However, things did gradually change as far as attitudes and prejudices evolve across generations. My mother would tell us that when she was growing up (mid 1920—mid-1940), it was not allowed that Catholic and Protestant children socialized together. This was not so during my youth. We did go to separate schools, but we very much mixed socially. We were at the tail end of the Hippie generation, and all kids back there went to the same parties. As teenagers, we were more interested in the music and the cultural revolution of the 60's and the early 70's. In social circles, we did not pay much attention to whether one was Catholic or Protestant. Give me a break! We were more concerned with how many cases of beer we could buy after we pooled our meager allowances. The more people to throw in to the pot, the better! As we sat around camp fires toasting each other and singing off key but heartfelt tributes to the Stones or Joe Cocker, our laughter and our spirituality were focused on a single thing. We were pretty big on living in the moment. We had a deep appreciation for the irreverent and joyous moments of our youth. Our parents probably took more note of the social piece, in a gossipy, small town sort of way. I never knew anyone who was not allowed to hang out with someone else based on religion. Getting married outside of the Catholic Church would be a hurdle for many of our parents; not an insurmountable one, but a hurdle nevertheless.

The nuns always seated us in classes alphabetically. So your life friends and classmates ended up being determined by the first letter of one's last name. Most of my closest girl friends had surnames that ranged from R—W my entire school life. As our teachers went down the roster, there was Richard, Rossiter (me), Rumbolt, St. George, and the wisest on of them all, Wiseman, at the end of the roll. We, "end of the alphabet girls", have remained friends for half a century. Catholic students went to separate schools by gender as well as by religion after elementary school. I attended an all girls' public school in junior school and high school, as did my mother and my sister. We were taught by Catholic nuns (Presentation nuns for my sister and me, and Mercy nuns for our mother). The nuns were very stern, and they had very high, academic expectations. Obviously, it was not even a consideration that girls could not do math. We were expected and required to perform. Likewise, our fathers and brothers attended the all boys' public schools, which were run by the Jesuit Brothers from America. They were reported to be very strict and enforced discipline harshly. However, I have never known a male of my generation or my father's, who ever had a bad word for the Jesuits. They spoke very highly of their school days. There was a heavy emphasis on academics and sports for the boys. There were great rivalries between hockey teams. The boys from St. Bon's and Gonzaga spiritually honored their hockey more reverently than mandatory attendance at Mass. I am sure more prayers were said for a "win" than in salvation of their poor souls.

My father did not go to college after high school. Like most Newfoundland boys, college was not an option in the 1940's. He had to work to support himself and to help out with the family. Also, Newfoundland men were fighting in World War II since 1939. There were not many frills or nonsense, such as entitlement and privilege for my parent's generation. That was life back there. People were proud but poor in an economic sense. The first generation of college students was that of my generation for most families. Newfoundland men, who were a few years older than my father, were fighting in World War II, as part of the Newfoundland Regiment. My mother's older brother fought in Germany. He told me later in life that he fought in the Battle of the Bulge, and he knew the Ardennes well. My mother was shocked that he shared any memories of World War II with me, as he never spoke of the war when he came back.

The United States opened four bases in Newfoundland after Pearl

Harbor. My father began working for the American government at Fort Pepperrell in 1942 at the age of 18 as a Supply clerk, making $1500 / year. He worked with the US Military in the Northeast Air Command until a Reduction in Forces eliminated his position in the fall of 1958. At that time, he was the Director of Civilian Personnel, with a salary of $5553 /year, as a LGS-10, step 4. He was very proud of his work with the Americans, and he felt that he had been treated very fairly during his years with them. The salary was actually good for that time and place. In effect, he worked for the US government for over 16 years, his first job out of high school until his mid -30's.

This was an exciting and wonderful segment of my father's life. He traveled to San Antonio, Texas for training in 1950, at the age of 26. Throughout his life, my father lit up when he spoke of his work with the Americans. He loved their easy - laid back style within an effective work ethic, the personalities he met, and the challenges and experiences that he had. Most of all, he loved the people. He related to the American outlook, and the American way of life. I think Americans exhibited a carefree and open passion for every day living. They brought to Newfoundland the hope of a better life for the average person. My mother also loved talking about St. John's in the 40's and the 50's when the American Bases were in full swing. Most of my mother's stories were about social things—dances, chocolates, nylons, and cigarettes. These were extravagant items, unavailable to the locals at that time. My parents were in their 20's and early 30's. The impression of these years validated their very beings and shaped the aspirations of their lives throughout their adulthood, and for their children. The Americans brought sunshine and laughter to a people who appreciated humor and wisdom, but who had only known a harsh way of life—survival, making ends meet, and faith in the after life.

A world of possibilities had been opened for my father—a world that he could only dream about as a young boy from Calvert. He was educated by Jesuit brothers from America and worked for the American government until he was 34 years old. At the same time, Newfoundland was struggling to find its own identity in the world stage. Local Newfoundland politics within the context of global politics haunted my father his entire life, and at the same time impassioned him to be a very involved and informed citizen. He saw civic responsibility as a mandate for living his life.

I saw an inner conflict in my father. He was a critical thinker, self-educated, and a whiz on geo-politics. He read Time Magazine from cover to cover every week. He would advocate that staying on top of world affairs was as important as a college education, and more attainable on a poor man's budget. He possessed a deep passion for learning and exploring, and yet he had a great contempt for the elitist, college educated type who displayed an arrogant indifference to the contributions and worthiness of your "average Joe". My father valued the wisdom in knowing and honoring the story of people from all walks of life. He loathed anyone who thought that they were better than someone else, based on the happen stance of their birth. The "let me enlighten you, patronizing type" really got my father's goat. They triggered a raw nerve; igniting an anger deep inside of him. He did not suffer fools lightly. He dismissed anyone who thought they were entitled to the golden calf. He had a very sharp Irish wit, and he could lance arrogance with a quick retort, often tinged with humor, but always slicing and to the point.

I believe the experience of working with the Americans during the formative years of his young adulthood validated and expanded his own personal sense of right and wrong, of justice and injustice, of possibility and future. The same can not be said for his personal experience and perception of the British. The Irish ancestors of Newfoundland settlers were the poorest of Ireland's poor, indentured servants who were brought to the New World to attend to the whims of their British masters. The American Revolution and the Constitution of the United States were sacred mantra to my father and his friends. After World War II, while my father and many other Newfoundlanders were working for the American government on sacred Newfoundland soil, the Republic of Newfoundland was determining the course of its future as a nation.

Newfoundland fell under the Stature of Westminster (1931) which established the foundation of the modern-day British Commonwealth. Australia, New Zealand, South Africa, Ireland, and Newfoundland were all considered "Dominion Status". The premise was that the Dominions would be autonomous, independent in external and domestic affairs, and share a common allegiance to the Crown. The outcome for the people across the British Dominions was poverty. The self-determined government of Newfoundland was bankrupt prior to the Second World War. The British did not want to be responsible for Newfoundland after the war, even though the men of Newfoundland had valiantly spilled blood in Europe from 1939—1945. By 1948, the options in Newfoundland had come down to two choices for the people to determine through the electoral process: Confederation (become the 10th province of Canada) or Responsible Government (independent nation state with economic union with the US). Confederation won by a small margin of votes.

This outcome and the election of 1948 are debated to this day among Newfoundland historians and politicians. My father was one of those people who never accepted the decision. He would never call himself a Canadian, even in his later years. He proudly and stubbornly called himself a Newfoundlander, a citizen of the Republic of Newfoundland. I remember being in the ICU of Humana Hospital in Fort Walton Beach, Florida in 1985. I had just recently moved to The States and to The South. A very old man was lying in the ICU, dying, with a Confederate hat on his head. The hat was worn and very dirty. It always reminded me of my father and how he felt about Confederation with Canada. Emotions and beliefs that are rock solid and formed early in life against our personal experiences and our personal truths become embedded and resistant to change when the passion for the belief is stronger than time. My father was very passionate in his belief that the people of Newfoundland would have achieved more honor and success as an independent Republic, with economic ties to the United States. He believed this until his death in 2002.

Whether my father was right or wrong will never be known. The course of history has taken Newfoundland to be the tenth Canadian province. Economically, it has remained poor. The people continue to live rich, personal lives within their every day struggles and triumphs. Newfoundlanders have always gotten on with plain living, taking hardship and disappointments in stride. My father chose to become a very involved citizen, and fought hard for positive change within the system, despite his personal feelings. I believe that he was a visionary, and that his personal vision was shaped within the context of the ideals of the American Constitution.

My parents' understanding and love of the democratic process was passed on to their children. Both my mother and my father had very strong opinions about politics, and they loved an intelligent discussion on issues that mattered to them. They were card carrying members of the Progressive Conservative Party in Canada. The dinner table was always full of conversations about local and international politics, and world events. Our generation was that of "children are seen but not heard." Hence, we often just listened as my father and my mother dissected current events from home and abroad. Geo-politics was standard fare at our kitchen table; as standard as bread and butter, and boiled potatoes. As my mother poured tea, she tut-tutted over the escapades of Margaret Trudeau and Mick Jagger, Jackie and Aristotle Onassis, John Lennon & Yoko Ono, or the current local political scandal of the day. My father paid close attention to Watergate, the Arab—Israeli Wars, the British—IRA conflict, Central America, Vietnam, Civil Rights, US and Canadian elections, and especially local politics. Looking back, we were exposed to very rich conversations despite the geographical remoteness of our lives in the context of the world stage.

As a young adult, I spent several months in the Yasawa Island Group, Fiji. The Fijians on the outer islands had no electricity. They had very little physical contact with the outside world in the early 80's. Since then, cruise ships visit the Yasawa chain, so maybe this has changed. But back then, the atolls were still with darkness and calmness after the sun went down. Very few tourists found their way there. Every evening the local people would sit around in a large circle, sometimes drinking yagona, but always listening to huge radios that would pick up broadcasts from around the world. They would have the greatest discussions on issues such as the Israeli-Palestinian conflict, how the Parliamentary system is different than the Representative System in the US, the World Cup, and events such as the eruption of Mount St. Helen, or whatever was current across the airwaves that night.

I was humbled and awed by the depth of their interest and insight into world events and places far beyond the reach of their small island boats. I have come to believe that ordinary people who are raised on isolated islands, geographically separated from mainland populations, tend to intellectually explore places and events that they read or hear about, from an innate need to be connected to the larger populations of the world. It's a paradox, as people who sometimes have the greatest access to information and events are not as interested in exploring, probing, and questioning for deeper insights and clarity of understanding.

Perhaps, I generalize too much, but it makes one wonder. I have worked with Americans who did not know that Canada is a country on their northern border. I will never forget my first day on the job in a hospital in Florida, when a coworker was asking me about where I was from. When I told her that I was from Canada, she really had no clue where that was. She asked me if it was the same as Boston. At first, I thought she was joking. The conversation moved on, and other people joined in, all Americans. They sort of filled her in, as I stood there wondering if she was putting me on or something. She wasn't, nor was she embarrassed.

For the most part, I was the only person shocked. At one point, we were talking about London, and she said that she would like to drive there someday. I again silently processed, "Am I being put on here?" However, she really had no idea that one could not drive to London from America. As I responded to her that there was the small problem of the Atlantic Ocean, she told me that I did not understand America. She just knew that from somewhere in America there had to be a bridge—that I just did not know where it was. I believe I remained silent but I am sure that my eyes were rolling to the back of my head as I walked away. It's a bad trait of mine, inherited from my Irish ancestors.

She is an extreme example but I have worked with and have had conversations with many Americans who have little interest in geography or world issues. Jay Leno addresses Americans' knowledge of basic geography and current events on the *Tonight Show*, as one of his pet peeves in an attempt to either highlight or shame his audience into awareness. I am not implying that most Americans do not know basic world history and geography. But, it has been my personal experience, that if I were to pick one area that American school children and adults tend to lag behind their peers in other Western countries, it is in both the knowledge and the curiosity of geography, both domestic and world; and in the nuances of geopolitics. It is the curiosity part that stands out for me.

I am not convinced that American kids are behind the rest of the world in math and science, as we are often told. The comparisons are not apples to apples. I think that this myth is promoted and validated by a political agenda that endorses the outsourcing of American jobs to poor countries. Cheap labor feeds greed and absurd corporate profits. It is easier to rationalize the practice of screwing your own workers if you convince yourself and others that the American engineers or the American network specialists are deficient in knowledge relative to their peers in a third world country.

Personally, I have been very satisfied with the Public School System in the United States, which is the victim of very bad press and misinformation. The public school systems that I have had first hand experience with in Florida and in Virginia have very rigorous curriculums, and the teachers range from "as good as it gets" to "as bad as it gets", as they do everywhere. I think one of the greatest gifts that we can give our children is teaching them to survive and learn from their least favorite teacher. It's the whole discipline of learning and endurance that was hammered into us by the Catholic nuns on a daily basis.

Self-discipline and ownership of our responses allows children to maximize their school outcome. Today, we are always trying to fix every little school problem for our children. The result has been that teachers are always on the defensive, and our children do not honor their educators as we did at that age. In Newfoundland in the 60's, no one questioned a teacher or, God forbid, a principal. We had play clothes, church clothes, and school clothes. Everything about school was placed in a framework of discipline, honor, and allegiance to the whole school experience. It was very much a part of the culture and the time. Education was the path to a better life. And yes, the nuns were always stern and often mean, but they were also respected and smart. Some were more fair and kinder than others. But, they all challenged us to rise to their expectations and standards of conduct.

I have had discussions, as an adult, with childhood friends about our experiences with the Catholic nuns. My memories are not as negative as that of some of my friends. The good sisters did not tolerate wrong answers with any sense of humor or empathy. A hard ruler to the knuckles was standard fare as early as first and second grade if we did not know our math facts. I always knew mine. The incentive of the combination of humility and fear did inspire a discipline for practice and rote learning of the basic fundamentals of reading, writing, and arithmetic. In college classes, I would learn that this is called vicarious learning. At the time, I did not know what it was called, but it was a "no brainer" relative to survival during our early years under the sharp, hawkish eyes of the hovering sisters.

The nuns were hard on us, but for the most part, the range of students in the classroom did learn addition, subtraction, multiplication, and division at the end of the nuns' rulers. We were served well in our high school years. For example, it is hard to master Algebraic Equations if you can't multiply and divide fractions. It is hard to study literature if your reading skills are not developed. I have never agreed with the current crisis with reading as a distinct subject beyond the elementary years. Shouldn't it be taken for granted that the fundamentals of reading are mastered, and that any reading practice for fluency would be gained through studying text books across core academic subjects? The emphasis in our adolescent years was on studying—religion, history, biology, grammar, literature, foreign language. The ability to read was a given; a gift delivered at the whack of a ruler by the Catholic nuns or with the sting of a strap form the Jesuit brothers.

The nun's favorite period outside of academics was choir. Now, I hated choir! I had to attend choir for thirty minutes every day of my entire school life. I hated it with a passion. The nuns were as intolerant with those of us who could not carry a note as they were with those who lagged in the academic arena. Talk about self-discipline and endurance! My mind would wander to vast ranges of my imagination and thought processing as I sat quiet in my seat, invisible; as the "on tune" voices sang sweetly and strongly around me. One time, I got kicked out of choir for laughing. I was sent to the library for punishment. I will never forget how happy I was to have free time in the library to look through the Encyclopedia Section.

Only rich families had the privilege of owning a private set of *Encyclopedia Britannica*. My parents often talked of perhaps we could afford a set "next year". Of course, next year never came as there was always the car to be fixed, or storm windows that needed to be replaced, or groceries to buy. But we always had the dream and the hope for next year. A click of the mouse has reframed all of that for our children. They take for granted their easy access to facts and world history. But, the access is only as valuable as the curiosity and the inquiry. We were trained to be curious about the world. Our culture demanded that we not waste an opportunity to learn, to make an honorable life for ourselves. I sat quietly and happily in my punishment, probing the pages of those thick reference books. They were expensive. We had to be very respectful and careful. We dare not tear one of those fine, thick, gold-trimmed pages. The beady eyes of the nun as librarian pierced through the back of our heads from behind the check-out desk. You could feel the unflinching stare boring through your occipital lobe, as she listened as hard as she looked for a reverent and gentle turn of the page. No dogs ears in those books!

The pendulum swings. My generation of parents is more inclined to coddle our children. We have shifted our expectation from a responsibility of the child to a blame of the teacher or the school. We advocate for our children's right to learn. We disrespect teachers and we question their skill. We listen to our students' version of the facts and we blindly march in to set it right. During my school years, the nuns took for granted every students' right to learn. What else would they be doing? The wise and good sisters bull-dozed straight into the discipline of learning and the hard work of learning. Our parents and our media did not question or demean our educators.

Religion was taught to us for thirty minutes every day. The nuns and the occasional priest were well versed in the theology of the Roman Catholic faith. We were drilled on the meaning of sin, and types of sin from lying to murder. There were cardinal sins and mortal sins. Murder was definitely a mortal sin. Are lies always sins? We had great philosophical discussions with the nuns, even though we moaned our way through the period on most days. We were raised on 'knowing right from wrong', the Ten Commandments, helping the poor, and the merit of penance and forgiveness. The inevitable direction of our souls towards a future in heaven, hell, or purgatory was discussed on a daily basis, especially when the nuns thought that the deep estuaries of our souls were in immediate need of divine insights and interventions.

For example, if a girl was seen smoking outside of school, and especially in her school uniform, we were going to hear about it in no uncertain terms. These mindless girls were definitely on the path to hell in a hand basket. Such a report would send the nuns into immediate and emphatic teachable moments. We were drilled that drugs would destroy brain cells and cause irreversible damage to our God given, healthy bodies. Above all, the negative image offered to the public of "Presentation students" could not be tolerated. We were ambassadors in those uniforms and we were not to represent our school in a dishonorable way. The local mall would actually call the front office and report to the good Sisters if they saw any young ladies dressed in green and gold behaving mischievously or smoking after school or during lunch. Needless to say, every spirited girl that I knew was very eager to get out of the green and gold calling cards before we left the building. We would tear our uniforms off in front of our lockers as soon as the bell rang, and squeeze into our faded Levis as naturally as breathing. We had already learned to compartmentalize our lives.

Vatican II had begun in 1962 and continued until 1965 with a range of modern reforms for the Catholic Church, sanctioned by the Pope. I started school in 1962 at the age of 4. I would turn 5 that November. My school experience and that of my friends was grounded in moral instruction as much as in learning our A-B-C's and the three R's. My mother told us that prior to Vatican II, the format of the Mass service was removed from that of the congregation. Masses had been said in Latin. The ritual of the celebration of the Sacrament of Communion did not engage the people. The reforms of Vatican II were revolutionary to my parents' generation. The changes stimulated much discussion in our classes with the nuns, and in our homes. We attended Mass during the school day for any and every reason. My birthday is a Holy Day of Obligation. Every year on my birthday, we had to attend Mass the first thing in the morning. My sister's birthday was on Nov 11th, Veteran's Day, always a school holiday. Growing up, I thought that I got the short end of the stick in that deal. Catholic instruction was a dominant part of our school life from elementary through high school. As children, we were not at all impressed, but we developed great life skills in the domain of self-discipline.

One of the major reforms of Vatican 11 imprinted on us by the nuns and the priests was the teaching of tolerance and the acceptance of other religions. We were taught in depth that the process of living your life as an Ambassador of God's love and compassion was the litmus test of Christianity. It did not matter what church, mosque, temple, or synagogue one attended. It was how you lived on a daily basis that counted. Those who walked the walk did not need to convince others of their piousness and their status as Christians. How often did the nuns and our parents remind us that actions speak louder than words? Spending time verbalizing how Christian you were would kind of defeat the purpose, especially if you compared yourself to others. We were drilled to understand that we were not holier or better than anyone else, no matter where they came from or what they believed. What we were taught was that we would be more accountable at the Pearly Gates because we had the privilege of a very fine Catholic education; that is, we "knew right from wrong". There would be no excuses for us on Judgment Day.

We were taught that our humanity brought us into the world as sinners. Our rules to live by were to treat others as we wanted to be treated; to reach out an empathic hand to those less fortunate; and to do the best that we could in tough situations. As we lived the Golden Rule of charity, kindness, and fairness, our love and honor for God would be self-evident. We could not treat others poorly and say that we loved God. That would be hypocritical and the worst sin of all. These lectures were repeated and reinforced daily throughout our entire home and school experience from kindergarten to graduation. Unless one was a total moron, there was no missing the point for us.

We definitely would not brag that we were one of the "good Christians", owning the moral high road so to speak. No, that would be very shameful in the culture of our teachers and our parents. One might have to polish the church pews in Penance to bring that sense of entitlement down a peg or two, to trim your sails so to speak. There is nothing like manual labor to help put lofty ideals of self-righteousness into perspective. He who lives in glass houses can not throw stones. We were taught to worry about our own glass houses, and not to judge others. That would be God's job. Our job was to get our own house ready in a dignified and humble way.

We were kids like kids anywhere. We were usually tortured to sit through these discussions and lectures every day in school and in church on Holy Days of Obligation and on Sundays; and then in our homes whenever the need arose. I experience Mass differently than during the endurance training sessions of my childhood. A Catholic will tell you that the meat of the Mass is in the sermon. Priests inspire greatly or they disappoint greatly. Of course, such talk would be forbidden when I was a child. But it really is true. Most people go to Mass to hear a really good sermon. If that does not happen, then we find comfort in the internal acceptance of the presence of our faith. In the ceremony of the Mass, most Catholics feel a sense of peace and nourishment from the traditions and Communion with God. We find simple comfort by spending a short time in the hushed dignity of God's house. But always, Catholics are hoping for a sermon that inspires us or at least one that keeps us awake.

Newfoundland's relationship with America during my childhood was also heavily linked to the Catholic Church. The Jesuit presence was so strong there. John F. Kennedy was loved and admired greatly. His Presidency was a part of our connection to the world. Everyone was inspired by the power of his words. Kennedy's easy charm and powerful speeches transcended borders and inspired us to do better in our lives. His message was reinforced by our parents and our teachers in the values of Newfoundland culture.

I remember sitting in my first grade classroom, watching his funeral on a black and white, 12 inch TV. We never had TV in school prior to that day or after that day, as far as I can remember. Skinny Sister Louise, who would be described as sour by her six-year old class, had brought the small TV into the classroom. She cried through the entire funeral, which only accentuated the large, black circles that were always noticeable in her hollowed, shrunken face. My six year old memory of her was that you could practically see her skull underneath a thin, yellow layer of fragile skin, always stark and haunted looking against her black habit. The shock and horror of Kennedy's death imprinted on us as it did on America. I think the innocence of possibility and hope was adjusted by his assassination. There was an overwhelming sadness. My mother can not watch footage of his funeral to this day without tearing up.

After Kennedy, there followed the turmoil of the 60's and the 70's.

The baby boomers in Newfoundland grew up with the same news that American kids did. We viewed from the outside the Civil Rights struggle, Vietnam, Watergate, the assassinations of Martin Luther King and Robert Kennedy, Woodstock, and Kent State. At the same time, Pierre Trudeau was quite the personality in Canadian politics, and terrorist groups such as the PLO, the Red Brigades, the IRA, Black September, and the FLQ were followed closely in the Canadian press. The Arab—Israeli Wars were covered. It seemed like the world was in turmoil everywhere, except in our humble haven in Newfoundland.

We had no crime back then. Police officers did not even carry guns. There was no need. It was quite acceptable for kids to hitch-hike. When I attended college in the mid-70's many college students, who lived outside of St. John's, hitch-hiked across the province on weekends or university breaks. Kids were not attacked or murdered, nor did they threaten the drivers who picked them up. Are you kidding? We were so grateful for a ride to get out of the wind, the rain, and the dampness of our climate. I can remember hitch-hiking after midnight when I was in college. Maybe we were pushing it a little bit, but we were young and invincible.

Life was simple and safe in that time and place. We were not wary of strangers. Instead, we embraced meeting anyone from away, and we opened our lives to them quite freely, as did our parents, and their parents before them. A hot cup of tea, or something a bit stiffer, and a bit of something to eat would always be offered to guests at any time of the day or night. This tradition still lives in Newfoundland. But today, kids don't hitch-hike, and there is more crime. It's all relative. For the most part, Newfoundland is still a very safe place to observe the world's problems from, and to grow up in. A friend of mine in Florida often asked me why people would stay in Newfoundland. He thought the climate and the isolation would be unbearable. My answer to him was that it is the same story for people all over the world. People are from places. Belonging is belonging. People are not from Newfoundland. They belong to Newfoundland. At the same time, my nephew in Newfoundland would ask me how anyone could stand living in Florida. He thought the heat and the humidity were unbearable there. I always smile inside at the give and take of what is known and what is honored from the experiences of our lives.

Chapter 2

HOW DID I GET HERE

IT WAS IN THE MIDDLE of the night of an ordinary week day in February, 1982. I groggily and slowly woke up to find myself lying on a cold floor in the bathroom of my small apartment on a Royal Saudi Air Base in Khamis Mushayt, Asir Region. As I realized in a hazy, spotty sort of way where I was, my mind drifted to how the hell I had gotten here in the first place. I did not have the energy to grope my way up off the floor. For another hour or so, my conscious memory grasped for some sense of reality through the fog of my thoughts as I slowly came to, lying white as a ghost on the concrete floor of my tiny bathroom.

I guess my journey to Saudi Arabia really started back in the spring of 1978 when I made a conscious decision to leave Newfoundland, to work outside the province. I had graduated from the College of Trades & Technology after completing a three-year course to be an X-Ray Technologist. I never really wanted to work in a hospital, and I had no great passion to enter a Technical College at the end of high school in 1974. The problem was that I did not know what I wanted to do, and my options were limited from a financial perspective, as were those of most of my friends. The emphasis in Newfoundland in 1974 was that it was taken for granted that kids would continue their education after high school, with the focus towards employment rather than higher education for the sake of higher education. Older siblings were graduating with college degrees and were unable to find jobs. In the town where I grew up, I knew several boys who graduated from Memorial University with Accounting Degrees, but ended up working back in the Pulp and Paper Mill with their fathers. Everyone knew young people who had teaching degrees, but who could not find work in the province.

The focus for our parents and for the government was towards a secondary education that would result in employment. A Liberal Arts education was not offered as an option to the class of 1974 in our all girls' high school. To my knowledge, not a single person from my graduating class went on to university, but many girls were channeled into nursing programs, technical programs, and secretarial programs. There was no guidance or encouragement from school personnel or our parents to enroll in a traditional Bachelor's Degree program. For the most part, our parents trusted our educators to do right by us. Considering the employment options in the province, there was some short-term merit to the focus of their direction for us. They were guided by the reality of time and place.

I had a cousin who was an X-Ray Technologist. She was smart and successful, and my mother thought it looked like a good career choice for me. I didn't have a better answer, so there I was. I knew in the first two months of the three year commitment that I would not work in a hospital in Radiology for the rest of my life. But, back there, you didn't quit, or even waste the first year. I decided to finish it up, always with the thought that I would do something else after I could support myself with a career. I would use X-Ray Technology as a vehicle to get me somewhere else.

I also wanted to travel and see places. That was a passion of mine. I did not want to wait until I was older to travel. I always thought I needed to explore afar and exotic places when I was young. I rationalized that you can never know where the future will bring you, or if you will have the health to travel if you wait until you are older. I don't know where this outlook came from or why I had such a need to travel, as none of my friends were of the same mind. I think I was always affected by my friend, Elizabeth.

She died when I was about 11 or 12 years old. She had been in the hospital for a lot of her life, either on dialysis, or waiting to be on dialysis, or post-dialysis. I never quite understood the specifics back then. She just always appeared to be weak and tired. My sister and I spent several summers visiting her in the hospital almost every day. I hated the smell of that hospital. We used to enter from a lower level. The hospital seemed so cold, dark, and damp to me, and the smell was always with me. I remember when she died that we had to get permission from the nuns to go to her funeral because it was in the Anglican Church. The nuns were very kind about that. My sister, another girl from our street, and I met in the hallway of school and waited for permission as the nuns gravely whispered among themselves about the tragedy of her death. Even though the nuns taught us about faith and life after death daily in religion classes, they seemed to be at as much of a loss as the rest of us in dealing with the human side of death; grief, and the immense sadness of the death of a child.

That was one of those life changing experiences for me. My memory of Elizabeth is that she was like an angel, at peace with the world. She was so kind and gentle. She never said a bad word about anyone or complained about being sick. She loved cheesies! She would spend about 20 minutes carefully brushing off all of the orange on the outside, as she was not allowed to eat salt. She would gently and meticulously rub one lonely cheesie down to a narrow white core before she nibbled slowly and methodically on the pitiful, remaining, thin strip. She just ate a couple at a time. Elizabeth stretched out the process of eating a single cheesie for a half an hour or so. It was quite the production. She waited for us to come; sharing this rebel event with us. The nurses allowed the minor infraction with a lot of tut-tutting and moaning when they walked in.

It was this simple, fun thing that she sneaked with us, but not really. The conspiracy was more that we did not want to engage the ongoing lecture from her nurses of eating just a couple, and brushing all the salt off. Elizabeth knew all that, and she was diligent in her task. She liked to stretch out the pleasure of eating that cheesie as long as she could. She gave us her chocolate bars and chips. People were always bringing her things that she was not allowed to eat. We would talk and laugh, and waste away hours in her hospital room. We would probably eat an entire five-cent bag of chips while Elizabeth worked on a single cheesie. She was so happy and content to share her drawer of candy and chips with us. My sister and I always felt very helpless and sad for Elizabeth when we walked home and knew that we were leaving her there. It was this life lesson that we did not understand very well. I think Elizabeth taught me to live in the present, and to be at peace with things that are out of my control. Our friendship is one of those gifts that was brief in time, but is stored forever deep in my soul.

Years later, as an adult, I had a dream about Elizabeth out of nowhere. I had not thought about her for a long time. But the memory was so vivid! The experience was very real for me when it happened. The dream brought it all flooding back. Elizabeth had been given a very chic and expensive cashmere wool pant suit. I seem to remember that an adult sister had bought it for her in Toronto. This was the early 70's. Twiggy was very popular, and she was often sporting one of those pant suits. It was a deep burgundy color, and it was nicer than anything we had ever seen in our local stores.

Elizabeth had it wrapped in plastic in the drawer of her night stand, next to her hospital bed. She would take it out, gently unwrap and unfold it, and we would drool over it together. It seemed like an outfit that you would see on a fashion magazine cover. I loved it as much as she did. Elizabeth knew that I adored her expensive, cashmere pant suit. She told me that she would wear it when she got better. But, if she did not get to wear it then I could have it. She never got to wear it. When she died, I never got her pant suit. I wanted it so badly. I actually remember sitting in the church during her funeral, looking at her closed casket, and wondering if her mother had chosen that pant suit to dress her in. I guess I never saw her in the open casket. Perhaps the adults thought that would be too much for us. The stupid pant suit was such a big thing in my mind.

My parents and her mother had no idea of our little pact, and I would never ask for it, or tell anyone back then. I was very shy to verbalize a want for myself. I did not want to appear selfish and heartless in the midst of the tragedy of her death. But here I was, about 25 years later, startled awake in the middle of the night, with the memory of Elizabeth and her cherished burgundy pant suit so vivid, and still wishing that I had been given the soft, wool top and pants. I knew that I would have never worn her outfit. I would have kept it wrapped in the same plastic, taking it out gently to unfold and refold, whenever I thought of her. I wanted so bad to be a good steward of her beloved pant suit. It is funny where all of these life events go in the recesses of our minds, and how they come flooding back to us, and what, if anything, they mean when they do come back.

I think my exploratory spirit was also impacted by my clinical training. I remember clearly the first time that I walked into an ICU with a male technician to do the daily round of portable chest x-rays. I was seventeen at the time. My mentor was very aware of me; my newness to the horrors of the ICU. He was as gentle with me as he was with all of his patients. There was a young man who had been badly burned. His charred skin and yellow puss clung to the pillow case that we used to wrap our cassette. The blend of black skin cells streaked with yellow and red against the white of the cotton cloth have remain imprinted in the visual cortex of my brain to this day. Just moving him, and having to place the metal case under his body was one of those life changing moments, when you move from a child to an adult with a single event. He was in so much pain, and our brief work was necessary, but we were inflicting more pain in the process, no matter how gentle we tried to be. Then, there was the first dead person that I had to X-Ray. He was only about 21, ran over by a drunk driver the night before. Hospital workers are the best of the best. They deal with so much day in and day out, and for the most part, they are able to compartmentalize, to take joy in the healing, and to honor the sorrow. I learned to live in the present with an eye to the future and a healthy respect for the past through the jokes and the compassion of my friends and mentors.

Hence, within the framework of living in the present, I set out to explore the world in the spring of 1978, at the age of 19. I also knew in my heart that if I accepted the job offer that I had been given to work at the Health Sciences Complex, a brand new hospital opening in St. John's in the spring of '78, that I would probably never leave there. I would settle into the easy rhythm of life and work, slowly aging and growing comfortable in the sameness of my employment the rest of my life, safe and secure in a world that was familiar and known. I was probably right. My fellow students who did take jobs in St. John's are still there, content in their mid-life stage, easing towards the prospects of retirement in 2008. Thirty years of faithful and dutiful work looms in their very near future.

Back then, I was restless inside myself, and within the boundaries of my world. The security to leave rested in the fact that I always knew that my home was there to return to, with no questions asked, and no explanations needed at any time. It remains so today, the solid and steady rock of Newfoundland, anchored over time and distance in the freezing waters of the North Atlantic, but forever welcoming to those who were raised in her bosom. I headed to Edmonton in Western Canada. Alberta was known to be a far richer province than Newfoundland, and work was rumored to be plentiful there in the spring of 1978. I had a friend in Edmonton and I felt confident that I could find a job there—in the way that young people are not afraid of that which scares us later in life. Wayne Gretzky was a rising star with the Edmonton Oilers. I attended my first professional football game in sub-zero temperatures to watch Edmonton win the Grey Cup that fall. I think the game was against the Ottawa Rough Riders. I should know that for a fact, but the details of some memories escape me. I always worry about the memory thing. I hope it is just a matter of too many inputs verses a symptom of early dementia. I do remember the numbing cold frosting the breath of the screaming Edmontonians. The die-hard fans wore ski-doo suits to sit in the bleachers; sipping on spiked concoctions in their thermoses to keep the blood circulating; or at least to thin it with the most common diuretic of all; the purer the ethanol, the better that day.

In Edmonton, I came to realize that the more reserved personalities of Canadians from the Prairie Provinces were distinct from the openness of the sea-faring descendents of the Maritime Provinces. It bothered me at first, but I began to understand that the initial aloofness of Edmontonians was a function of their culture rather than a function of me. It was the beginning of my life analysis into how people think, what they have been taught, and what they value as a product of their culture. My fondest impression of the land of Western Canada remains the canvas of the spectacular majesty of the area surrounding Banff, Lake Louise, and the Rocky Mountains that slice through Alberta into the interior of British Columbia. Words can not describe the work of God's hand in shaping the immense beauty of the Canadian Rockies. I stood on the top of Sulphur Mountain, looking around, and thinking that I was as close to heaven as I could ever be in my human state of being.

I worked in Edmonton for thirteen months at the Royal Alexandra Hospital. Two treasured girlfriends; Chris, Laurie, and I made a covenant to save $10,000 each in one year. We decided the amount was a comfortable sum to finance a year long back-packing adventure through the South Pacific. We discussed Europe as a possible destination, but we felt that Europe would be somewhere we could visit when we were older. The South Pacific was warm and exotic, and appealed to our youthful desire to explore a world removed from that of our own. Laurie was tall and brunette. Chris was average height and blond. I was the shortest with red hair. We were an interesting threesome, or so we were often told. We had a kindred spirit; always finding laughter and easy fun in the passage of our days.

We set out from Vancouver in June, 1979. We had purchased return air tickets in advance with open-ended dates for travel. We did not want to lock into a set schedule. We were going to take one destination at a time, playing the itinerary by air. We were young and innocent, but we weren't all together clueless. We planned out our route, and we read about the places that we would visit. We knew from the get go, that whatever might happen or if we ran out of money, that we had tickets to get back home. Those return airfares were our safety net, providing insurance that we could get back to the familiarity of Canadian soil if something went wrong. We had a trust in ourselves and a trust in each other. Life was simple and inviting; waiting to be tasted and discovered; no expectations beyond exploration, fun, and adventure in the moment. That was the scope of our itinerary.

The rules of the airfare allowed us to have three open-ended stops between Vancouver and Australia. After much discussion and pondering over maps, we chose Honolulu, Nadi, and Auckland enroute to Sydney. The year was wonderful! We had so many different experiences with people and cultures. We loved Hawaii. That was our first and most expensive destination. We managed to balance a frugal budget with spirited exploration and laughter, always honoring the priorities of our youth. We were determined to soak in as much of Hawaii as we could, and at the same time to make our money stretch towards the unknown but anticipated adventures yet to come.

A wonderful travel agent in Edmonton had found us a deal in Hawaii for the entire month. We rented very nice two-bedroom condominiums at three different resorts: two weeks on Oahu, one week on Maui, and one week on Kauai. The rate was $45 / night, and it included a car with unlimited mileage. That worked out to $15 each a night over 30 nights. Our main expense in Hawaii for a month—long visit cost us $450 each. We covered every inch of those three islands in our rental cars. From the lush tropical wonder of Kaui to the northern shores of Oahu, pausing in the emotion of the SS Arizona, and reveling in early morning jogs along Waikiki. We chewed to the core of the pineapple and easily swallowed the delicious beauty of Hawaii. Our accommodations were fairly plush, easing us into our adventure without too much emotional stress, to say the least. Actually, the world was at our feet during that time, and we paced fluently and eagerly from one experience to the next.

We were always very pragmatic and open to unexpected opportunities. For example, one evening we splurged for a movie and we went to see *The Deer Hunter*. It had just come out and everyone was toting it as a "must see". A night at the movies had to be budgeted into our schedule and expenses. We decided that we could quietly close out the rest of our evening budget on a single Spanish Coffee, as we were determined to spend no more than $5 after the luxury of the movie. And, let's face it; *The Deer Hunter* had left us in a more somber, reflective state than we were accustomed to in this open and carefree world of ours. We walked into a small, quiet looking establishment to order our special coffees, and to linger over our easy conversation. Immediately, the bar tender asked us if we were crazy. They had $1 Margaritas. We quickly calculated five Margaritas verses a single coffee and Kahlua. The nuns had made the math easy; hence there was not a whole lot of brain power needed to quickly set a different evening in gear for us. Our serious post *Deer Hunter* mood quickly dissolved in the abandonment of our youth, and the reckless pursuit of a good time. We managed to stay within our $5 budget despite ourselves, and despite our hangovers the next day. My last memory of that evening is of Laurie smiling widely and laughing loudly as she mixed drinks behind the bar. I was sitting across from her wondering how I was going to get myself down off of my stool and accomplish the task of walking out of there.

After Hawaii, we spent several months in Figi. We saw police men in skirts directing traffic in Nadi. We saw native women selling papaya in open air markets. We rode in buses with no windows along unpaved, winding mountain roads. We swam and snorkeled in the barrier reefs around some of the most beautiful atolls in the South Pacific. Children with big smiles would chase us, laughing as they skipped along with us. We learned to carry candy in our backpacks to share with the little ones. They were so happy with the smallest of gestures from us. They viewed us to be rich and very worldly. It's all relative. Looking back on that time, we had chosen to live very rich, easy lives in the eager ramblings of our days. We hung out for weeks at a time on Beach Comber Island. Many back packers found their way to the absolute serenity and beauty of this atoll.

Beach Comber Island was a resort which provided dormitory style accommodations for budget travelers in addition to more upscale and pricey thatched roof bungalows for more affluent guests. Three meals and snacks were included for about $22 / day at the dorm rate. Many nights, a group of us would sleep on the beach in our sleeping bags rather than in the dorms. I had grown up camping in Newfoundland. It was the only vacation that we could afford. It was very natural for my friends and me to fall into the lazy pace of life on Beach Comber Island. We were lulled to sleep by the steady rhythm of the ocean waves, and awaken every morning by the golden—orange canvas of the tropical sky melting into the calm blue of the South Pacific. And then there was the rich smell of coffee brewing! All was right with our world.

One of my fondest memories is of meeting Charlie. He was from California. He looked like he had just walked out of the Haight Ashbury scene or Woodstock into the mystical world of an island paradise. Charlie waded in the water up to his knees in worn jeans and a very faded grey T-shirt to greet our boat. The coral reef prevented the small boats from reaching the shore. Charlie sported a thick, black beard on a bronzed, suntanned face. He had the widest and easiest smile; a welcome party onto himself. He was extremely skinny; tall, and gangly. His wet jeans were weighing him down. He laughed through the soaking mess of his greeting.

With white teeth flashing through the large grin on his face, he told us to take off our watches. Charlie told us, "Just listen for the drums. That's all you need here. Listen for the drums." We quickly learned that the drums called visitors across the atoll to meals. He was right. In that time and place we did not need to track time. We would pick tropical flowers and put them in our hair as we walked along the path to the outdoor dining area for the evening meal. Life was about pacing our days and our lifestyle; back gammon in the shade of a thatched roof from the heat of the afternoon sun; lazing on the beach or snorkeling in the mornings; and dancing and laughing the evenings away. Our senses were filled with the gentle brush of the ocean breezes, and the stark beauty of a tropical island. The constant backdrop echoed the lyrical sounds of joyous laughter from the Fijian workers. We passed alive, wondrous days on Beach Comber without a care in the world.

We loved the native Fijians! They had this great philosophy on living in the moment, and bringing laughter into whatever job they were doing. They valued the land they were born into, and they valued quality of life from a playful perspective. Fiji is actually divided in population between native born Fijians and descendents from India. They were brought to the Pacific Islands by the British to work the sugar plantations in the 18th century. A Fijian citizen explained to me that the Indian-half of the population controlled most of the businesses and possessed more personal wealth in hard currency than the average Fijian native. But, he said that the Fijians owned all of the land. They had never sold any of it. Ownership and reverence for their native land was the priority for the South Pacific Island natives. He stated that the value of the Fijian culture was for the land itself. They did not worry about money as long as they had their land. This man told me that the rift of values would cause future problems in Fiji. This was hard to imagine in the peaceful world that we witnessed Fiji to be in the early 80's, but it has played out since then.

The Fijians were great teasers. They were child-like in their ability to incorporate humor and laughter into their every day jobs. They loved sports, especially beach volleyball. They would have games setting up teams, always *Fiji* verses *The World*. A combination of tourists from anywhere else would form a team against the Fijians. The native workers would set the other team up, acting the fool and clueless, especially if they had a bunch of jocks such as a Rugby team from Australia. They always won in a big, playful way after allowing the opposing team to get a few points to start out. If the opposition was weak, they held back, playing to the level of the lesser team. If the opposing team was cocky and rude, the Fijians would come back and slam them mercilessly. It was great fun to sit back and watch.

We met so many people in Fiji from all over the world. We made contact with many other back packers. The back pack scene became a sort of family of its own. Travelers would tell each other of where they had come from, giving information of where to stay, what to do, what to avoid. The conversation was always friendly, informational, and very carefree. Use the information or not. It was there to be had, no worries. Then there was the backdrop and the culture of the South Pacific to frame our overall experience. In Fiji, we learned to handle stress with the phrase, "Maybe tomorrow!"

We waited at a dock for a boat that would carry passengers from one island to another. The local people waited there also. Often the boat would not show up at all. The Fijians would just shrug their shoulders after waiting for hours, and say, "Maybe tomorrow. Maybe it will be here tomorrow." They would then give us a big, belly-type laugh, and walk back to return the next day to wait again. Every time that I am in an airport to this day, and my flight is inevitably delayed, I think of the simplicity of the Fijian outlook. I try to remember the peaceful feeling of that place and time, especially when I am in the middle of Atlanta airport, where my flights are always delayed, and the staff is less than helpful. I remind myself that it's not so bad to be forced to slow down, to have time to mull over a good book or a magazine article. I learned from the Fijians the inner peace of owning our reactions to the interruptions and frustrations of our scheduled lives.

New Zealand was the next stop for us. From the top of the North Island to the very bottom of the South Island, we covered the rich and varied landscape of this beautiful country. We did a lot of hitch—hiking in New Zealand. It was very acceptable, and we had the greatest experiences with families. Men and women, who were my parents' age, would offer to bring us home to meet their children; ordinary folk from ordinary places like Timaru and Paihia. They seemed fascinated that three young girls from Canada were spending a period of time traveling through New

Zealand. A single word to describe our New Zealand experience would be wholesome. It was a country that inspired us to know the land and the people intimately.

We hiked glaciers on the South Island. We trekked through tall forests and bathed in extremely hot geysers near Rotorua. We visited a sheep farm on the North Island, and we walked through bountiful English gardens in Christchurch. We crossed a very choppy body of water between the North Island and the South Island. If I remember right, it is where the Pacific Ocean meets the Tasman Sea. The strong, unforgiving currents reminded me of the ferry crossing from Newfoundland to Nova Scotia. In Wellington, we guided our way through the natural habitat of hundreds of seals bathing on the mammoth, grey rocks along the coast. In Paihia, at the top of the North Island, our gentle hostess treated us to "sconce and tea"; after a day of painting and laughing over our never ending nonsense. Her niece lent the three of us, Chris, Laurie, and I, clothes to go out in the evening. It was an event in itself, with our different heights and sizes. We could make an event out of anything in the moments of our journey.

The scenery of New Zealand was like a mini-version of Canada. I think our wanderings in Hawaii and Fiji had opened us to continue our communion with nature. The New Zealand coast line was rugged and pure, as steep cliffs were smashed clean by the fury of ocean waves. The land was full of contrasts from the rolling, green farmland of the North Island to the breathless fiords found in the interior of the South Island. We had a great adventure at the Lake Tekapo Youth Hostel. There was a group of us there from several countries. The weather was not cooperating to allow us to see the majesty of the fiords of Milford Sound. Instead, we had a wonderful time passing the couple of days with guitars, spoons, pots and pans; and a character of a local warden to entertain ourselves through our wait. And entertain ourselves, we did! We never did see Milford Sound. The weather never lifted. In the end, we bought a post card. We got pretty close. We accepted the outcome as we moved on to our next destination.

Young Kiwis, whom we had met in Fiji, were always happy to put us up, and to share their friends and their world with us. Many single adults in Auckland had room mates, as it was too expensive to rent individual apartments. Our peers complained of how high their taxes were, and that it was hard to get ahead on an individual salary. They did seem to live a more frugal lifestyle than we had known in the same generation in

Canada. As a people, they also tended to have some mixed feelings of their relationship with the British Commonwealth. I remember a shirt that someone was wearing. It said "Do your country a favor, punch a pomme today." I asked the young guy what a pomme was. He just laughed and said it was a slang term for a British citizen. I guess my father had some company scattered across the old Dominion status countries.

My take on New Zealand was that if you were from there, then there was nowhere else you would want to live. It was very beautiful, and the pace of life was relaxed in a familiar sort of way. Overall, the people appeared to be very practical, hard working, happy, and content in the boundaries of their dual-island nation. The distance to travel was quite small compared to the physical size of other countries. The climate was very temperate. The winters were mild enough that the locals did not have central heat in their homes. We were in New Zealand during the end of their winter, into their early spring months. We were usually freezing in New Zealand, even though the temperatures were nothing close to the frigid cold of our Canadian winters. The difference was in the interior temperatures.

The Kiwis would open the windows to air their houses out in the middle of the day when it was about 50-60 degrees Farenhieght. In the evening the temps would drop lower, and all they would do was close the windows. No heat!!!! We really had a hard time with that. The New Zealanders would laugh at our weak constitution, especially since we were Canadians. They got quite a kick out of the whole thing, but we were genuinely freezing a lot of the time. I guess it didn't help that we had spent the last three months in Hawaii and Fiji. Whatever hardy constitution we had from Canada had ebbed away with the hypnotizing lull of the tropical breezes. We definitely had thin blood relative to that of our hosts.

The native people of New Zealand are the Maoris. We spent a weekend with a gracious Maori lady and her family in Rotorua. The Maori values and culture reminded me of the Native American story in Canada and America verses the South Pacific Islander experience that I had witnessed in Fiji. The Maoris displayed a spiritual connection with nature, and their place in nature. They did not seem as carefree and content with daily living as the Fijians did. The Maoris appeared to be more restless and resentful, distrustful, and discontented with their lives and existence in mainstream New Zealand. That was my impression. The Maoris struggled to maintain their dignity and a sense of purpose in the modern democracy of New Zealand. I may be totally wrong, but I sensed that the Maori experience in New Zealand was a quiet but deep schism within the outwardly, steady, and complacent order of this spectacular country.

After the quaintness of New Zealand, we were primed for the crazy cosmopolitan lifestyle of Australia's cities. Cities such as Sydney and Melbourne pulse with a brash and confident aura of aliveness. Aussies work hard and they play hard. They revel in the sunshine of their days, and they seem to rush to soak up the world through all of their senses. If they smoke, then they smoke cigars. If they drink, then they will probably get drunk. If they play sports, then they play to win. If they party, then they will take it to the wee hours of the morning. If they are your friend, then they are your loyal friend for life. If they work, then they put in an honest shift. If they swim, then they break through the water like a submarine. That is my perception of Australia and its people—full force ahead, and no turning back.

Culturally, Australia was very liberal against our conservative, Canadian lifestyles. Sydney reminded me of a mix between Los Angeles and Paris, sort of a blend of the best and the worst of both worlds. At that time, I had never been to either Paris or Southern California. It was my impression of these cities that came to life for me in Sydney. All of the beaches were topless. They did not even sell the tops of two-piece bathing suits in department stores. There was a huge and very open gay population in Sydney. At that time in Canada, the gay scene was very quiet and under the radar of mainstream behavior. Not so in Sydney! Business men in fine, expensive suits would meet for lunch in downtown Sydney and display the sexuality of their relationships very openly. The night life was nonstop, 24 hours, and the raunchier the better. *The Rose* with Bet Midler had just come out. Men would line up for miles to get a ticket to see the movie. Bet Midler was adored by thousands of gay men in Sydney in the summer of 1980. I soaked it all in, quietly observing the vastness of the human condition, and growing within myself along the way.

Beyond the spirit of the Australian people are the expanses of space, which stretch for thousands of miles between the great cities of Australia. My memories of this vast land include the herds of emus that ran with my train across the Nullabor Plains, the majesty of Ayers Rock as it arises from the desert heat of the Outback, the beaches of the Gold Coast stretching from Brisbane to Cairns, and the white sands of the Indian Ocean that form the wide shores of Perth. We were constantly meeting kindred spirits in our travels. For example, Chris and I were quite impressed with a character who we met in the middle of the Outback, as we hiked Ayers Rock (no easy feat). Even though we were pretty fit in those days, we were huffing and puffing and sweating profusely, as we labored in the early morning heat to conquer the steep ascent.

Ayers Rock is one of those places that it's a hell of a journey to get there. If you are fool hardy enough to think that you have to see it in real life, then you might as well climb it; as that would be the point, wouldn't it. Never mind that it's hot as hell and the flies are thicker than the air you're breathing. Never mind all that. If you don't climb the beast of a rock, you could have saved yourself the bother; bought a post card, and checked it off your must-do list in Australia. The experience of getting there, driving through hundreds if not thousands of miles of dirt road, and of swallowing large, black flies with every breath after you survived the slow, hot, tedious trip would have been missed. Oh, the joy of the Australian Outback! I can compare it to going to Canada and thinking that you have to visit Goose Bay. The local Aussies thought we were as crazy to go to Ayers Rock in the middle of the summer as the average Newfoundlander would view the common sense factor of a tourist visiting Labrador in February.

A fragile looking gentleman was keeping pace with Chris and I as we dragged ourselves up the side of the bare rock, hanging on to chains to overcome gravity and our own slippery footing; trying to get the better of the sheer face of the monster. Our comrade appeared to be older than seventy, ancient to us. The longevity of his years was not evidenced in the spryness of his step, nor by the taut muscles of his upper arms. The old man's easy gait put us in our place as we made eye contact with each other. It was obvious that he was neither breathing as heavy nor sweating as profusely as we were. Anyway, we got to talking with him. His story was a great inspiration to us. His name was Jim and he was from Scotland. He told us his last name was *Chivas*. I always wondered about that one. Was he having a moment with us? He was a pretty regal fellow.

Jim Chivas from Scotland was traveling alone. He told us that he was on the 'tour of his lifetime'. He had bought a passage on *The QE 11* (cheapest berth based on occupancy of 4). He said he did not mind sharing a berth on the lowest level, which made the fare quite reasonable. He then used the single passage fare to travel for a year. Apparently, the majestic ship sailed the same route every three months or something like that. He would get off at the Port, travel all through the region, and get back on the great ship when she came back to Port the next time around. He would do this at every stop along the way. We were quite impressed with his nomadic spirit and his sense of adventure. He was a great story teller. His vigor and his humor touched us and made us smile. We were both locking away his story; storing the insight and the wisdom for the possibility of our future.

Australia is a very large country, both in geographical size and in the personality of its people. Later on, I would work with some Aussies in Saudi Arabia, and their raw spirit would be challenged. By April, 1980, Chris, Laurie, and I would go different directions. We had been together for almost a year in our adventure. We loved each other. The friendship had only gotten stronger. We never had any real problems. By Australia, we had begun to drift more independently. We would separate for a few days or weeks and meet up again, with the comfort of knowing that we had each other as back-up at any time. Laurie had started to work in a small hospital north of Sydney. She would actually stay on in Australia, work for a year or so, and then travel through Indonesia before returning to Canada. Chris had decided to go back to Edmonton to enter a brand new Ultrasound training program that the Royal Alexandra was starting. She was looking into her future direction from a career perspective. By April, I was ready to leave Australia. I had been there four months. I had traveled south to north, east to west. I had seen a lot of the country. But it was huge and the cities were high paced. I had connected more with the simplicity of the island life in Fiji. I decided to go back there for a few months before I returned to Canada. You had to love those open-ended airline tickets, even though they had cost us a fortune when we bought them.

Chris flew to Fiji with me, and we both went back to Beachcomber Island, our resort paradise for a week or so. Chris wanted to end her adventure with one last taste of "no worries, no hassles, and listen for the drums." I stayed on after she left with a desire to see more of the non-tourist places in Fiji. This was not that common or easy to do, as the outer islands were not serviced by passenger boats. They were not accessible for the most part. But, where there is a will there is a way. My first journey was to go to Suva which was on the other side of the main island from the airport. I traveled there in an open air bus. It was a long drive over the red, clay roads. My backpack would get covered in this rich red dust. They have the same rich, red-colored earth in Prince Edward Island. The local people on the bus were very friendly and they would laugh at the red covering layered onto our meager belongings.

I found my way to a guest house in Suva. A young girl, who was staying there over night, asked me if I would like to go to her village with her. She was about my age. She was studying in Suva, which was rare for females from the more remote villages. Anyway, I was thrilled for the invitation. We traveled by bus, and drove for hours and hours high up in the mountains to her village in the interior of Viti Levu. When we got there, it was an experience of experiences. They had no electricity. They lived as they had for hundreds of years. Most of the villagers did not speak English. The Fijians in Nadi, Lautoka, and Suva did speak English in their jobs. English was actually the official language in the cities from the days of the British Empire. Also, many American service men spent time in the port city of Suva during World War II. The hustle and bustle of Suva was a world removed from the native village life that I would come to know in Fiji.

Generations of native Fijians never left their villages. Many of them, especially the women, had never ventured into the cities. A few select members would take products to market on the weekends, but only a few. It was like walking into another time and place. The children would follow me everywhere. The girl who brought me there told me that I was the first white person who had ever been to her village. I am not sure if this was true, but I was definitely a novelty. The older women would touch my hair and talk quickly to each other. The same shade of red is seen in their people, and they were amazed that mine was the exact color. They brought out a baby for me to hold so that they could compare our hair color close up. The women were really amazed at the match of the shade of red. The children would eat raw sugar cane which grew everywhere. They grew their food, hunted, and fished. They had lots of natural fruit; coconuts, bananas, and papaya were plentiful.

The culture of the villages was that the men would often leave to work in the cities, mostly in tourism, and they would send supplies back to their village. Some of them had wives in the villages, and lived a separate life in the cities. A Fijian man told me that this was normal, and that the native women in the villages did not mind. ????? I never discussed his explanation with the village women, as I was a guest. I did not want to offend, and I did not know the boundaries of such a conversation. I was one to observe and to take the interaction and the experience where I was led. The women in the village did seem very happy and easy going in the simplicity of their days. I would delve into all of that a little more at my present age. But back then, I just thought, Oh really? I have always been one for the rest of the story, even if the query was only in my head. There are times to verbalize, and there are times to sit back and absorb; add the tidbits to your bag of tricks for future reference and pondering on a rainy day.

The Port of Suva was my next option to venture farther out into the lesser known and less traveled islands of the Lau Group. I met a young British couple. We were told that the only way to get to the outer islands was by cargo boat. We could go down to the Port to inquire if a Captain had any extra berths that they might open to passengers. I would not have been brave enough to do this on my own, but it was easy with the three of us. We did find an old, rusted cargo boat Captain who begrudgingly agreed to take us. His boat, *The Al Sekula*, was even more rusted than he was. He informed us that we would have no option but to go with the schedule of the boat, which could change depending on weather and cargo. He was trying to talk us out of the adventure. He did not want to be saddled with us, but he tolerated our request on his conditions. Of course, we said no problem. We were so grateful to have the opportunity. We had been warned that our chances were slim. It was unlikely that we would find someone willing to transport tourists. Lady Luck in the form of a grizzly cargo boat captain was on our side.

The first island that he took us to was Tavenuni. It is a beautiful island, no major cities, just a tiny town. We walked through the roads and explored the peaceful country side, as the crew loaded and unloaded the island's supplies. We were told that the main contact with the outside world in the past was through the interaction of the native Fijians with the American Peace Corps. They had served as teachers to young children in years gone by. The cargo boat also stopped at islands that were privately owned. Raymond Burr had an island in Fiji. I walked on the beaches of his private island. Forbes also owned an island in the Lau Chain, the island of Locaula. I remember that there were two bicycles sitting on the pier. It was unusual to see new, shiny bikes in Fiji, so they stuck out in my mind. The tennis court was also not the norm. The private islands usually had a Plantation, which was worked by the native people, and overseen by a foreman. They made their living off of the coconuts. The copra was the source of income for the people. The locals seemed happy and content. They told me that their rich and famous bosses only visited the islands several times a year, and that the people lived their lives as they would on any Fijian island in the outer groups. They were very hospitable to us, and surprised to see the three of us on their shores.

My last and best Fijian experience was in the Yasawa Island Group. This chain of atolls is beautiful. The movie, *Blue Lagoon,* was shot there. I know this because the movie crew left behind a generator. It was the only source of electricity on a single atoll among a group of small islands. This time I met a Polish lady. She was older than me, probably close to 50. She was traveling by herself, and she also wanted to get into the outer islands. The Yasawa Chain did not have any cargo boats that we could solicit. A local person told us to go to the wharf on Saturdays, when the outer island boats came in with their market goods. Perhaps, we could find a captain willing to take us back to an island village for a price. We were willing to try anything.

After several unsuccessful attempts, we were directed to a small boat (no bigger than a fishing dory in Newfoundland). A large, friendly looking man was unloading fruit and vegetables with two younger guys. We introduced ourselves. He spoke English. He listened. He shook his head at first, sort of to himself, as he appeared to be contemplating the whole thing. We waited quietly; pleading with our eyes for a positive outcome. He finally agreed to take us with him. He told us to come back at the end of the day, to buy some groceries to contribute to the village as a gift. He said that we would have to stay the week, as they only come back and forth to market on Saturdays. We were so excited and happy. We quickly skirted off to buy some supplies; canned food for the women, candy for the kids, and small packets of cigarettes for the men. These were our peace offerings, our gestures of gratitude.

It took us many hours to reach the Yasawa Group in that small boat. I look back on that now. We were in the middle of the Pacific Ocean in a very small boat with no life jackets. I guess not that it would have mattered. There were plenty of sharks in those waters. And that was before the word "tsunami" tarnished any thought of such an adventure for me in the present. But here we were; an older Polish women and a young Canadian girl who hardly knew each other; heading out to an unknown atoll on a small boat with a crew of three—only one who spoke English. It sounds crazy and irresponsible, but it was one of the most amazing experiences of my life. The calmness of the ocean and the beauty of that boat trip are impossible to describe in mere words. We would skim our hands through the crystal blue water as the boat lazily puttered along. We had a great conversation with the Captain. He would translate for the younger guys. We all asked questions, laughed at each others' comments and responses, and talked easily back and forth throughout the travel. No worries! Actually, the Captain was very educated, and he was true to his word, except for one minor detail. He was not taking us to his atoll.

He said the women of his village would not be happy if he brought us there. He was really serious and respectful of the culture of his village about that. He did not tell us this minor fact until we were many hours and miles from the shores of Lautoka. There was no turning back. However, he had a hand written letter of introduction (as he called it) ready for us to hand to a lady on a neighboring atoll. He explained to us that she used to run a boarding house in Suva during World War II; that she was very used to Americans and tourists, and he knew that she would not mind. Apparently, her family owned this island. There was no village on it—just her family members; all of whom had private homes on the island. He said that we should pay her something. We had already expected to pay his village for their hospitality. He would not take any money from us; for getting us thus far, or for his part in all of this. He had a twinkle in his eye. He was enjoying our reaction, and he was proud that he had arranged such an adventure for us.

We were quite taken aback when we arrived at the atoll. A coral reef would not let his boat go all the way to shore. He had one of the young guys carry our grocery bags and our back packs, and he bid us a good visit. He stayed with the boat. We pleaded with him to come with us; to explain our presence. He told us not to worry. We had his hand written "letter of introduction", which he had meticulously crafted and carefully folded. He assured us that the letter was adequate. It was all that we would need. He would be back for us the next Saturday. He adamantly stated that we would be very welcome here. He was very kind and almost fatherly to us. It was sort of like sending your kids off to college. We wanted to debark, but the hesitation and initial fear were holding us back. I guess it was a little late for us to be fearful.

The young man left us on the shore after he had taken us to a narrow path. They waved good-bye to us. We stood on the beach of the atoll, letter in hand, and not a person in sight. We looked at each other with eyes that said, "Holy shit!" We did not even know each other that well, but each of us was very grateful to have the other one's company. It's not so bad when there are two of you. At least there was small comfort in that. And, she was older than me. I was young, idealistic, and stupid. Gosh only knows what was racing through her mind. She never said much. She just kind of muttered under her breath, shook her head, and pointed up the path. We looked back for one last look. Perhaps, he was joking and he would be back. But he was waving largely, smiling, as his boat headed away from us. He yelled out, "Just ask for Auntie Lucy. Everyone calls her Auntie Lucy." His voice and his laughter faded as the distance lengthened between us.

We took a deep breath, looked at each other, and tenderly started up the path. After just a short distance, we rounded a bend to see an amazing sight in that time and place. All of the women in Fiji wore very traditional long cotton skirts or dresses; beautiful batik patterns and colorful cottons. Even in the cities in their jobs, the working women dressed very traditional. It was quite charming. So, we were shocked to see an older lady with grey-white hair, sitting on a small stool, puffing on a corn cob pipe, peeling kasava, dressed in cut-off khaki shorts (very short), a faded cotton shirt with the sleeves cut out, a worn baseball hat turned to the side, barefoot, and leathered. She looked up at us, and without missing a beat she said, "What are you standing there staring at. Come over and lay those heavy bags down. Goodness gracious, what do you have in those bags anyway?" That was it. She was not at all fazed to see two strangers on her island path, appearing out of nowhere. We gave her the letter, which she skimmed pretty fast. She laughed at what the Captain had written. She said he was a character. We had already figured that out. Gosh only knows what he had written about us. It didn't matter. Auntie Lucy was a treasure. Captain Bokini of a small atoll in the Yasawa Group really had done right by us.

The Polish lady and I stayed the week with Auntie Lucy. Our gracious host and I really connected; it was like we had known each other our entire lives. Her name was Lucy Doughty. She was probably mid-late 70. I was 22. It did not matter. We fit together like a glove and mitt. I returned to Auntie Lucy's island and stayed another two weeks with her before I left Fiji. I had never grown up with any grandparents. Both of my mother's parents had died before I was born. My father's father had passed when I was a child. I never knew him. My family visited him several times. He had some stage of dementia, and I was a little afraid of him as a child. My mother always talked about what a "hard man" he was, even when he was younger. My father's mother had died when he was young. I did have a step grand-mother. She was very nice and kind, but we lived far away from them. Auntie Lucy never had any children. I think that she and I needed each other in a very human, comfortable way.

Sharon Richardson

I sort of gained part of my soul in Fiji on this island paradise with Auntie Lucy. She was so wise and she had this great sense of humor. She really had run a bar in Suva during World War II. She had the greatest stories. She could color her vocabulary in a very non-offensive way. She was very apt at the use of fitting descriptors to nail home a tale or two. Her home was a quaint cabin with three bedrooms. She took care of her elderly sister who was well over 80 years old. Her sister, Stella, did not speak English nor was she very communicative. Auntie Lucy tended to her and loved her. They appeared to have a very simple and peaceful existence. I think Auntie Lucy was as thrilled for our company as much as we were grateful for hers. The atoll was privately owned by her family, which consisted of an older brother, the sister, and herself. Her brother had a son, who lived there with a young wife. They all lived in different areas on the atoll. The only dwelling that I ever saw was Auntie Lucy's. The other family members would come over to visit and talk quite often, but they always came to us.

Auntie Lucy was the only one who had led such a colorful and non-traditional life. She loved people. She charged us $2 / night to stay there. She would not take any more. When I went back the second time, she told me that I was not to pay her. By then, I was her personal guest and we were friends. Payment would be an insult to her. I bought as much groceries as I could carry. She laughed at that. The window of my bedroom opened up to the most picture perfect, red-orange sunrises. You could see the blue of the ocean and the white of the beach against the crimson sky peeking through the palm trees around her cabin home. A most breath taking view of paradise was my alarm clock! That and we went to bed very early as there was no electricity.

I fell so easily and completely into the island lifestyle. Fresh fish, rice, flour, kasava, and fruit were the main stay of the diet. Auntie Lucy would pick lemon grass. She made the best tea that I have ever tasted from that lemon grass. We had her delicious tea with fresh, home-baked rolls, and tree-picked papaya for breakfast every morning. I would walk for miles on the beach, circling the atoll. In the early mornings, I would make my way to a beautiful lagoon where I would hang out by myself for hours at a time. I would read, swim in the small lagoon, and just laze in the spirituality of the place. By late morning, I would stroll back and join the family members as they worked the copra. That was their only source of income. They gathered the coconuts, dried them, scraped the meat from the inside, and discarded the husks in a huge pile for market. The Fijians harvested every part of the coconut. This was hard work, but it was paced in the easy pulse of a tropical island.

We would sit in circles with these powerful radios, listening to the news of the world, laughing and talking, as we scraped the coconut shells. Men and women, young and old; everyone sat together, stripping the bountiful supply of coconuts as the conversation and the laughter naturally flowed. The afternoons would pass easily in the lull of our work and our comrade. A simple meal of fresh fish that had been speared in the lagoon by Auntie Lucy's nephew was cooked in a variety of different spices and sauces. Of course, there was a coconut sauce for the fish. Fresh meat was scarce and considered a rarity; a real, luxury item. Every now and then, someone went to market on Saturday and obtained a single meal of meat. But for the most part, the taste and the smell of meat was only a savory dream on their tongues, and a sweet but desired memory in their minds. They would have discussions of their longing for meat; laughing at themselves in their wish for more of it, and knowing that the reality was a world away from their simple island lifestyle. But, it was fun talking about it! The Fijians have a great ability to laugh at themselves and their needs.

In all of my travel that year, it was bitter sweet to say good-bye to Auntie Lucy. I knew from her age that I would probably never see her again. She knew that also. Neither of us spoke this aloud. Neither she nor I cried. We were not about that. I think we both knew that our experience together would stay in our hearts for ever. There was no need to try and put it into words. She actually offered to sell me some of her land for $2000. I am sure that was quite the bargain. The Fijians very rarely sell their land, so her generous offer will always be locked deep in the sanctuary of my soul. Her gift for the taking was not about the money. It was a gesture of trust and love. I felt overwhelmed and humbled by the power of her quiet words to me; an outward expression of kinship and acceptance. We both knew where the decision was coming from.

Even if I could afford it; the reality of the geography! I was neither a famous actress nor a millionaire. I couldn't jet back there on a whim. I rationalized these self-arguments at the time. I did know that I could come up with the money when I got back to reality in my near future. Aunt Lucy said that she knew I did not have the money in the moment; to think about it, and to know it was there for me. She was so kind and wise. We would tuck each other away forever; the connection of two spirits blended into one; young and old; North Atlantic and South Pacific;

resilient islander and resilient islander. That was us, plain and simple. The year was winding down. I was heading home to work and to make my way. On reflection, it was not the cost but my own limitations. As the years have passed, I have wondered about my choice, the ceiling that I imposed on a possibility. I often think of going back to Fiji, but can I ever match my memory of my journey there. I wonder if it's better to leave some experiences in the quiet reaches of your soul; there to guide you and to anchor you without marring the depth of the meaning from the distance and the strength of the memory. But then again, perhaps one day, maybe tomorrow!

It is the fall of 1981, and I am living in Victoria, the capitol of British Columbia. I have been back in Canada a little over a year from my South Pacific adventure. I am working at the Royal Jubilee Hospital. It has been a little hard to settle back into a routine, but I am in a good place mentally. I love Victoria. It suits me much better than Edmonton. I missed the smell of the ocean in Edmonton. The land was too barren. I did not want to live there again. I would have stayed in St. John's when I retuned in June of 1980, but I could not find a full-time job there after the summer hiring season. I wanted to stay home for a while, as I had not been home for Christmas for the past two years. Instead, I left Newfoundland in September. I could not let myself collect unemployment insurance after my summer job. My independent nature and my pride would not allow that. This time I left because I could not find employment. My wandering ways were catching up with me; that, and the reality of the economy of Newfoundland. Many of my friends from Corner Brook were scattered across Canada. I remember a doctor who I worked with that summer remarking that Newfoundland was losing its best resources; its young people, as many of my generation left the province to find work else where.

Perhaps, it was time to settle down. I was ready for that and I loved Victoria. To this day, I think Victoria is the prettiest city that I have ever lived in. When I got hired on at the Royal Jubilee, I was very content in Victoria and with my life. I loved the Pacific Northwest, the San Juan Islands, and the parks and the harbor of downtown Victoria. I would jog for miles along James Bay when I got off work, and I was very much at ease in the pace and the climate of Vancouver Island. It was strange because I had not lived in Victoria long, and I did not really know a lot of people. I was content with myself, not searching for whatever it was that I had left Newfoundland to find a few years earlier. I had always been an outwardly happy enough kid growing up, going with the flow, but I realized that I was always restless on the inside. I was able to understand that, accept it, and to find a sense of peace with my inner stirrings after Australia.

It happened on a remote beach, about halfway between Brisbane and Cairns. I was camping at this beach. I had met an Australian group who were also camping there. They had invited me to join them. I was in a solitude mood that night, and as I sat away from them, watching the sunset on the isolated beach, I had this overwhelming sense of inner peace. I can feel it to this day. It was almost as if God had laid a hand on my shoulder, reaching out of the sky, across the endless expanse of empty beach and ocean to say be still, be free to be you, be at peace to wander and to quest. At the time, I had a conscious awareness that I did not need to keep searching for that "meaning in life". It was like the prism of my mind was finally at peace with the ebb and flow of my internal estuary. The salt water and the fresh water had stopped swirling around each other. The tide of my soul was calmer, more reflective, less conflicted by my restlessness. I guess I had become okay with the puzzle of me.

I always wanted to see new places, and experience new things because I had this sense that life would pass me by in a mundane existence. Then, that evening in Australia, sitting by myself on the wide, endless merge of white sand and blue water, a calm spirituality washed over me that brought me inner peace. I don't know from where or why, but I felt it strongly, and I have been more or less content with myself ever since. I think that people who are never happy or who are always searching for something else never experience that peace or awareness within themselves. On that beach, I came to know that I would honor my nomadic soul by accepting it rather than seeing it as something that I had to solve. I came to know that my need or inner drive is in the quest itself. I would always have a curiosity for deeper knowledge and new experiences. I came to be okay with me.

So, here I was, content and wiser in Victoria. I had a game plan also. The only thing I hated about my life was coming back to Canada flat broke. I had spent every cent of my sacred $10, 000. I had saved that amount in one year, and I could do it again, but the discipline of it all. I had to start from scratch. I promised myself that I would never let myself be in such a financial hole again. My new priority was to save enough to get myself enrolled in the University of British Columbia and to eventually apply for Law School. I planned to speak to my director at the hospital about working full-time hours with weekend and evening shifts, so that I could free my days up to enroll in classes. I was very content with this plan. I loved the city, and I could happily balance study and work with jogs along the beach, and strolls through the city parks and downtown shops.

Does fate intersect with freedom of choice? Are our lives predestined, within the parameters of our decisions and our actions? We often had these discussions in religion classes with the nuns when I was growing up. The good sisters were always drilling into us the responsibility of our actions against the mystery of faith and destiny. Looking back on the fall of 1981, I am not sure of the balance of free choice and fate, but something outside of my plan unfolded to alter my life direction. A girl, who I worked with and who I did not know very well, asked me to go with her the next weekend to a seminar in the lobby of a Vancouver hotel. She had an ad from the paper, recruiting medical workers to seek out information regarding working in Saudi Arabia.

I told her that I had no interest in working there. I did not know a lot about Saudi Arabia, except that I had no desire to travel there. I had read the biographies of Golda Meir and Moshe Dayan, and I always had a fascination with the State of Israel. I read a lot of Leon Uris back then. I very much admired the tenacity and the will of the Jewish people. My father had always followed the history of Israel, the British fiasco after World War II, statehood in 1948, the Six Day War, the conflict with Egypt in 1972, the chaos of Beirut and Lebanon, and the US hostages in Iran. He was always one to verbally explore and intimately know current events. I was one to listen; to absorb it like a sponge. I had no desire to go to the Mid-East. She pleaded with me to go to the information seminar with her. I thought, "Why not?" I liked the idea of taking the ferry to Vancouver on a Saturday. I didn't know the city of Vancouver that well, but I wanted to. Her request presented as an opportunity to explore Vancouver more than anything else. Perhaps we would see some whales splashing around on the trip over.

I guess the rest is history. The recruiter from Whittaker Corporation offered me a job and not my friend. I turned it down. Whittaker wanted employees to sign a two-year contract. From the day of the seminar, over a course of a couple of weeks, the guy contacted me back and forth. He was very knowledgeable about Saudi Arabia, very professional, and he negotiated with me. On my part, the money thing was more of a burden than I had anticipated. It was harder to save ahead for college in the short term. I was impatient to manage the expense of full-time college against supporting myself. I had bought a new car. I needed it to work shifts. Also, I wanted to rent a place of my own. I had a room mate, but I felt myself moving in my own direction. I really wanted to enroll in classes, and I wanted the freedom of my own space to pursue my dreams. The most recent Whittaker offer was very tempting and offered a short-term solution to my dilemma.

He offered me a one-year contract. He explained that Whittaker ran four hospitals in different cities in Saudi Arabia on Royal Saudi Air Bases. He recommended employment in the hospitals in Tabuk or Khamis Mushayt because of the climate. He told me that the heat in Jeddah and Riyahd were unbearable. I weighed it all out. I loved Victoria and I did not want to leave. But, I also wanted very much to enroll in the university, and it had not been as easy as I had hoped from a financial perspective. My decision was that it did not matter how restrictive life would be in Saudi Arabia. I did know that women were not allowed to drive there, and that they did not have as many rights as men.

I thought I could handle anything for one year. I would read books in my free time, work, and save as much as possible to finance my goal. My plan was to return to Victoria in one year, get my job back at the Royal Jubilee, and have saved a cushion to get me started on my journey to Law School. In the end, the decision was easy, and I was at peace with it. Besides, the Whittaker people sent me a ticket. Hotel reservations and airport transfers in Arlington, VA were arranged. I was to meet up with a group, with whom I would travel to Saudi Arabia. My girl friends and I had been totally responsible for ourselves during our South Pacific adventure. The actual journey to the Mid-East did not frighten me at all, once I had made the commitment to go. Logistically, it was all relatively painless and simple from my end.

My first experience with Americans in a group was traveling with a gaggle of about fifteen middle-aged women from Arlington, Virginia to Jeddah, Saudi Arabia. They were all older and louder than me. I was so conscious of the noise of them. I was embarrassed and a little annoyed to be in their midst. The women had spent several days at the Marriott Key Bridge prior to my arrival from Vancouver. I was the only Canadian in the bunch, and the only person less than forty. I must have gotten added on to the group at the last minute. The Americans already had gotten to know each other. They had three days of orientation before leaving Arlington. They were having a ball, and they were letting everyone know it, the louder the better.

I landed late in the evening after flying all day to get there. I think I was routed from Victoria to Vancouver to Chicago to Washington with a plane change at every airport. I am not sure Dulles or Reagan. I did not get in until the evening, and we had to leave very early in the morning to connect with a short flight from Washington to New York. We then had a direct flight from New York to Jeddah with Air Saudia, sixteen hours non-stop on that leg of my journey. I did not even get a meal in Arlington, and I really had no time to meet any of my fellow travelers. I had to listen to this trail of women going on and on about the food at the hotel over the course of their three-day stay, and their endless loud chit-chat. I was so tired from the back to back flights that it really did not matter. I just wished that they would shut up, and stop drawing so much attention to our group. We really stood out on the Air Saudia flight, or at least I thought we did.

I sat away from my group on the large plane for our long haul across time zones and calendar days, one of those airbus type planes with about ten seats across the middle, and a row on each side with about five seats each .I guess someone was looking out for me, as I felt quite a relief when my boarding pass directed me to a row away from the gaggle of squawking geese. An attractive, well-dressed, sophisticated looking, young woman did sit in the seat next to me. The flight was long, so we had several conversations over the course of our journey. She was a Saudi national. She told me that she had lived and worked in Washington for several years with her husband, who was a business man. He was not traveling with her. I have since learned how unusual it was for her to be traveling without her husband, but at the time, I thought nothing of it. She was articulate, charming, and appeared very well-educated. Before we landed in Jeddah, she went into the bathroom of the plane, and came out covered from head to toe in a black abaya. She enlightened me with the word for the traditional and mandatory public dress of Saudi women.

This beautiful, graceful lady had disappeared behind a cascading shroud of secrecy and darkness. She told me that this was the custom in her country, and that she was quite comfortable to have to cover herself with the black abaya before she landed. She said it made her feel safe and she liked it. I am sure she could read the puzzled expression on my face. I told her that I could understand all of this if she had never known anything else, but she had lived for several years in a modern, American city. And, she also appeared to me to be very comfortable and confident in her chic, fashionable clothes prior to our descent into Jeddah.

She said she knew that it was hard for me to understand, but that she was legitimately comfortable with the different roles she could lead in America and in Saudi Arabia. We landed in Jeddah and bid each other a fond good-bye before we departed the plane. She was excited to see her sisters. I was just very tired, and I wanted to find my hotel room. I had no idea that this would be the only time that I would have the luxury of having a real conversation with a Saudi woman. In the following sixteen months of living and working in Saudi Arabia, I would never have this opportunity again. I was about to step off of that plane into the most unbearable heat that I had ever known, and into a world that challenged every moral value that I knew to be my truth.

Chapter 3

SAUDI ARABIA

THE HEAT COULD BE SEEN rising in waves from the desert sand and across the tarmac as we entered the terminal. Jeddah has a combination of humidity and heat that permeates through every ounce of your being, straining your lungs, and smothering your chest cavity. It is like walking into a sauna, except it's all around you in the air you breathe, not concentrated nor restricted in a controlled space from which you can escape. The airport was ultra modern and busy. Two nurses from Australia joined us in Jeddah airport. They had landed just ahead of us, and they were added to our group. Immediately, I gravitated to them. They were older than me, very kind and open with a quiet dignity that I was immediately drawn to. We quickly formed a trio within the larger group. In the airport, there was a sea of crisp white robes and elaborate head gear on the men, and always the black abaya on the women. You could tell class and status by the material in the abaya, and the elaborate details of the face veil, but the color was always plain black, no trim nor accent color. Most Westerners will spend years in Saudi Arabia and never see a Saudi woman's face, except her eyes. On TV news from the Mid-East, we often see women in Iraq or the West Bank with anguished or angry expressions on their faces. This would never be allowed in Saudi Arabia. To view a Saudi women's face is *harraam* (forbidden) and the law is totally and strictly enforced.

As we arrived at our hotel in Jeddah, there was a very large, emerald green Rolls Royce parked immediately in front of the main entrance. I don't remember the name of the hotel, but it was new, modern, and first class. By then, I had punched in over twenty-five hours of flying time and gotten probably five hours of sleep in Arlington between the flights from Victoria to Virginia and then from Arlington to Jeddah. The hotel details remain fuzzy. But, I have a vivid memory of the shiny, green hugeness of the Rolls Royce, with the hot sun bouncing unchecked off the chrome and the metal. I had never seen a Rolls Royce before. This one was huge. Our limousine driver told us that the glitzy monstrosity of a car belonged to Idi Amin, and that he occupied a suite in the hotel. Well, I about fell out of my seat, the *Butcher of Uganda*. I had read the book, *Idi Amin, Dada*, which described in graphic horror the atrocities of his dictatorship in Uganda. I could not believe that Idi Amin was living the life of royalty here in Jeddah, sleeping in the same hotel that I would be staying in. I needed a reality check. I remember clearly the surreal feeling of that moment. It was like I had to step back and view the event of the shiny green Rolls Royce in front of me through some sort of filter, like watching a movie, but this was no movie. The only filter that I had at that moment was overwhelming jet lag.

I was told that Idi Amin was granted a pardon and asylum in Saudi Arabia by King Fahd because he was a Moslem brother. This made no sense to me. What did that have to do with right and wrong? Pardoning Idi Amin was like pardoning Hitler in my mind. This was my introduction to the many rationalizations that do not make sense to the Western mind, as we try to integrate our schemas of thinking with that of the Arab mind. Idi Amin was foreshadowing for the clash of cultural values and the hypocrisy of social justice that I would encounter in the Kingdom of Saudi Arabia. Over the next several days, my skin crawled every time I walked by the metal obscenity of the emerald green Rolls Royce, which remained in front of the hotel doors. One time, I made eye contact with a very overweight, dark-skinned man as he got in the elevator. He was dressed in a suit; not your typical, Saudi dress. I quickly looked away as I feared that it might have been him. I think I felt a little like Dorothy, plucked out of Kansas, and landing in the middle of OZ, which is a pretty good metaphor for the Arabian Desert Kingdom. And I guess in a way the streets of Saudi Arabia are paved with the spoils of gold, black gold that is; or at the very least, lined with gold suugs. I would need more than a pair of shiny red slippers to navigate the lay of the land here, both literally and figuratively.

My group would spend several days in Jeddah for orientation. I slept through most of the sessions due to jet lag. I could not sleep at night and I could not keep my eyes open in the middle of the day. We were given hand outs of the rules and expectations of conduct. We were to honor the traditions and laws of Saudi Arabia, as would be expected of a visitor to any country. That is why I am so amazed that Americans and

Canadians often bend their own cultural norms beyond what is necessary for foreign guests and immigrants. I think each country's customs
should be honored in a bi-directional relationship. In the West, we can
be overly accommodating, blurring the lines of appropriate behavior as
the host country. When in Rome...

The human resource people of Whittaker Corporation explained our
benefits as well as the rules. We would be allowed approximately forty
days of leave/year. Do the math. We got two months of paid leave. We
would also earn a stipend called the R&R by those in the know, or the
Rest and Recuperation benefit. That meant that we would be paid a bonus of $1000 after five months of employment to use in a manner of
our choice. The stipend required us to rest from the toils of daily labor
for at least a week every five months. To receive the R & R payment, an
employee had to take five days leave. Employees did not have to leave the
country during this time, but they did have to burn up a minimum of five
days off. At the anniversary of the employee's hire, the company would
pay the employee a cash amount equivalent to round—trip economy fare
from the post of assignment to the point of hire. For me, the dollar value
of the fly miles would add up between Khamis Mushayt and Victoria. I
would be paid every two weeks in US dollars, which added a little more
to my Canadian bank account in the exchange. I thought, so far, so good.
I can do this. My college tuition fund looked more promising, and the
labor requirements were a walk in the park. Two months of leave a year!
I thought I could handle that. Employees would also be given Arabic
language instruction at their site. We were paid in Saudi Riyals, SR 1,200
per year for lessons. I learned enough words to communicate basic instructions to patients. We were compensated for our honest attempts at
communication. Fluency was not a factor.

The employee benefits were to be offset by the rules of conduct. For
every yin, there is a yang. Rather than attempting to summarize the
Ministry of Defense and Aviation's rules for adult conduct, I have written
them here verbatim. I would not want to lose any meaning or details in a
narrative summary. I had to sign the following rules prior to my hire, and
they were explained and reviewed in depth at the orientation in Jeddah.
I listened. I absorbed. I contemplated. I concluded. I would not have a
problem. I would keep my nose clean, do my job, read in my spare time,
and save. The Presentation Sisters had prepared me well to be an ambassador of compliancy in following similar rules throughout my adolescent
and teenage years under their tutelage. Never mind that working, con-

senting adults from all across the globe were expected to follow the rules of a Catholic school girl in uniform.

Regulations Governing the Conduct of Hospital Employees at Khamis Mushayt and Tabuk Medical Services Department Ministry of Defense and Aviation

All personnel employed at Whittaker Corp. who are not Saudi Arabian Nationals, are reminded that as visitors to the Kingdom of Saudi Arabia neither Whittaker nor the diplomatic representatives of the country in which any employee holds citizenship are able to intervene on behalf of the employee in the due process of the enforcement of the laws of the Kingdom.

All employees are reminded that the following regulations governing conduct of Whittaker employees are hereby issued by the Ministry of Defense and Aviation, Medical Services Department, to insure that all Whittaker employees conduct themselves in a manner which is compatible with the laws, customs, and traditions of the Kingdom:

1. *The manufacture or possession of any alcoholic beverages is strictly forbidden.*
2. *Mixing of unmarried men and women in housing is forbidden.*
3. *Females will only leave the base and return to the base when accompanied by an authorized individual or by Whitaker furnished transportation.*
4. *During periods of darkness females should not venture beyond the housing/hospital area unaccompanied.*
5. *A Whittaker employed gateman will be posted at the entrance to the single female apartments to insure the safety of female personnel.*
6. *If a single female desires to have a single member of the opposite sex visit her quarters, there must always be a married couple present. Visits to female single quarters by males will not otherwise be allowed.*
7. *Single females are not permitted to visit the single male quarters unless accompanied at all times by a married couple.*
8. *Single male and female personnel may visit married couples or families in the family quarters.*
9. *Married quarters will be occupied by married physicians and other senior staff members whose spouse is residing at the base. Exceptions to this will require joint approval by the Director General of M.S.D., and the Whittaker Project Manager.*

10. *If married quarters are assigned to be shared by two or more single physicians or senior staff members of the same sex, single visitors of the opposite sex will not be permitted unless accompanied at all times by a married couple.*

11. *Any housing quarters that may be temporarily vacant due to the absence of the assigned "tenants" will not be occupied by anyone else unless written permission is granted by the "tenant" and approved by the Hospital Liaison Officer.*

12. *All visitors to the military base are subject to base security regulations established by the respective Base or Area Commanders.*

Twenty-five years later, my take on all of this can be expressed in, **"o9endak ishal?",** translated, **"Do you have diarrhea?"** At the time, I focused on the end game.

In just a few days, we left the concrete vastness of Jeddah behind, and boarded a small plane to take us to Abha, the closest town and airport to the Whittaker Hospital in Khamis Mushayt. The women from our Jeddah group had been dispersed between the hospitals of Jeddah, Riyadh, Tabuk, and Khamis Mushayt. There were only a few of us who were headed to the mountains of the Asir Region, which stretches south from Taif to Yemen, bordered by the Red Sea on one side of the mountain chain and vast reaches of inhospitable desert on the other. Khamis Mushayt was south of Abha, about twenty miles from the Yemen border. My two Australian friends were also employed at Khamis Mushayt. I said a silent Hail Mary of thanks on that one.

Any prayers would be silent and invisible for the next sixteen months. I publicly obeyed the Shariah Laws of the Kingdom. We all did. It is illegal for anyone to outwardly display any form of Christian worship, Jewish worship, or even traditional Islam worship in Saudi Arabia. It is also illegal to practice Christian worship in the privacy of your home. Any form of religion other than the Wahhabi interpretation of Islam is forbidden in the Kingdom. Discretion would rule as laws were complied with externally. Internal matters of the heart and the soul did prevail, and were called on many times to get us through the cultural shock of living in Saudi Arabia. For example, my coworkers and I silently asked for forgiveness in breaking the spirit of the Shariah Laws of the Kingdom when we washed down dry pieces of home-made bread with dry, home-made wine in the privacy of a Scottish doctor's home on Easter Sunday and Christmas Day. There was honor and a proud dignity in the simple

Communion of our Lay Services, and in the passive aggressive satisfaction that we derived from daring to perform our heartfelt reflection behind closed doors.

My first day in Khamis Mushayt remains a blur of being driven from the airport to the base, a distance of perhaps thirty miles or so, being shown the hospital, and being assigned an apartment. It was apparent that the set-up was very similar to that of a university campus; college apartments, tight with a postage stamp of a kitchen, and very basic quarters relative to living space, bedroom, and bathroom. But, it was more than fine for me. We did not have to pay any stipend at all for these apartments, and electricity and water were free. The only thing that we needed to spend our paychecks on was food. I had no issue with my accommodations. It was actually better than I expected. I passed many open doors as I walked along the path to my apartment. Young women, many close to my own age, would smile or shout a warm welcome in a variety of accents from every corner of the globe. The sun was beginning to shine through the fog of the past few days.

Geographically, the area was more appealing than that of Jeddah. There was a stir of freshness in the air. The stifling heat of the desert had dissipated to a bearable level in this mountainous region. Mountains are all relative. It was not the Canadian Rockies, but the elevations provided a stark beauty of plateau type scenery, polished boulders dotted with sparse green weeds, and some areas of wild flowers. Everything else was flat and barren, dusty and empty. The Asir Mountain Region did bring needed relief from the oppressive, humid heat of Jeddah, and the overwhelming dry heat of Riyadh. Whittaker Corporation had provided a pool, a library, and a work-out room in the recreation center of our housing complex, which was a very short walk from my apartment. The uneasiness of my Idi Amin introduction to Saudi Arabia was lessened with every bright smile and friendly greeting that I encountered on my first day.

The polarity of worlds that existed for Westerners employed in the Kingdom of Saudi Arabia was only beginning to unravel itself for me, one thread at a time, one day at a time, one experience at a time—until it became forever entangled and choked within a tight ball of weak connections, both positive and negative. It was as if the electrons of an atom had become unstable, erratically firing at each other, while trying to come together at the same time. I don't remember the intricacies of nuclear fission, but I think my understanding of electrochemical imbalance begins to explain the clash of cultures that Westerners encountered on a daily basis in the Kingdom in the spring of 1982. I think the unbridled energy of opposing forces that I witnessed and sensed in this mountainous, tribal area of Saudi Arabia exploded on the world stage on 9/11. Since then, tremors and after shocks boil and ferment under a very thin and brittle layer of misunderstanding, half-truths, and hypocrisy, constantly bubbling over and clashing in the utter chaos of the present decade.

I believe that the magnitude of the current world crisis mirrors the frustrations of individual people of good will, who know personal truths very differently. When I say people of good will, I am not talking about terrorists. I am talking about your average Mid-East citizen. No single country or culture has the monopoly on truth. As citizens of nation states, we have all been taught relevant truths in a historical context across generations. Then, within the boundaries of our neighborhoods and homes, and through our life experiences, we refine what we know and what we have been taught.

In Saudi Arabia, my personal knowledge was affronted in a way that I had never prior experienced. It is hard to articulate my cognitive assimilation of this period of my life. However, I feel that I must attempt to voice my humble understanding of the clash of cultures that appears to be rolling out of control, with no end in sight. We keep trying to stop the train from pummeling off the tracks, yet we do not know where to find the brakes, let alone how to apply them. It's as if every action causes a reaction that pits us further and further into a bottomless, black hole that threatens to swallow us deeper and deeper into the oblivion of its cavity.

The most unanticipated benefit of my employment with Whittaker Corporation would be the genuine fun and comrade of working with a cross-section of middle class, hospital employees, who came together from across the globe as the staff of a relatively small hospital on a remote Saudi Air Base in Khamis Mushayt. The sad reality would be that this wonderful mix of cultures and friendship would remain separate, and forbidden from interacting socially with the people of our host country. We lived and worked within walled compounds, not to keep the Arabs out, but to keep us from mixing with and contaminating the Saudi nationals with our Western ways and beliefs. The Saudis were our patients. A very narrow and professional relationship was as close as we were permitted to get to communicating with the citizens of Saudi Arabia.

I remember a single incident when I had a brief, personal connection with a female patient. Our short exchange remains imprinted in my memory as if it was yesterday. I was on call in the middle of the night. I was paged by Labor & Delivery to do a Pelvimetry on a young mother. A Pelvimetry is simply a bi-directional X-Ray of the woman's abdomen; done in such a way that doctors can measure the size of the baby's head against the size of the pelvic outlet to see if a C-Section is needed to deliver the baby safely. It is usually done after a long and difficult labor. These exams have become obsolete after the advances of Ultrasound, but in 1982, they were still fairly common.

Anyway, a nurse from Labor & Delivery had accompanied the Saudi girl to X-Ray. There was only the three of us around in the emptiness of the middle of the night. I had to turn lights on as we entered the X-Ray Department and the Diagnostic room. The nurse and I said a few words. The patient was quiet and compliant, turning as we asked her to, and holding her breath when instructed. She looked away to the side, which was a common response to interactions between Saudi women and the foreign staff of the hospital. The Saudi women always looked away if we initiated eye contact, or spoke directly to them in a normal patient-care-giver communication. The word *normal* is definitely relative in describing our working interactions in Saudi Arabia. I went in the darkroom to develop my films, and when I came out a few minutes later, the nurse was not there. The Saudi girl was alone, lying on the hard X-Ray table in a pool of blood that glistened and soaked into the hospital green sheet underneath her. Tears were streaming down her face.

It took me a few seconds to realize that the baby had come while I was developing the films. The blood of the placenta and after-birth was dripping down the side of the sheet onto the floor. So much for the C-Section! In a way that hospital employees can mask panic with quiet deliberation, I tried to console her in my horrible Arabic, as I worked to contain the blood and to assess if she was physically okay. I tried to communicate that the baby was with the nurse and in good care. Silently, I was wishing that a nurse or doctor would barge into the room at any second, as I was out of my element in the birthing process. Trauma, back boards, neck and head injuries, and broken bones were no problem for me in the middle of the night. But this! I had no experience with labor and delivery.

This young Saudi girl, pretty, with huge brown eyes, thick wavy hair, and nice skin slowly turned to look at me. In perfect English and in a calm voice, she asked me how old I was. I told her that I was 24. She then asked me if I was married. I told her no. She asked me if I had any children. I told her no. She then said very slowly and quietly, in a matter of fact kind of way, "You are 24 and you have a life. I am your age, and this is my sixth child. I have no life for me. I don't want another baby." She then looked away, as the tears continued to stream down her face. She never said another word. What was there for me to say? Two nurses arrived a few seconds later. As we were moving her onto the stretcher, I made eye contact with her. She held it while the nurses wheeled her stretcher across the room and out the door. I will always remember the imploring, resigned look in her eyes, and the heavy silence of my response to her.

Other than the conversation with the Saudi woman on the plane from New York, I would never again have an opportunity to connect in a real way with a female Saudi national. The paradox was that I did have wonderful experiences and connections with females from all over the world in Saudi Arabia. I did not appreciate the reality of working in an internationally staffed hospital until I was in the middle of it. Doctors, nurses, technicians, translators, orderlies, cooks, dental hygienists, therapists; we were all in the same boat. We were foreign nationals who had found our way to this distant land for whatever reason, living apart from known expectations, separated from family and friends. Despite our country of origin, we were all thrown into a culture that was qualitatively different than what we knew to be a normal, 20th century existence. We walked on eggshells through a country that employed us but did not welcome us. We were in effect servants, of a class apart from the laborers who we saw everywhere, but very much employed workers, distinct and inferior to the elite status of a Saudi national. This was the reality of our shared story.

English was the business language of the hospital, so all employees spoke English. The only people who not did speak English were the majority of our patients. Hence, in our housing area and off duty, English was the language of communication. Every accent imaginable were represented as single girls from countries such as Germany, France, Ireland, England, Scotland, Sweden, Denmark, Jamaica, Australia, Canada, and America shared an immediate and close bond of easy companionship. There was no taking a couple of weeks to get to know your neighbors. Within the first hour of my arrival, many of the other girls had stopped by, giving me advice, and inviting me to their apartment or to town with them. These women already knew what I did not yet. Our relationship with each other would be the life blood of our experience in Saudi Arabia.

Within this society of total oppression of local women, our compound of Western women would exist in a world of freedom and fun. The life that I had expected to lead in Saudi Arabia, that of quiet reading and early to bed, would be replaced with the frivolity, laughter, and excitement of a Friday night on a college campus after mid-term exams. The spirit of this group of women was one of immense passion for living life in the moment, exploring every nuance of their daily experience, and laughing together about the absurd. And there was much that we viewed as absurd in Saudi Arabia. I believe that the personalities that came together from across the globe provide a window of hope into the possibilities of the human spirit. Most of the single women had an inner passion for exploration and adventure to have traveled to that part of the world in the first place. So there was always a "time to be had" no matter how mundane the day or the evening may start out to be.

The golden rules of actual behavior relative to the restrictive laws of the Kingdom were explained to me over and over again by anyone who had spent any length of time in Saudi Arabia. The bottom line was that the Saudis would leave Westerners alone as far as "adult behavior" went, as long as it was left on Western compounds, and that it **never** spilled over to include interactions with Saudi nationals of either sex. No social interaction what-so-ever with the Saudis. That ran the gamut from lunch in one's apartment to socializing in the evening. We were often invited to social gatherings on other Western compounds. Women are not allowed to drive in Saudi Arabia. That really was not a problem, because transportation was provided for us any time of the day or night with no questions asked. And we were allowed to drive with married couples. We had a wonderful Scottish couple in my apartment complex, who were always available to provide "escort service" if a single woman needed that. The Saudis' driving habits are haphazard, reckless, and beyond imagination. I did not mind being chauffeured while I was over there.

Some women made wine or lemon gin in their apartments, usually in the bathroom, with IV drips pacing the liquid through the process. Making lemon gin appealed to women who loved to cook, as they played with recipes that called for the peels of oranges, lemons, and potatoes to be thrown into the mix. I was raised in an Irish culture, so I immediately understood the benefit of this enterprise. However, the Laws of the Kingdom were fresh in my mind, and I could not bring myself to that level of risk. Anyway, lemon gin and home-made wine were always available in our small world. Many Westerners in Saudi Arabia, especially males, drank a home-made brew called *Sedike*, which is Arabic for friend. But, Sedike is nobody's friend. It is an extremely, strong, gut-rotting, white lightning excuse of a passable, social drink. I tasted it once. I immediately spat it out. It was awful! I heard that guys who never had drinking problems became alcoholics in Saudi Arabia. The Sedike was pure ethanol. They did not have access to anything else.

Most days after work, a group of us would gather in someone's apartment and hash out the experiences of the day. We had great stories and tales. Medical workers have great stories anywhere. Every idiosyncrasy of the human condition finds its way into hospital emergency rooms and outpatient clinics on a regular basis throughout the world. But the clash of cultures was so "in your face" in Saudi Arabia. The warped sense of humor of your average hospital worker enabled us to survive with laughter rather than tears. The hardest thing for most of the women I knew was an acute awareness that we were visitors here against the reality for Saudi women. We would all leave at some point. We knew that the Saudi women had no choices, and that most of them would never leave. I am not saying that all Saudi women are miserable. We did not know that because we could not have a conversation with any of them. Can you imagine that alone? But from our Western perspectives, the choices for women were so limited and so restricted in Saudi Arabia. It was hard for strong, independent women, who were natural caregivers to process the reality for women in Saudi Arabia. It ate away at you. Our only role was to observe the narrow and oppressive existence for Saudi females. We had no power to effect a change.

So, it is my second or third afternoon in Khamis Mushayt. A tall girl, who I had met briefly, popped her head in my door and invited me to go into town with a couple of girls. She was leaving the Kingdom in the near future. Her two-year contract was about to be up. She wanted to do a little shopping before she left. I had not been off the Air Base since I got there. It sounded like a great idea. We would meet in an hour to catch a van into town. She reminded me to wear a long skirt or loose fitting clothes. We did not have to cover up as the Saudi women did, but we were briefed to dress conservatively. We all did. It is not a problem for most women to be told that they have to wear loose fitting clothes.

Sometime that evening, we passed a vendor on the street, cooking a pancake looking thing. The girls all bought several of these. They looked very greasy to me. I did not buy any. The girls assured me that they were wonderful. They appeared to be woofing them down with pleasure. The tall girl nagged me to at least taste one. She broke off a piece and I ate it. I did not really like it. It tasted as it looked to me, bland and greasy, with the taste of old oil or bad lard. I am not usually fussy about trying new things, but these pancakes reminded me of when I was in college, and we had run out of groceries. My room mates and I were known to mix a batter of flour, sugar, and water, and fry it, when we had nothing else in the cupboard. I had been there and done that.

After we returned home I was very sick in less than an hour. I remember going into the bathroom to throw up several times. My next memory is of waking up sometime in the middle of the night on that cold, cement floor. Whatever food poisoning or intestinal bug I had picked up did a number on me. I was very sick for several days. I actually lost about fifteen pounds from that ordeal. It was almost a month before I could eat normally again. The other girls never got sick. Perhaps my immune system was compromised from the physical pace of the prior week. Whatever the reason, my first couple of weeks in Khamis Mushayt were spent in the bathroom, trying to purge my body back to a semblance of my usual hearty self. As I came to, in the middle of that cold night, many thoughts drifted in and out of my consciousness. I slowly and sporadically became aware of where I was.

I was a little like Tom Hanks in the movie, *Volunteers*. He wakes up in Indonesia from a huge hangover, and realizes that he is overseas with the Peace Corps, in a world far removed from his prior, known, privileged life. He does not realize where he is at first. He stumbles onto the deck in the early morning, bleary-eyed, groggy, and unaware. He takes one step too many, and lands flat on his face in the mud. As I became more aware of my situation, I felt a little like Tom Hank's character, except this was no comedy. This was the real thing, and here I was. Oh, yes, Saudi Arabia. Now I remember! I had to be careful of my steps, wary of taking one too many. I may have passed out on my bathroom floor from food poisoning. A lot of rest and hydration, and that nonsense would be behind me. My wariness was of what lay ahead of me. I would tread cautiously. I did not want to land on my face in the dry, hard mud of the desert floor. Now, to scrape myself off the cement floor; my goal is no more than that in the moment.

Chapter 4

DIALOGUE & FRIENDSHIP

THE RADIOLOGY DEPARTMENT WAS STAFFED with another Canadian, four Americans, a Scottish nurse, a Palestinian, and a Saudi national. The nurse and three of the technicians were female, including me. We had a female Radiologist of Philipino descent from America. Her medical skills were awful. She definitely would not be employed in an accredited hospital anywhere in the Western world. We were all shocked at her level of incompetence. The male Radiologist was an Egyptian. He did not interact that much with the staff other than from a working, professional relationship. He did not bother to engage his command of the English language to chit-chat with those of us who did not speak Arabic. For the most part, he was fine to work with, just not one to get to know.

The good doctor's temperament could be described as explosive; very passionate and short on patience. Most mornings, we were entertained as he shouted crazily at our patients in Arabic. They boldly and openly ignored his directions on a routine basis. He in turn would shout louder in frustration; very animated and emphatic. It was quite amusing to us, as we knew what would be coming next. The Saudis' usual reaction to the initial taste of Barium was to spit it in his face, rather than to swallow as directed. We knew to stand back, out of spitting range. I have seen thousands of patients over the years who also hated the taste of Barium, but it was only in Saudi Arabia that our patients expressed their dissatisfaction so blatantly and so honestly. There was never a dull moment. It was even more fun when the translators had to explain the highlights of a Barium Enema. You want me to do what? Let the games begin.

The Director of our Department was an extremely, quiet, dignified American from Phoenix. He never said a cross word to anyone or raised his voice the entire time I worked there. We had a dynamic mix of personalities in our department. He validated everyone with a calm presence no matter how crazy it got. He watched out for his staff, making sure that everyone got breaks and help when they needed it. He had been a POW in the Korean War for a span of years. He never talked of it. He never spoke much about anything. He listened very intently and smiled quietly in response. He was a chain smoker and he always had a cup of black coffee in his hand. Everyone respected him and understood the reality of his quiet being.

The other Canadian in the bunch was pleasant, quiet, and conservative. He left a few months after I got there. I really did not know him all that well. I mostly worked with a mix of Americans and Mid-Easterners, with always the sparkle of our Scottish nurse to anchor us. She was older than all of us. Her husband was an Emergency Room doctor. She would bring in cookies and treats all the time. We all loved her. She was kind of a parent to the group of us. She had a pretty face, a wonderful smile, and she creased it with laughter often.

One of the American girls, a very pretty girl about my age, was the most angry, negative, and reactive person that I have ever worked with. She hated Saudi Arabia and its people with a passion. She screamed her frustrations, cursing like a sailor throughout the day. She was angry at the world. She called the Saudis "F------ Rag-Heads" to their faces, and she despised everything about the country. I never understood why she was over there because she appeared so miserable and angry all the time. She seemed to hate anyone or anything that was not American. I felt her sting directed at me as much as at my Mid-East coworkers. At times, they tolerated her disdain through counter arguments, but often they would just walk away from her tirades. She responded to conversations or events very heatedly in a crude, outspoken, and often vulgar tone.

I learned to keep my distance from her, and she had no problem with that. She could not be bothered to give me the time of day. She would come out with vindictive and hateful remarks in reaction to a Saudi law or custom. She always exploded reactively without being able to put the constant affronts to our Western culture in any kind of framework to deal with it. It was sort of poetic justice in that she would exhibit a negative and unattractive image of Western women as she was screaming in frustration to denounce the injustice of the very same image. My Saudi co-worker would quietly shake his head. The Palestinian would often argue back with her. He could not contain himself to ignore her. They would get in these loud shouting matches, neither one backing down.

I now realize that she did not know how to handle living in Saudi

Arabia. She was a judgmental personality type. She was unable to put the clash of culture in any kind of perspective. She appeared to be mad at the world. Her stated mission was to pay off her home and to renovate it, but she resented enduring the means to the end. She had made a choice to complete the two years of her contract. She hated herself for it, and everyone else who crossed her path. I am sure that she had a lot of inner demons beyond the experience of Saudi Arabia. She often said things that were true, but screaming her reactions to the Arab mind in a manner dotted with F--- and other descriptive adjectives did not lend itself to any kind of middle road in a working relationship with Arabs. I learned in a short time that many foreign laborers and Westerners grew to hate working in Saudi Arabia. She was an extreme case as she was not able to contain her disgust in her daily interactions at work.

One thing that I did notice about her was that she got along okay with the other Americans. They weren't like her, but they understood her, and their presence would calm her down. The male tech from Seattle made us all laugh. He was really funny, and he never seemed to let anything bother him over there. He was focused on a mission to save as much money as he could in his time in country. He was frugal to the point of ridiculous. He was smarter than any of us in his nonchalant, casual, eccentric way. He took everyone else's call for the extra money. Several of us never wanted or needed the call. We had more cash than we knew what to do with in that time and place. He had a purpose and he was extremely disciplined in achieving his goal. And he was so disarmingly witty about it all.

At this point, I am going to put in fictional names of my three coworkers who helped me to understand the complicated web of experiences and world events that had transpired in our separate lives as we passed from children to young adults. We became friends within the boundaries of passionate dialogue, each one trying to explain to the other his or her thinking and perspective on similar events. Cognitive and cultural schemas that understood world events very differently were explored and challenged in an atmosphere of openness and probing for clarity. I don't know that we solved the world's problems or created an effective change on personal truths, but we all gained broader knowledge and insight into each others' lives. And we all liked each other.

The first person who greeted me on the job, and who would become a dear friend of mine for the duration of my stay in Saudi Arabia was Hamdam. He was a teddy bear type, about late 20's, very boisterous in expression, happy with a zest for life, and very political. He introduced himself as a Palestinian. From the first time that we met he very much wanted me to understand that he was a good person, that Palestinians were good people. I admit that I knew about as much as your average 24 year old Canadian did about Palestine in early 1982.

I knew that Palestine bordered Israel, and that it was in conflict due to the loss of its land to Israel during the Six Day War in 1967. I associated "Palestinian" with the PLO and Yassar Arafat. I had a very disdainful and apprehensive view about the PLO. In Canada, we had hosted the Montreal Olympics in 1976. There was great fear and news coverage of the assassinations of the Israeli athletes at the Munich Olympics by the PLO in 1972. The Canadian authorities and the press discussed in length the possibility that a similar incident might happen during the Montreal Olympics. I knew the PLO to be a terrorist organization; some very, very bad guys. There had been plane hijackings, bombings, always violence and war.

So, I was a little startled when Hamdam told me that the PLO was a legitimate government organization, greatly supported and respected in the Mid-East. That would be the basis for many future discussions and debates throughout the next sixteen months. Hamdam told me that his mother still lived in Palestine and that he and his brothers could never go back there. He was the youngest brother in the family. I naturally wanted to know why they could not go back, as my mind is clicking away…terrorist??? He told me that he was not a member of the PLO, but that an older brother was. The Israelis had deported all the males in his family several years prior linked to the involvement of his brother. This information was a little too close for comfort.

However, I never felt threatened by Hamdam then, or ever; despite the polarity of his view from mine; despite the collision of our worlds. Actually, he and I got along famously. We had a great working relationship. He kept up his part of the work load. We joked together all the time. He was a playful, teasing type; never in a mean way. He loved to laugh as loudly and as often as he wore his broken heart on his sleeve. His heartache was for the plight of his family and his people. He was completely open and impassioned in his discussions to strongly promote my awareness and understanding of his Palestinian story. Hamdam introduced me to a worldview that directly challenged many of my own assumptions and beliefs.

Hamdam told me that he had been deported to Jordan. He carried a Jordanian passport. He explained that the Palestinians were not welcome in Jordan, and that they were discriminated against. He appeared angry, resentful, and hurt when he spoke of the Palestinian treatment in Jordan, which he perceived to be that of second class citizens. He told me that the Jordanians' support of the Palestinians was focused towards getting them out of Jordan and back to Palestine. He would say these things to our Saudi co-worker, directly, angrily, almost daring him to stop his tirade. He was vehemently angry with the Jordanian government. He did not feel any real ownership of his Jordanian passport because he shouted that he did not enjoy the benefits and privileges of Jordanian citizenship. He said the only point of the passport was to enable the Jordanians to get him out of the country, to work in Saudi Arabia. He saw his homeland as Palestine. His heart was aching to return there and to see his mother. He very much wanted to tell me all of this, and for me to hear his story before I met Tammy. Tammy was the other American who was not in the country my first week of work. She was due back in a few days. Hamdam playfully called her "Tammy Begin"; Begin pronounced as in Menachem Begin. You could tell from his voice that he adored her, but that she drove him crazy with her support of Israel.

Khaled was a very unassuming, humble, and calm Saudi national. He was a member of the Royal Saudi Air Force. He usually wore military fatigues to work underneath his white lab coat. He was a reflective type, a good listener. His quiet demeanor balanced the intensity of Hamdam's passion for debate and discussion. Khaled often hung back, listening intently to heated interactions between us. I always sensed that he was a lot like me. He was an observant listener, the type of person who can incorporate the points of views of others without the fear of losing themselves in the process. When he articulated a position, he appeared genuine and introspective. He usually spoke in a hushed manner, sort of guarded in who he would open himself up to. In contrast, Hamdam was anything but guarded.

Hamdam was an ordinary person with a robust passion for living. He was caught up in a world that had spun out of his control. He shouted from the rafters for all to hear the reality, as he knew it, of the human tragedy of the Palestinian story. Khaled had great empathy for Hamdam's emotional turmoil. However, he was the citizen of a country that did not recognize the existence of the State of Israel in 1982. Khaled was reluctant to articulate a reaction to Israel. How could he respond to something that did not exist? He was more inclined to discuss Iran. The Iranian Revolution and the US hostage incident were world events that he understood very differently than I did. Khaled was a Shia. He was cautious but intent to express his views, which were that of a suppressed minority in the Kingdom of Saudi Arabia. Khaled was always looking around, aware of who else might be listening when our discussions were lively. He held back; deliberately weighing time and place; then speaking softly, humbly, and thoughtfully in the company of our very, small core group. I got the feeling that he was always looking over his shoulder when he spoke.

I remember the first time that I heard of Saddam Hussein. His name was not known to me prior to my employment in Saudi Arabia. I was probing Khaled with my knowledge of Iran and its people. I viewed Iranians as fundamentalist, reactive, explosive, and closed to any kind of dialogue or relationship with the Western world. Khaled had very strong and quiet opinions that differed greatly from mine. He discussed the reign of the Shah, as America's puppet. His view was that the Shaw and his Secret Police had squelched the rights and the beliefs of traditional, intellectual, moderate, and fundamentalist citizens in Iran. Khaled told me that the people of the region viewed the Western support of the Shah to be criminal and anti-Islam. He said that this went back to the aftermath of World War II, first the British and then the Americans.

From his perspective, the people of Iran had been plundered and treated badly by the colliding forces of the world's superpowers. The British, the Americans, and the Russians juggled to control the oil market; literally exploiting the Iranian workers through impoverished working conditions and slave wages. In other words, as Western economies flourished, the Iranians remained locked in poverty with dismal living conditions. The Shah's wealth and pro-Western policies angered the Iranians for the quarter century of his reign. The fundamentalists gained in strength as the traditional tribal cultures and the established hierarchies of power were dismantled under the Shaw. The angry clerics became a voice for the oppressed masses, both rich and poor, both liberal and fundamentalist. The people of Iran lost the grounding of their long and colorful history. Although, Khaled never condoned violence, he felt that the Iranian hostage incident was justified as a reaction to the injustices imposed by the Shah, who blatantly represented an extension of Western arrogance and domination. Khaled was as passionate in discussing Iran as Hamdam was in discussing Palestine.

Khaled quietly told me that the most dangerous Arab country was not Iran but Iraq, and that Saddam Hussein was a very dangerous leader and a very bad guy. I did not know much of the politics or the intricacies of the Iraq-Iran War. I admit. I had never heard of Saddam Hussein before Khaled spoke his name to me in 1982. We heard a lot of Ayatollah Khomeini in the news coverage in Canada in the late 70's and the early 80's. But Saddam Who? I knew more of the history of the Israeli-Arab conflicts. As long as I could remember, there were on-going wars and violence in the Mid-East. I did not understand half of it. It always seemed as if the region was chaotic and brutal; carnage after carnage blaring into our living rooms from our black and white TV screens, day in, day out.

Later, I was to understand more of Khaled's guardedness in discussing political issues. At the time that he was educating me from his Shia perspective of Mid-East politics and conflicts, the official policy of the government of the Kingdom of Saudi Arabia was to back Iraq against Iran. This was also the policy of America. I was beginning to be exposed to the multi—ethnic layers of complexity and allegiance that have collided to create mistrust, anger, and rage throughout the region from both internal and external sources. Khaled would not utter a word against his government. It was often in what he did not say.

For example, he called me to the side one day. Out of the blue, he told me not to travel south of Khamis Mushayt towards the Yemen border, which was only about twenty miles from us. I asked him why. He just shook his head. He was very determined to impress upon me not to go there, but he hesitated to explain more. He finally told me very quietly that the local people from that area did not like any Westerners, and that it would not be safe for a young, Western female to drive towards the Yemen border period. He said that there were very dangerous people, who would be very hostile to a young, Western female. He was embarrassed to say these things, but he was determined to warn me. Khaled also expressed that most Saudis were not like that, but that the border region with Yemen was extremely dangerous for Western women. At the time, I was struck by how sincere and intense he was in his very quiet and humble way. I listened to him. He was so serious. I could tell it worried him. I never drove that direction from our base with anyone, ever.

Both Khaled and Hamdam were very happy to introduce me to Tammy. You could tell that they really liked and respected her. Tammy was a true ambassador for everything that is wonderful about the United States. She displayed confidence and competence in a very carefree, easy way. She was not condescending nor was she overly humble. She loved America. She was very patriotic. She also loved the human experience of people from all over the world. She expressed her opinions openly. She debated Hamdam and Khaled all the time, but she never dismissed them. She was the most well-traveled person I had ever met, and she had a keen mind with great insight into many areas of the world. Tammy had worked at a refugee camp in Cambodia. She had spent several months on a Kibbutz in Israel. She had trekked several times through Nepal and the Himalayas. This was her second tour in Saudi Arabia. Previously, she had worked in Riyadh. In a way, she was bigger than life, but in reality, she was an ordinary girl from Tallahassee, Florida.

She had a great sense of humor. She would entertain us with her tales of working in Disney World as "Winnie the Pooh" when she was in college. She could sail, dive, and water-ski. The first time that I saw her, she was very sun-tanned. She was wearing this bright orange sweater over her hospital scrubs. She had sun-streaked hair pulled back in a pony tail. She had the biggest smile. People who are not raised in America have an image of an "American lifestyle", sort of based on Hollywood movies, the Beach Boys music, California Girl, and all that. Tammy was that image, and she was the genuine thing. Everyone in our X-Ray Department loved her. She was a force to be reckoned with.

Tammy would become my mentor and my friend. She knew so much about Saudi Arabia that I did not. She was never afraid to verbally challenge the rules and the customs of the Kingdom, even though she complied with them, as we all did. We really had no choice. Tammy would drive Hamdam and Khaled to near tears at times with her outspoken world view, but her delivery was so decent and honoring of others that they could not remain angry at her for any length of time. Tammy was very pro-Israel. I was always fascinated with the State of Israel and the courage of its people, but I had never been there. She has spent several months on a Kibbutz. She loved that experience and the people with whom she lived.

Tammy also knew how deeply the official Saudi government hated Israel. I did not know as much about that. In any book store in the modern, shiny malls of Jeddah or Riyadh, you could not purchase any publications or books that even mentioned the word *Israel*. There were rigid laws of censoring in Saudi Arabia, so that freedom of the press did not exist. If you were to buy a world map in Saudi Arabia, the state censors would have already opened it, and placed a large, black dot with a felt tip marker to block out the area on the map that represented the State of Israel. The official policy of the Kingdom of Saudi Arabia in 1982 was that the State of Israel did not exist. They attempted to erase the reality of a nation state with a fat, black, felt tip marker. Tammy told me about this. I unfolded several maps in book stores in malls in both Jeddah and Riyadh to check this out for myself. I saw the black blots each time. My reaction was that it was so ridiculous that it was almost funny.

The censors impacted much more than black dots on world maps. Tammy would educate me on the realities of Shariah Law in Saudi Arabia. Beyond the total restriction on freedom of worship, the actual laws of the land were based and enforced from a fundamentalist, rigid, and closed interpretation of Islam. The enforcers or religious police were headed by the League for the Encouragement of Virtue and Prevention of Vice, under whom the Public Morals Committee would recruit local volunteers to report suspicion of banned activity from the streets of the cities and towns. What this meant in reality was that the population and especially the female half of the population tread very lightly and guardedly as they maneuvered through the realities of their daily lives.

In the market areas and public places, the religious police or mutafahs would walk around with canes. They would chase people, yelling at them as they waved the canes in the air, and sometimes whacking individuals with the canes for infractions of their rigid interpretation of the Islamic Law. For example, the mutafahs may berate a Saudi woman if her ankles were showing as she walked along the street, or if her veil had slipped showing any of her face. During these incidents, several males would be simultaneously yelling and screaming at the poor woman as she struggled to adjust her abaya from exposing any skin. This would include the males in her company and the religious police and their party. I witnessed several of these incidents on the streets of Riyadh and Khamis Mushayt. I always felt so sorry for the women, as they seemed to shrink further into the blackness that shielded any public expression of themselves.

I, personally, did not have any experience crossing with the cane swinging, angry bearded enforcers of Shariah. I was in downtown Khamis Mushayt late one afternoon with a bus load of women from the hospital. People had split up into smaller groups, shopping among the gold suugs, the carpet shops, the brass and copper shops, and the myriad of small shops that were available. When we were waiting for our transportation at the scheduled time to return to our housing complex, a small group of three or four women came running up, short of breath, and laughing in relief as one does after experiencing the adrenaline rush of a scary experience. They were laughing and a little shaken at the same time.

Apparently, they had walked by an open door of a dark room in which Arab men would gather to smoke their pipes and to hang out. I never knew what was in those pipes, but Arab males had their own form of adult indulgence in mood altering therapy; even though they did not have access to the liquid nectar of traditional lounges and bars. Anyway, these Western ladies took it upon themselves to wander in the establishment to check it out, and they were even cheeky enough to sit down at one of the low tables. I am sure that they had not thought it through to what they would actually do once they sat down. The enticement to enter and dare to linger was thrilling enough by itself.

It was a very short time before the mutafah showed up with his entourage, and chased them out, screaming and waving his cane as they high tailed it up the street. There were many of these types of stories from Westerners who worked and lived for any length of time in the Kingdom. But for many, it was an oddity, sometimes even a lark to challenge the absurdity from the position of our values, and acceptable adult behavior. The extent of most rebellion was impulsive and reactionary as Western women struggled to absorb the overall experience within the relative safety of our visitor status. The expectations of strict compliance were somewhat altered for us, as we were viewed as Western prostitutes anyway. For the Saudi women, the restrictions on behavior were severe and the punishments were very real, and there was no future escape into a more moderate world.

Tammy recommended a book for me to read. It was a pretty good story of the history of the House of Saud in the 20th century. The tribal piece, the formation of alliances between clans, and the total oppression of moderate and tolerant Islam laid the foundation of rule in this Desert Kingdom. I had to borrow Tammy's copy as this book and many other historical fiction or factual books were censored. In effect, Saudi nationals had very limited exposure to Western thought and alternate views, or even more traditional expressions of Islam. The only news in the Kingdom was State run. From a freedom of the press perspective, Saudi Arabia was a totalitarian state in 1982. I am not sure how much the internet has challenged this control in the present, but we still see no open coverage of Saudi Arabia in the Western press. Somehow, our own media seems to have given our staunchest allies a ride on this fact. After 9/11, you think that we would actually discuss the phenomena of a free press relative to real world outcomes.

It was against the backdrop of living in Saudi Arabia that Tammy,

Hamdam, Khaled, and I would discuss and explore our daily experiences. For the most part, we worked together to perform the basic duties of a routine, diagnostic X-Ray Department. It would be throughout the day, often in reaction to a patient or a personal experience, that we would explore each others thought processes. People really do see the same things differently, especially when their prior life experiences are so fundamentally different. Our patients were the family members and active duty personnel of the Royal Saudi Air Force assigned to the Asir Region, and also the local civilian population. Our hospital was the only hospital in that area, which is not a heavily populated region of Saudi Arabia.

We had Bedouin patients. The Bedouin women appeared to be uneducated and they led very simple lives. I always felt charmed by them, as they were more open than your average Saudi women. The Bedouins never spoke a word of English, so our direct communication was always gestures, nods, and smiles. They would smile back, laugh, and sometimes bow down with gratitude. They would hold your face in their hands in a way that was very honoring of your work and your interaction with them. I felt humbled in the presence of the older Bedouin women. They treated us as if we had saved their lives or that of their children, when we had just performed a routine exam, that was purely diagnostic and not treatment based. Their gratitude was genuine in its simplicity.

It was an event getting our Bedouin patients changed. The Bedouin women would wear about five layers of dresses underneath their black shrouds. Usually, it was apparent that they had not taken off the layers of clothing for days, possibly even weeks. It was a struggle to get the heavy weight of the fabrics over their head. We often had to help them, as the task was too burdensome for independent success. It was like being in a cramped dressing room in a department store, and trying on an article of clothing that you realize is too tight after you have squeezed into it. The challenge would be to get out of the garment without tearing the seams, and without squeezing the oxygen out of your lungs as your ribs are restricted from natural expansion. The Bedouin women with their wrinkled, henna-dyed hands would shrug their shoulders and laugh at the helplessness of their undressing ability.

In contrast, other Saudi women would quietly go into the dressing rooms after they received instructions for changing. The instructions were always given in Arabic by male translators, either directly to the women or through her husband, which was usually the case. The men would lead their wives back to the dressing area. These exchanges would start out fairly calmly, with the directions being explained matter-of-factly and professionally. Often the husband would question the directions. It was common for the husband to begin arguing back, and then the translator's voice would rise, the husband's voice would rise louder, and it would go back and forth.

In the end, the spouse rescinded, usually muttering under his breath and shaking his head. I was always amazed that the husbands would then appear to take out their frustration with their loss of control in the situation by turning around and screaming at their wives. Prior to this, the woman had been silent, standing behind her husband, waiting for the okay. By the time that her husband gave in to the conditions of "changing", he would be so angry that he would take it out on the silent spouse; who had been patiently waiting, with head down, while men argued about her level of undressing for a medical exam. It was like adding insult to injury.

The experience of undressing for a medical procedure is not comfortable for patients anywhere in the world. It's the vulnerability of the whole thing, having to remove ones underwear and get into a hospital gown with unusual and gaping openings. We all know the feeling. But in Saudi Arabia, the vulnerability of self-exposure was intense for the women in a way that was unique and in response to the Shariah Laws that ruled their very existence. First of all, our gowns were those disposable, blue contraptions that tear easily. They had huge armholes and an opening that went the entire length of the gown, without the comfort of ties that are usually on cloth gowns. The disposable gowns do not offer even a false sense of cover, as they are stiff and resistant to wrapping around the body. Patients, everywhere, complained about those disposable gowns.

Most of our female patients would quietly go into the dressing rooms. Some of them would stay in there, half ready. They would go no further, and they would just sit down silently, not wanting to come out. Then the husbands would start shouting at them again. In other instances, they would come out, but they would have the gown on backwards with it wide open, and the black veil still covering their faces. This was the hardest part for them. They were less afraid of showing their breasts than their face. They remained resistant to exposing their faces, even after they were behind closed doors in the X-Ray room. Well, it's darn near impossible to drink Barium through a face veil, or keep it in place as one lies in different positions for multiple views of the organ system or bones of interest. Our translators would end up shouting at these women before they would shyly and pitifully remove the veil.

I remember one day in particular. A female patient was in the dressing room changing. This time, her husband was seated in the waiting area, not hovering outside the changing room. I was standing in the high traffic area in the middle of the department, in front of the X-Ray view boxes. This area is usually in the middle of an X-Ray Department, as most diagnostic rooms feed into the work area. The films are reviewed there by the technicians and doctors before patients are dismissed in case more views are needed. The dressing rooms are usually close by, along some internal corridor in the department.

Anyway, several of us were working in there, sorting our films, chit-chatting about nothing special, pacing routinely through our morning. Out of the blue, Hamdam began screaming loudly and shrilly in Arabic at someone behind me. I could sense a tone of more panic than anger in the intensity of his voice. I turned around to see our next patient, standing there, not saying a word, just waiting on us; stark naked with the stiff, blue hospital gown shaped into a veil that she somehow managed to balance on her head, covering her face. Hamdam was near hysterical, looking around as he tried to impress upon her to get back into the dressing room, and to not look at her as he frantically screamed his instructions. He knew the implications for her and for his position within the punitive and unforgiving Shariah Laws.

I can't imagine that woman's need to keep her face covered. She would have been totally vulnerable to and embarrassed by any level of undressing. These are women that can't allow their ankles to be seen in public. But, to be so humiliated at the idea of unveiling her face that she would stand in the middle of our work area stark naked is so telling. Obviously, our female, Western reactions to an incident such as this one would stimulate great discussion among us. I am sure Hamdam, who probably never had a drink of alcohol in his life, would have gladly swallowed a stiff drink or two that day. He was visibly shaken. I think he was so afraid that her husband would round the corner at any second, and he could only imagine the level of wrath that would be bestowed upon the woman and on him.

I talk a lot about female patients. For the most part, our male patients did not have any more problem with changing and undergoing diagnostic exams than men do anywhere. They all hate it. The main difference is that the Saudi males would argue passionately with the translators and the doctors before inevitably complying with the instructions. Men in the Western world resist things out of their control about as much. They just don't scream about it so blatantly. Western men are more likely to keep talking about how they can handle pain, and how they are not wimps, as they are standing there sweating bullets at the thought of a needle or having a tube inserted into a body cavity. The Arab men would yell not only 'No", but "Hell No", to be followed by a several lines of graphic and colorful phrases in Arabic. Western men tend to try to rationalize their natural resistance, where as the Saudis would just spit it at you in no uncertain terms.

Discussions would gravitate to the effects of culture and education on how we think, what we know, and what we value. The only Western women employed in the Asir Region were those of us working at the hospital. All of the other foreign workers around there were males who worked for a variety of defense contractors linked to the Saudi Air Base. These male contractors from many different countries did not have their wives or families with them. So the hospital females were the only Western women to come into the Asir region of Saudi Arabia. We were it; nurses, technicians, physical therapists, dental hygienists, and pharmacists. We were the only women outside of Saudi nationals to walk the narrow streets of the few towns or bazaars. We were young and old, black and white, short and tall, blond and brunette; and we were all educated, middle class, hospital employees. We were respected and honored in our profession in our native countries.

It was hard to understand and to absorb the following truth. All Western women (that would be us) were described as prostitutes and whores by the religious clerics and imans. The young Saudi boys in the religious schools were taught that we were unclean whores, the deliverers of Satan. We listened and pondered as we sat on the curb of the street in the shopping area of Khamis Mushayt, waiting for the stores to reopen after the afternoon or evening call to prayer. The speakers blaring from the mosque across the square often included a message describing Westerners and infidels in very derogatory, disgusting terms. This was a fact of life for all of us. It didn't matter if you were Irish, Swedish, Canadian, American, Australian, Jamaican, or British. It didn't matter if you were a nurse, a doctor, a medical technician, a therapist, or a cook. We were all prostitutes and whores. We were described as unclean infidels, dirty and vulgar. We posed a threat to contaminate the purity of the Saudi nationals. We were definitely not welcome and barely tolerated by the religious clerics of Saudi Arabia.

I remember sitting on the curb of the street, listening to those speakers, and then silently seeking to probe into the minds of the Arab men as they came back into the streets. I was 24 years old when I went there. I used to wonder about the thoughts of the young men, who would be about my age. They had been educated and raised listening to their teachers and clerics describe Western women as whores and prostitutes on a regular basis. I wondered about how they must view us. I pondered about how they must think. They had no opportunity for alternate views or independent exposure from media or a free press. It was something to reflect on as we sat in the square, in the midst of a world forbidden from us in any real sense.

I can tell you that the young men would never look at us. Older Saudi men were more comfortable with that. The older men never leered at us. I actually expected that type of response since the Saudi women are so hidden from view. We were really sort of an oddity in Khamis Mushayt. The Western females from the hospital stood out like a sore thumb in the shopping area of the small downtown. It was my experience that older Saudi men were polite for the most part. They sometimes made eye-contact. They would nod or greet you in an appropriate manner if they paid attention to you at all.

The younger men were different. They more or less ignored us, as if we were a non-entity. They did not look at us sideways or underneath their eye lids when they thought we weren't looking. They just plainly ignored us. Young men of a similar age to a group of young women in their 20's and 30's did not acknowledge our existence among them. They did not hassle us. They left us completely alone. Their faces were impassive. If they were walking towards us, they looked past us as if our very presence was invisible to them. Or, they would cross the street to put more distance between us, keeping their eyes focused beyond us, staring ahead, never flinching in recognition of our presence. At the time, it was not unnerving; more puzzling. We never went into town by ourselves, always in groups and always in the daylight or early evening.

On weekends, groups of us would sometimes go camping at the Red Sea. We really did have good times with the mix of people who worked in Saudi Arabia. Several vehicles would travel together in a caravan. There was always a married couple or two, who could act as chaperones for the single people in the group. Yes, we were adults, but the mixing of sexes was very much a reality that we dealt with over there on a daily basis. We were very sensitive to the laws of the land. And, no one wanted to end up being flogged prior to being thrown in a Saudi jail for any reason.

We had to take everything, as there were no camping facilities, cabins, or hotels to be had. Water was the primary requirement. We would transport it by the gallons. The Red Sea is beautiful. There was great opportunity for water sports, diving, snorkeling, and sailing. The stars at night are amazing. They appear to be so bright and so clear in the sky there. One time, a small herd of wild camels slowly wandered by us, walking in a straight line across the desert, close to the beach. They did not bother us. They just sort of strolled along at a steady pace. As they were passing us, one of the camels stopped, and a few seconds later, a calf fell out of her. It was the most amazing thing. Within a few seconds, the baby had gotten up on wobbly legs, and the mom continued to follow the herd with the baby struggling to walk behind her. Just like that! A Scottish friend of mine found a huge turtle shell on the beach. The Red Sea had a stark beauty that was appreciated against the journey to get there safely. The drive down the escarpment was half the adventure of going to the Red Sea.

I can describe the narrow, mountain road that wound its way from the top of the Asir Mountain Range to the base at the Red Sea as similar to the Hana Road in Maui. The main difference is that the escarpment route would include the wild driving behavior of Arab truckers, who challenged powerful Mercedes Benz engines to accelerate their decorated trucks on the weight of two wheels around extremely tight and narrow mountain curves. Coming around a hair pin turn at high speeds, the out of control truck and driver would come hurtling towards your vehicle, hogging the only bit of road to be had. Your choice was to hug the boulders and cliffs rising up from the road and pray, or to pummel over the side of the bottomless, steep drop on the other side of the road. From the view of the mountain road, the ground far below was littered with the skeletal remains of vehicles of many shapes and sizes whose luck was not with them on the fateful day of their demise. It was always with a sigh of relief that I would arrive home safely from the driving adventure of a weekend at the Red Sea.

As we drove through the region, I could not help but notice the living quarters of workers from third world countries who are employed by the thousands in Saudi Arabia; to perform every level of service job and manual labor. There were Thai, Vietnamese, Sinhalese, Pakistani, and Korean workers living in tin shacks in the middle of nowhere; suffering the desert heat in unbearable living conditions. These squalid shelters could be seen from the road. It came up one day at work after I had a conversation with a Philipino worker during an evening shift. He was polishing the floor as I came out of a room with the portable X-Ray machine. He very politely walked up to the machine and asked me if he could look at it. He asked me about the kilo voltage. I knew from his interest and his questions that he knew something about the machine. He was trained, and he told me that he had worked with the same machine in the Philippines. I asked him why he was not doing X-Ray work verses cleaning the floors. He explained to me the concept and the rules of block visas. I had never heard of them before that.

In Saudi Arabia, third world workers are hired through block visas which control their salaries and the type of work that they can do. A citizen of the Philippines could only be employed as a laborer. Even though the wages were low against Western standards, they were still better than what he would make at home. Many of the women in my complex would pay Philipino hospital workers to clean their small apartments. For the most part, the women did not really need this service as much as it helped to supplement the wages of the Philipinos, who were respected and well liked. We would talk about the obvious difference in living conditions for workers from third world countries with Hamdam and Khaled. They were not comfortable with the disparity anymore than we were. I recently read that slavery was legal in Saudi Arabia until the 1960's. If this is true, it would not surprise me. Think about that. Slavery! The living conditions that I saw for the workers of poor countries was horrible, and unnecessary in a country as rich as Saudi Arabia.

This would bring us to talking about our own wages at work. Hamdam and Khaled did not feel as satisfied with their compensation as I did. Not that Canadians and Americans made huge bucks in our field of work, but most of us were satisfied with the living expenses that were provided, and the benefit of not having to pay state or federal taxes. Hamdam and Khaled told me that they both paid a hefty tax. They called it the PLO tax. They said that every Mid-East worker had to pay a portion of their salary to support the PLO. This was automatically taken out of their pay in the same way that we pay our state and federal taxes. So, while the Western world viewed the PLO as a terrorist organization, every wage earner in the Mid-East paid a percentage of their income to support the legitimate, government organization. I really didn't have a clue. The framework of the Palestinian situation and that of the PLO were seen so differently by my Arab co-workers and their countrymen.

The one thing that I got out of our discussions with both Hamdam and Khaled was that they viewed hostile actions as a legitimate forum of expression of the needs and views of the citizens of the Mid-East to the Western world. Khaled viewed Iran as a country in which traditional Islamic values and highly educated scholars had been suppressed under the reign of the Shah. He felt that the Iranian Revolution was justified, and the US Hostage incident provided a means for the Iranians to have a voice on the world stage. Hamdam desperately wanted the plight of the Palestinian people to be understood by the Western world. He also felt that the actions of the PLO were justified against the injustices to his people.

As they both never directly condoned the violence, they would quickly try to dismiss our focus on terrorism and violence as side issues. They felt that we always missed the point. The issue for them was that the actions of the Iranians and the PLO during the past decade were a valid and legitimate means of getting the world's attention on the underlying problem, as they saw it. They truly felt that the Western world, which was represented by the power of America, dismissed the Arab side of the story across the Mid-East. They were frustrated and angry that they did not have a voice on the world stage. The perception of dismissal of their voice in the process, as a people, fueled their anger and frustration.

The bright note from all of this was that a group of middle class workers could hash through and spiritedly explore opposing view points, and at the end of the day walk away as friends; joking, and looking forward to the next day at work. It all comes down to the basics. We worked together and we respected one another. Even though we constantly disagreed, we listened before we argued back. We saw each other as decent human beings. We watched out for one another. We took good care of our patients through all the shouting and the antics of our unique working situation. A sense of humor and a compassion for the plight of our patients helped us to overcome the most bizarre situations .Whatever it took to get it done, we did together. We laughed a lot on the job. We had a very good working relationship. We were all just ordinary folk who had come from different worlds. Our common bond was the human experience that draws people together as we came to know each other as decent people.

Chapter 5

WHAT I CAME TO KNOW

A S I SAID EARLIER, THERE comes a time when Westerners become aware that the clash of culture can not be overcome in Saudi Arabia. Some foreign workers hang on for a long time because of the money. It takes hold of you, and it's hard to walk away from it. I met nurses and contractors from a variety of countries who had been in Kingdom for eight years or more. Without a fail, they hated Saudi Arabia. They were negative about everyone and everything that had any association with their host country. I could never understand the thinking of the long term group. They would acknowledge that they had met their original financial goal, perhaps paying off their house, helping their families, paying cash for new vehicles—whatever. But it was never enough. There was always one more thing, one more possession to be gained, and one more…In addition to the house and the new cars, there was the nest egg in cash that would be needed to go along with it. In the meantime, they lived miserably in the present over a period of years.

I can pinpoint two experiences that, in the middle of each experience, I stopped and looked around, and had a conscious awareness that I thought differently than the Arabs around me, and that the differences were qualitatively significant. I knew for sure on Dec 31, 1982, after I had been in country for almost a year that I would need to leave soon. As I looked around on the escarpment, I thought about how our Western values conflicted so deeply with the Saudi way of life. I felt that we could never come together to accommodate each other as a society in any meaningful way. Our Western social and cultural values insulted the Saudis, and their social and cultural laws insulted us. It was as simple as that.

The specific moment was late afternoon on New Year's Eve. We had camped at the Red Sea. I think it was my third time to the Red Sea. I was becoming an old hat at it. Anyway, the group in my vehicle had decided to leave fairly early to get back by mid-afternoon. An Irish couple was hosting a New Year's Eve party and we wanted to get back for it—the Blarney Stone and all of that. Also, the husband was a great chef, and a very funny, witty host. There was nowhere else we would rather be on New Year's Eve than in the company of this wonderful, friendly couple. Anyway, we were about two-thirds of the way up the escarpment. The road was very steep, narrow, windy, and treacherous. There are no guard rails, and the cliff drops away into nothingness all along that part of the road. As we rounded a sharp turn, we came to traffic that was backed up in front of us. We slowed down, coming to a complete stop. We witnessed a driving nightmare unfold in front of our eyes in less than a couple of minutes, and we were totally entrapped in it.

What was causing the traffic to be backed up was the afternoon prayer call. About half of the cars and trucks had pulled over on the road. Their drivers had gotten out to pray. When I say pulled over, I really mean stopped, as there was no side to pull over to. The real problem arose when the other half of the Arab drivers, in high powered cars and the huge Mercedes trucks, started trying to get around the parked cars. There was nowhere to go, but they would bully and squeeze their vehicle into whatever inch of space they could find. This created a jigsaw of vehicles, angled in all different directions, which resulted in chaotic and complete grid lock. There was no option for anyone to move. These drivers then tried to force other drivers to back up, but cars were turned every which way, and there was no space to begin to undo the mess. We were in a vehicle with a standard shift, squeezed out to the edge of the cliff. I have never been so afraid in my life.

We sat there for what seemed like hours with the Arabs getting madder and madder with each other as the time wore on. Finally, we were told that the police had to close off the road at the top. The police then walked down the escarpment, and car by car, inch by inch, directed drivers to untangle their vehicles from the spider web of chaos. The problem got even worse as the traffic around us slowly started to move. Impatient Arab drivers would not wait for the car in front of them, or at an angle beside them to move. So, whenever an inch forward was to be gained, a hazardous driver would try to cut off other drivers with no regard for safety. It was cut throat to the extreme. Our vehicle was at a very steep angle, and hugging the cliff, so that all we could see was the drop, which appeared to be mere inches from our tires. The stop and go of the untangling—as vehicles would start only to be cut off, and the backward roll of the manual shift had me in tears.

Our driver fought intensely for a safer spot on the road. I finally got out of the SUV and walked over to the inside of the road, hugging the mountain, standing back, just sort of watching it. My fear was so real and reactive to every backward roll that it was not helping the situation for the rest of the people in my vehicle. As I stood and looked around at the angry mess of vehicles, my brain consciously processed the violent, entangled chaos as a metaphor of the clash of Arab culture from within Saudi Arabia; the reality of those who stopped to pray on a narrow, mountain road against the angry reaction of the Arabs who bullied to get themselves ahead. There appeared to be no middle ground. I realized that I was an outsider here. I did not belong. I had never felt like that before. I was always able to relate to people, to understand them. But here on the side of the escarpment, I knew that the best way that I could honor the Saudi culture was to leave it.

I never learned to hate Saudi Arabia like others did. I actually really liked our Bedouin patients. The old ladies always made us laugh. I enjoyed my days at work; the friends I had over there. However, I did learn that the values of our cultures were embedded in opposite fields of quicksand, each one sucking us further and further away from the other. Our cultures were driven by forces that were opposed to one another, and at the same time used each other. We were barely tolerated as annoying visitors; forbidden to have a voice at any level of honest or rational dialogue within the Kingdom. It was like the clash of values within the country was playing itself out here on the mountain road, the modern Arab and the fundamentalist. Neither side wanted to give an inch to accommodate the other side. A sheer battle for control and power had been born out on the treacherous road.

In the early 80's, Westerners were expected to humbly obey and observe. We were acutely aware that we were conspicuous outsiders on the treacherous incline of the escarpment drive. We had chanced into a foreshadowing of what would play out on the world stage about twenty years later. I don't know why, but as I watched all of this, I felt a very real and immediate sense of danger. It was a feeling in the way the hair rises up on the back of your neck and you're not sure why, but the adrenaline is flowing, and every human sense is in over drive. I sensed that I was viewing an event that had no rhyme or reason to it, but that it represented a very real danger to me personally in the present, and in the future as the values of my world could only clash with the values that I had come to know in Saudi Arabia. At the age of 25, I stood on that road, and realized that the way the Saudis think and the ways Westerners think are fundamentally different. My heart felt heavy and frozen as I processed all of this. Every single hair on my arms and neck prickled my skin with the urgency of the feeling. It wasn't just what we believed; it was how we thought, and how we rationalized things. The gridlock of cars represented opposing, hateful forces that kept pushing against each other, locking each other deeper and deeper into a black hole. There appeared to be no desire for anyone to give an inch, to allow an opening out of the entangled mess.

The other incident had happened September 10, 1982. I had learned about Ramadan from my co-workers. They talked about it a lot in the months leading up to it. During Ramadan, Muslims from all over the world would make a Hajj to Mecca, a pilgrimage to deepen and honor their beliefs. I was told that the religious observance was a period of time in which Muslims fasted from sunrise to sunset. From a pragmatic perspective, it would greatly affect the routines of our daily work. The preps for exams that are linked to diet and fasting had to be considered differently during the month of Ramadan. For the most part, our work load was cut back in much the same way that routine procedures are cut back in Western hospitals over Thanksgiving and Christmas holiday seasons. Tammy told me that it would be a good time to go on vacation, and it was in the time frame for me to use my R&R anyway.

So, when I was flying back into Saudi Arabia from Sri Lanka, I did not think anything about a plane change in Kuwait. A plane change is a plane change anywhere, right? We landed in Kuwait airport in the dark, late evening. I found out after we landed that there would be no planes out of Kuwait until early the following morning. All passengers of connecting flights would stay in the terminal overnight. That was the routine there. There was not even an option to go to a hotel. They actually locked the airport up. Nobody got in or out after about 11:00 PM. I had my Fijian philosophy, "No Worries. Maybe Tomorrow." I had camped out in airports before. No big deal!

Within the first hour or so, several planes landed. It seemed like an influx of flights were coming in before the airport closed down for the night. As the planes unloaded, the terminal became extremely crowded with large groups of Muslim men, looking to be of Pakistani or Indian descent; dressed in nothing but knee-length, white, toga-looking, cloth garments. They were disembarking from charter flights on their way to

Mecca. I looked around and realized that I was the only Westerner in the airport, male or female. I glaringly stood out as the only female who was not covered from head to toe by the black abaya. The Pulitzer Prize winning-journalist, Steve Coll, reported in *Ghost Wars* that Saudi charities and wealthy patrons from the Gulf States built over 30,000 madrassas (Islamic schools) in Pakistan, many of them clustered along the Pakistan-Afghanistan border, by the mid-80's. I guess I can be thankful that I was not sporting a Russian passport in those days. It was all bad enough. To say that I did not feel comfortable or welcome in the terminal would be a definite under statement. I realized very fast that I was in a predicament.

Not only was I the only female without a black abaya, there were, in fact, very few females to be seen. I saw a Saudi couple who had a little girl with them. I sat across from them as I was very self-conscious of my plight. The men on Pilgrimage were openly scowling at me, and they were not discreet in moving close against my personal space. It seemed like there were hundreds of them, filling every space in the terminal. Before I saw the Saudi family, I had to keep moving, because if I stood still or sat down, a group of the toga-clad men would fill in the space around me, and they were neither smiling nor friendly.

I had gotten this stupid wicker elephant in a market in Colombo. I was carrying it with me. It was a plant stand. Anyway, I had sat across from the Saudi family for several minutes when the little girl, who was probably about ten years old, got out of her seat, walked over to me, and arrogantly snatched the elephant, which was next to my feet. She was brazen and rude. Her manner was neither cute nor appropriate for a child of her age. She knew exactly what she was doing. In the way that strangers in airports look to the parents of unruly children, I gently placed my hand on my wicker elephant, and looked across to the parents. The mother, as usual, did not make eye contact with me, nor did she say a word to the child.

The immaculately starched and well dressed father strolled over to me, standing over me as I was seated. He then pulled his wallet out, flicked a roll of bills in my face, and very disdainfully said to me, "She wants it. How much?" There was no question, no friendly tone, and no pretense of conversation to lead up to his words. It was not meant as a question. For him, it was an annoying demand. He was speaking to me like I was a servant. My pride was bigger than my brains that night. I told him that I had bought it for a gift (which was not true). I had bought it on a whim.

It had no great, personal value to me other than I could not let him treat me like that, and I was not about to give his bratty kid the satisfaction of getting her way when she had been so rude. I politely tried to tell him that it was not for sale. He became very quiet and rigid, staring at me. I thought he was actually going to hit me. He then said again, "But she really wants it." I just shook my head. He turned red. He was fuming. He then turned around, gathered up his wife and daughter, and stalked off. Well, that was pretty stupid of me. I had just messed up any chance of even a small, human connection in the terminal.

I went into the women's bathroom. As I opened the door, I had to step over a rather large group of older Arab women in their black shrouds, who were sitting in a circle on the bathroom floor, eating, gossiping, and hanging out in there. They were hunkered down for the night. It seemed like I had stepped back in time. The women had no expectation to sit in the chairs in the terminal. They did not look up at me. They kept talking among themselves. After a few minutes, I braced myself to go back out to the terminal. I could not bring myself to hang out in the bathroom for the next five hours. I could not sit on that floor. How could a simple plane change have turned into this? It was going to be a long night.

I found an empty seat. As I sat down, a group of togas walked over and stood around me. I really felt like they were trying to intimidate me. It was working. The whole thing had turned into a nightmare for me. All of a sudden, out of nowhere, someone tapped me on the shoulder. I looked back, irritated, thinking it was one of my smothering companions, venturing beyond just scowling at and crowding me. Instead, I saw the put-together face of a modern, chic, smiling, Western-dressed woman. She looked like an angel to me. She never spoke. She just nodded, and gestured for me to come with her. She did not have to tell me twice. She was a stewardess. I had forgotten that the airport had been locked up. The stewardesses from all the flights were in a separate room, sleeping in chairs for the night. She never said much to me. She didn't need to. We both knew why she got me. She went over to her group, snuggled up in a chair, and went to sleep. I was never so grateful in my life at the action of a stranger.

There is one more twist to my Kuwait experience. A bunch of planes boarded around the same time very early the next morning. Of course, I was going to Jeddah, so the sea of white togas was pushing onto my flight. However, I had an assigned seat, and the stewardess had let me board with her. I thought the worse was behind me. We lined up on the tarmac to take off. We could see a row of planes in front of us. We sat there without moving for several hours. It never fails right. The Captain finally came on and told us what had happened. A plane that was two planes ahead of us was being high-jacked. I am not kidding. You can't even make this stuff up. As we began to move, I saw a plane pulled off the runway. It had JAL on the side, Japanese Air Lines. It was surrounded by two tanks. As we took off in the sky, I thought, "Oh my God! Were those guys in the terminal with us all night?"

The Kuwait terminal experience moved me from a position on the sidelines.

This really was a time and a place that was not open to a comfortable relationship with Western culture. The airports of Kuwait and Jeddah were as modern as any in the world. But, all that glitters is not gold. There was so much tension and turmoil very close to the surface. There seemed to be this huge gap among internal forces. We will look power-ful, modern, and first class. At the same time, we will remain pure and uncontaminated by the Western world. We will look like the West on the outside, only better and more powerful, but we will not be like them. The yin and the yang were becoming more evident to me as time passed, and with each new experience. I had begun to realize that I could never understand it. It was not mine to understand. The cultural schemas of a young, Canadian woman could never be integrated into the cultural beliefs of Saudi Arabia and the Gulf States. These were my thoughts. I thought that the only way that I could honor this culture was to walk away from it. It was mine to observe. It was mine to ponder. It was mine to process. Through all of this, the bottom line became that it was mine to walk away from.

Before I left, I had the opportunity to travel within the country beyond our drives to the Red Sea or to Abha. Tammy knew lots of people. She was out going. She had previously worked in Riyadh. She had connec-tions. Everyone liked her. She had a spirit of adventure and curiosity. So, it was with her that I went to Riyadh for a few days, and also to Dhahran. Riyadh was a lot like Jeddah, except it was not humid like Jeddah. It was the sort of dry heat that I had known in the Outback of Australia. The buildings were big and modern. There were shopping malls and lots of smaller shops. The Saudis looked rich in Riyadh, richer than they looked in Khamis Mushayt. You could almost see the money oozing through the pores of their skin.

It was not uncommon to see small groups of Saudi women shopping together; walking and talking among each other. I was always amazed at how much they avoided any contact with us. They did not appear to have any curiosity what-so-ever to talk to women from other countries. They were not receptive to letting us into their world. Is this because it was forbidden? Or, did they truly have no interest in us? I was never able to figure that out, and I never had an opportunity to talk to a Saudi female beyond the poor girl with the baby to begin to have any insight.

They did like gold. We would see them shopping in the gold suugs. The gold was purchased by weight. It was soft, a flat yellow color, and of very high caret. Saudi women would try on bracelets over the black cloth. Sometimes, they would wear solid gold bracelets from their wrists to their elbows. As Western women, we were always amazed at the amount of money they paid for gold jewelry. We would buy a single bracelet or two. That was usually a big splurge, and often because we had nothing better to spend our money on. They would buy thousands of dollars in gold purchases in a single day.

Tammy could not wait to take me to Dhahran, nicknamed Little America. It is the home to AREMCO. It is a world of its own, within the Kingdom, but separate from it. Dhahran operates with a separate set of rules. Women drive within the borders of the town. Dhahran was originally built as a US Base after World War II, linked to the protection and the control of the oil industry. The Americans turned it over to the Royal Saudi Air Force in the mid-60's. The Americans have always maintained a strong presence there.

I was not overly impressed with the area. The scenery was pretty flat and empty, with huge sand dunes scattered across the emptiness. There was access to more American goods than we could get on a regular basis in Khamis Mushayt. I think that American executives spend time in Dhahran, and they see the lifestyle as somewhat moderate and progressive, in a relative sort of way. That is like staying in the Green Zone in Iraq, and thinking things are not so bad over there. Or like going to Disney, never leaving the property, and thinking everyone in America lives a magical life of Pixie Dust and make believe. The experience of the life of your average Saudi national is not represented by the lifestyle of Dhahran.

I came to know that I did not belong in Saudi Arabia. I could not stand the difference in living conditions for foreign workers of Western countries relative to the accommodations of workers from third world countries. I never understood why the leaders in the native country, who had negotiated the terms of the block visas, did not insist on more humane living conditions for their citizens. I never understood why the servant class and the laborers were treated so badly in Saudi Arabia. Every time that we drove by the tin-roofed shanty towns in the middle of a barren, dusty field on the side of the road, I felt like I do when I walk by a homeless person asleep on the cold ground. In the depths of your soul, you know how wrong it is. And like everyone else, I am paralyzed by inaction. My mind processes the injustice and the cruelty of the world for some of its citizens. But I walk by. I can find no peace with these thoughts. I continue to walk by. The unfairness always nags at me. The nuns warned us that we would have to answer for our actions or our inactions in the after life because we knew the difference of right and wrong. We had the benefit of that fine, Catholic education. The bar would be raised for us.

I came to know that Saudi Arabia did not have a middle class as we know it. There was not a working class of people in the Kingdom. Why did they need to import medical workers? The citizens of the third world countries built their roads, constructed their ultra modern buildings, cooked their meals, did their laundry, manicured their property, and swept their streets. Mid-Easterners from many other countries were employed in Saudi Arabia. Our personnel director was Lebanese. Hamdam carried a Jordanian passport. Our Radiologist was an Egyptian. The Sinhalese drove their taxis. The Pakistanis and many others worked in the small shops and bazaars.

On the streets of Khamis Mushayt, we always noticed how many young Saudi men of working age seemed to hang out in the daytime. They would go in and out of the mosque during calls to prayer. In between, they seemed to have no purpose to fill up the time of their day. Some appeared educated and relatively well dressed, as far as a white robe and a headdress can be described. They were immaculate. Their robes were pressed and starched. They were well groomed. They appeared to be resolute, calm, and somber. They did not smile a lot or joke among themselves. The older men in the bazaars would shout out to each other, joking and kidding, but the young Saudi men were more serious. This is my memory of them in that time and place.

I had decided that I would stay until the beginning of the summer in 1983. After my year was up, I could go from month to month. That was a very nice option. It was in March, 1983, that the Marine barracks were bombed in Lebanon. We were instructed not to leave our housing area on the Saudi Air Base for a couple of weeks. It seemed as if our hosts knew the dangers for us more than we did. For the most part, we did not feel physically threatened in Saudi Arabia. March became an uneasy time. This was mostly because the Arabs, who we worked with and saw around the Air Base on a regular basis, appeared agitated and unsettled.

I would walk by an apartment in which a Lebanese man lived. He was usually friendly. I would see him around the hospital all the time. He spoke perfect English, and he always had a friendly comment and a wave. Since the Beirut bombing, over a course of the last week or so, he would have a roomful of men in his apartment. They would have heated debates in Arabic; very loud as they were glued to the TV. You could not help but notice them as you walked by. His door was always open.

I was on my way home one day after work, walking the same route that I walked every day. It took me on the sidewalk in front of his building. When he saw me, he got out of his chair and very purposely closed the door as I approached. He knew that I would just walk by and wave as I always did. It was very weird and appeared very deliberate to shut me out. He had always been genuinely friendly and nice prior to that day. I wondered if he shut that door to protect me as much as to shut me out. Whatever the reason, it was a sobering incident. There it was again. I did not belong here. I was out of my element.

So, it was soon after Beirut, that I gave my notice to end my employment. It would take several weeks to process the paperwork. Saudi Arabia is the only country that I have ever traveled to that required one to apply in advance for a visa to exit. You can not get into Saudi Arabia without an entry visa; requiring an official sponsor and a reason for being there. You also could not leave without an exit visa. It is one of the most controlled border systems that I have ever traveled through. As foreign workers, family members and friends were not allowed to visit. Entry visas were only issued for official reasons. Your company of hire had to apply for your entry visa and your exit visa, and it did not happen overnight.

The exception was if a foreign national was being quickly whisked out of the country. Foreign workers were deported for even a minor infraction of a Saudi law, or sometimes for being in the wrong place at the wrong time. For example, an auto accident would usually get the Western driver deported, even if the accident was obviously caused by the Saudi driver. Their reasoning was that it was automatically the foreigner's fault. If he was not in the Kingdom the accident would not have happened in the first place. It was as simple as that. The reasoning made perfect sense to the Saudis. The procedure for the company was to get the employee

out very quickly, and to pay the Saudis an amount of money to compen-
sate for the problem. I knew two young Aussie girls who were deported
after they had been partying with a Saudi officer. They were in his vehicle
during a minor accident. They broke the cardinal rule, and mixed it up
with a Saudi national. It did not matter if they were invited and that he
was a person of relative power. The next day they were gone. It was the
way things were handled over there.

What I came to know from my brief experience in Saudi Arabia was
that this was not a country hospitable to people of other cultures and
places. Saudi Arabia is a police state for the most part. People will argue
this fact. We see the modern cities, the riches of the oil wealth, and the
polished, educated Saudis who travel the world. The ruling class has been
educated in some of the most elite universities of America and Great
Britain. The modern surface covers the reality for the average Saudi
citizen.

Powerful and rich Saudis live one life in the Western world and enforce
a different life for themselves and their citizens in Saudi Arabia. The core
of the country's rule imposes a very strict, punitive version of Islam on
its citizens. The Wahhabi version of Islam is not conservative in the way
that we understand conservative. The Shariah Laws of the Kingdom are
absolute and punitive in the style of Stalin. The reality is the suppression
of women and a restriction of freedom of the press, freedom of religion,
and freedom of expression. It is the control of the press and the denial of
the oil barons that has helped to contain a true knowledge of life in the
Kingdom from awareness in Western democracies.

Policy makers are quick to point out the evils of the rhetoric out of
Iran, anti-American, and very fundamentalist. This angry hatred against
Western interests and values fueled the exact sermons and messages
that we heard broadcasting from the mosque in Khamis Mushayt. The
Western world has been kept isolated from the closed society and the
realities within the Kingdom because journalists are not allowed to freely
travel or to report from the streets. Also, most Western contacts in Saudi
Arabia have been linked to the oil industry and the Saudi elite, who have
the capacity to operate from both sides of the coin. All of this is catching
up with both the Saudis and their American counterparts. You can't have
it both ways without major cracks and fissures erupting. Can you imagine a country in which a woman is caned if her ankles or any part of her
skin is seen in public? We shudder at these same images and reports out
of Afghanistan with the Taliban, but this has been and continues to be

the reality for women in Saudi Arabia over the course of the Kingdom's existence.

What I came to know was that I felt an underlying danger against my beliefs and values in Saudi Arabia. I felt physically safe as long as I tread carefully around the obstacles for a single, Western woman in Saudi Arabia. We felt protected on the Saudi Air Base. The blatant affronts to our culture were felt acutely when we ventured into the towns and the countryside. An independent and strong group of women from all corners of the world shouldered each other through this time and place. I did not know a single female who could put our experience there in any kind of perspective other than to shake our heads, and to know that this was a brief moment in time for us. We could not relate to the lives of the Saudi women who were forbidden from interacting with us.

I have read that it was the influence of women in Northern Ireland, both Protestant and Catholic, who were instrumental in effecting the process of dialogue and peace in that country in the late 80's and early 90's. The Irish mothers and wives were tired of burying their loved ones in the ongoing and long dispute. The voice of a mother's heart can offer perspective and clarity when the waters are muddied with anger and mistrust. My friend, Hamdam, longed to be reunited with his mother in Palestine. As a Catholic, I place a lot of faith in the power of a mother's love. I witnessed the total public suppression of a mother's voice and heart in Saudi Arabia.

What I came to know when I boarded my plane in Jeddah to say goodbye to Saudi Arabia was that my background had afforded me an innocence and a trust in the basic goodwill of people. This basic trust had gotten me through my experience in Saudi Arabia. I came to realize that the ability to trust is a learned human process that must be experienced and nurtured to be realized. My friendship with Hamdam and Khaled allow me to hope that the process of trust can be moved forward as individuals of good will are waiting for a better life for their children. I don't have the answer, but I believe the people across the region must find their way through the mistrust and the anger if peace is to be realized.

Chapter 6

LEGAL RESIDENT ALIEN

"You don't need to figure it all out before hand. Just go back, get started, enroll in a few classes, and it'll work its way out as you go." That is the best advice for education that I had ever been given in my life. It was probably in the fall of 1987. A co-worker of mine, a big, friendly, very smart guy from New Jersey cut it to the chase for me. Stop talking and fretting about the end result. Just begin the process and let the future play itself out. My whole life I had spent planning one stage to the next, independently setting a goal, and working towards reaching it. I could handle the side issues along the way, but I always had directed myself towards a tangible goal. The nuns had taught me sequential processing very well and at a very young age.

You see, there were no programs with a Law School in Fort Walton Beach or an easy commute from there. I was so focused on needing to find a Law School that I had locked myself out of starting the process. The problem was that I did not know how to begin the steps without having a clear plan from A to Z. Without the path, I hesitated. I fretted. I had not yet gained the wisdom to figure out that life learning is all about the process of learning, not some end result of learning. My burly New Jersey friend helped me past the mental block that I had created for myself.

I had begun working at Humana Hospital in Fort Walton Beach in the Panhandle of Florida in the fall of 1984. I had arrived in the Miracle Strip as many others had done before me. My husband was assigned to Eglin Air Force Base. I actually had met my husband in Saudi Arabia. I never returned to live in Victoria. We had spent a short time in New Mexico and Colorado, prior to our orders to Eglin. My life plan for my return to Victoria and higher education had been interrupted by marriage and a new life in the United States. I was employed as a legal resident alien. That meant that I could live and work permanently in the United States, but that I could not vote or work for the federal government. I could apply for U.S. citizenship after a number of years.

It is not an adjustment shock for a middle class Canadian to begin working among middle class Americans. We share most of the same values; probably every thing except gun ownership. There is a huge cultural difference on this single issue. I was shocked when I found out that several of my female co-workers, young girls just like me, girls I hung out with, carried handguns for protection; especially when they worked shift work. That would be unheard of in Canada. That's one of those things that I don't think much about any more, but it was definitely a phenomena to absorb and ponder in the beginning. Other than toting a gun in your purse, I fell into an easy rhythm with my friends at work. My fellow X-Ray techs and nurses had the same cynical but compassionate sense of humor that I was raised on in the Canadian health care system. The cynicism was directed at our corporate bosses in America and at the government in Canada. The compassion was evident in boat loads in both countries to ease the fear and diminish the pain of our patients' suffering. We worked equally hard in both systems of health care, which are vastly different in structure, but very similar in the human side of caring.

It is my opinion that both countries have huge problems with their respective health care systems relative to delivery of care. I want to emphasize that the delivery of care is different than the standard of care, which is extremely high in both systems. Medical workers and doctors really do care about their patients more than anything else. They work very hard and are usually under appreciated until patients experience first hand the benefit of their service and commitment. I was discussing the two systems with a Canadian friend of mine who is a doctor in a very busy hospital in Newfoundland. He summed it up this way, "In Canada, we have access but not enough resources. In America, they have plenty of resources but not enough access." To me, that is the heart of the issue for both countries.

The Canadian delivery model is not funded enough to provide optimal coverage for the needs of all of its citizens. The American model does not provide any coverage at all for many of its citizens. But it provides world class medical services for others of it citizens. The gap is getting larger and larger in the States, and the access for Canadians is also stretched to the limit. The frustration for the average person is that from a system perspective, both countries seem stuck in defending their own system as not as bad as the alternative.

The Canadian issue with the American system is that medical care is not equally distributed. The rich and the entitled benefit more than the less fortunate. Canadians see health care as a right of citizenship, equal access for all. Americans shudder at the tax burden of a more socialized delivery model. I have never understood the difference to the worker of paying taxes for health care verses the high cost of premiums. Money out is money out. I am not saying the solution is higher taxes. It just seems to me that dollars for services are being paid by workers in both countries. We just frame it differently. High premiums verses high taxes; from the workers' take home pay, the outcome is the same. As citizens of both countries plod through the muck of the mess, politicians get stuck in se-mantics and rhetoric. They can't see the forest for the trees.

I think that the American system is currently in a deeper crisis than the Canadian system. More and more middle class workers are being squeezed out of coverage, which equates to very limited access to services in America. For example, I have a good friend who is one of the best teachers that any parent or principal could wish to have for their stu-dents. She is as good as it gets. Her students love her and fear her at the same time. She challenges them to maximize their learning in her pres-ence. In other words, she forces them, or in politically correct terms, she empowers them to shake out the cobwebs and to think. She is a single, divorced mother of two. Like so many divorced mothers, her ex-husband does not even try to provide the child support which has been mandated by the court system. I have learned from her that there are many laws on the books regarding child support, but in reality, the enforcement is a joke, especially across state lines.

Anyway, she recently told me that she could not afford the premiums in the health care options offered by her school district to take out the family plan. She had no health care coverage for her sons. She is very smart and educated. I could not believe that the health care system had failed for her. A family health care plan for the three of them would cost over $400 /month. The financial burden of coverage pushed her sons out of the system. Many working, middle class workers have to cross their fingers that, for example, their football playing-age son is not a broken bone away from a $20,000 medical bill. The medical system is broken in America for many of its citizens. In Canada, it is stretched for all of its citizens. Surely, there is some compromise among thinkers of open and willing minds that could explore and incorporate the best of both sys-tems into a more patient access delivery system. In the meantime, health care providers slug away in both countries with kind and caring hearts.

I was lucky and grateful to be introduced to living in America through the friendship of my hospital coworkers and through the support of my husband's squadron and military friends. Of course, the sugary, white beaches of the Florida Panhandle and the climate were easy to take. We worked hard and we played hard. We lived for a Friday Happy Hour on an outside deck. A live band playing Buffet or the Stones, and dolphins splashing in the background were a happy and fitting end to our work week. We laughed over the highlights, or better still, the bizarre stories of our days. An order of Macho Nachos to share around a cold pitcher of draft gently eased us into a fitting start for our anticipated weekend.

We worked shift work, both my husband in his Air Force job and me in the hospital. I think working adults, who do not have the responsibility of raising children, enjoy a mix of shifts. There were always more Indians and fewer Chiefs. We liked that. Shift-work allowed for day time relaxation and laziness on the beaches of Okaloosa Island, which are world class. In the mid-80's, the Florida Panhandle had been free of major hurricane activity for a long time. People took for granted the splendor of the beaches for miles and miles. Life was easy there. It was a good place to be young and healthy.

If we got restless or bored in Ft. Walton Beach, there was always a road trip to New Orleans. The experience of the city stirred our lulled brains to absorb the aliveness of The Big Easy. It didn't matter if you loved New Orleans or you hated it. You would still describe it as alive. Our group of friends loved New Orleans. We reveled in the music, the food, the smells, the people, and the over whelming humanity of the city. Bubba Gump's, Café de Monde, Pat O'Brian's, Preservation Hall, and The French Market Café—we loved it all!

We could spend hours strolling through the Audubon Zoo and the gardens surrounding it. We rode on the streetcars that connected the Southern mansions of St. Charles Avenue to the jumbled throngs of the French Market. We took free rides on the ferry to Algiers, lazily soaking up the sun as the cumbersome car ferry moved in slow motion across the muddy Mississippi. We couldn't decide what we liked more; The French Quarter Festival or the Jazz Festival. Actually, I liked the French Quarter Festival more. It was smaller, less known, and less crowded. Royal Street had a selection of local talent on every corner; jamming and having fun with each other in the Big Easy rhythm of being.

For me, New Orleans was a city of locals and tourists who managed to fit together in a synchrony of give and take. It was a place to let things be; old and new, rich and poor, black and white, merchant and beggar, bus and limousine. It was not a place to judge others. It was a place to be one with your inner self, without worrying about the endless range of things that occupy our thoughts on a routine basis. From the enticing smells and tastes of Madeline's Bakery to the debauchery of Bourbon Street, New Orleans could wake up your senses like no where else on earth. There were some really strong smells in New Orleans, especially if you managed to get yourself out early on a Sunday morning. That odor was not so pleasant but it was oh so alive!

Before the streets were hosed down to begin it all over again, the morning aroma jolted your senses and your motor system to walk at a brisker pace towards a more soothing sense, such as coffee and beignets or better yet, fresh pralines for breakfast (my favorite)! John Denver sang clearly and harmoniously of his personal experience with the awakening of his senses in *Rocky Mountain High*. In a different sort of high, the local musicians blew the beat of the Big Easy into the tiny, connective fibers of our muscles; allowing the pulse of a human heart to become one with the heart beat of an urban city. For me, New Orleans was America and America was represented in the ebb and flow of The Big Easy. New Orleans had captured the soul of America.

Americans and Canadians across the middle class share the same dreams and face the same challenges. I think that America has a wider rift between the "have not's" and the "have way too much" polarities of society. Canada has a broader middle class. The poor are not as poor, and the rich are not as rich. The greed of corporate entitlements and profit is not to the degree of absurdity in Canada relative to that of America. Wealth appears to be distributed more evenly between workers and capitalists.

This is not because individuals in Canada have the high road on personal morals. I think it is linked to more equitable labor laws and better enforcement. Also, a more socialized mind set does not honor unreasonable greed on the backs of the lower class to the extent that has evolved in America. I am not an economist. I am not even sure if my personal observation is valid. But it appears to me that the culture of Canada embraces a little less profit at the top, and a fairer shake for the working class at all levels along the rungs of the ladder.

In contrast, I also think that the opportunity to get ahead is available to a greater degree in the United States. There are many more opportunities and resources in the States from both private and government sources. The problem, from my humble perspective, is that a segment of Americans make personal choices that restrict themselves from accessing opportunities that are available. Human psychology is very complicated. An attempt to understand how people think is like gently peeling off layers of an onion. Just as you are beginning to have success, the fragile layer tears apart beneath your fingers. There are no easy answers to the interlocking web of emotional layers that drive our reactions to the world around us. I think it has to do with intergenerational trust issues. If you do not trust that the system is legitimately available to you, then it is easier to resist the probability of a negative outcome from your position than to take a risk on a positive outcome.

I don't know anymore than anyone else. I only have a viewpoint based on my life experiences and observations. I tend to think about how events and people are connected; a sort of historical reflection of relationships and the evolution of personal stories. I can posit with the best of them or with the worst of them. I do know that the Catholic nuns taught me at a young age to own my education, to own my learning, and to own my choices.

Acquiring and exploring new knowledge was taught to be a function of self, not a function of anyone or anything else. So, if we are to say that a segment of society or a group of individuals are not partaking in a system that is available, where does the blame lie? Where does the answer lie? I think a beginning is to peel the onion, one thin layer at a time, and to keep going when the fragile tissue tears. The key is to keep looking for solutions and away from blame. I have seen and believe that the opportunity does exist in America for all. One has to trust that active engagement in the process will result in personal success and not failure or disappointment. This sounds simple but the vulnerability of our humanity can make the most basic life decisions very complicated.

My life in America as a legal resident alien was very similar to the life that I would have known as a young, working adult in Canada. I went through the Aerobics phase; always striving to balance my bountiful lifestyle with the intake of my calories. I have struggled with that one my entire life. I honored the beach in a very big way. I balanced work and play. I took vacations. Everyone who visited me wanted to go to Disney World. I did manage to get myself enrolled in a university program; the beginning steps in my future world of credit hours and tuition. Our group of friends lived the good life; that of young, working, middle class adults, blessed with good health and robust energy. The experience of

Saudi Arabia faded easily into my past. It probably gave me more layers of insight than I knew what to do with. It was easier to lock that away. It would stay deep and far from my conscious thoughts until it came rushing back in 2001. But all that is a long way from my present.

Chapter 7

RACING FORWARD

I GUESS THAT I CAN NOT talk of my life in America without discussing race. My husband is black. I am white. We have been married for almost a quarter of a century. A quirky little aside is that my mother was born on May 13, 1924 in her family's house in St. John's in the churning belly of the North Atlantic, in the middle of nowhere. My husband's mother was born on May 13, 1924 in a rural part of Kentucky. Both of them were born into very poor families. Who wasn't poor in 1924? We did not realize the fact of our mothers being born on the same day and in the same year until after we were married. The connection of their births is one of those twilight zone kind of things that you don't want to think too much about. I wonder how all the little things fit into the grand plan. The nuns impressed upon us to think about these deep things as early as our elementary years; no answers, just things to ponder.

So where does one begin when discussing race issues? I can only speak from my heart of my personal story. I grew up in a place where the only black Americans that we were exposed to were on our television screens; men like Martin Luther King, Sidney Poitier, Harry Belafonte, Nat King Cole, Mohammed Ali, Jesse Owens, Arthur Ash, and Sammy Davis Jr. What was there not to like? Everyone loved the Jesse Owens story. He had stuck it to Hitler with the quiet and dignified strength of his superior athleticism. His performance and strength of character jolted people of good will across the world to feel a sense of triumph and hope.

My mother cheered every time she saw a black and white clip of Jesse Owens crossing the finish line in Berlin; Hitler visibly flinching, as the superior performance of a black American athlete wiped the smug smirk off the Furher's Aryan face; for a brief but powerful moment for the world to witness. Mom would say, "Atta boy Jesse" every time she watched that footage, with a happy and gleeful expression on her face. She was like a young girl cheering her high school team on to victory. The use of the word *boy* in the culture of Newfoundland is not used to belittle or to rank a person as inferior to the speaker. Boy pronounced *Bye* is used affectionately and often in local lingo to express confirmation, encouragement, and approval, as in "Some good boy" or "Way to go boy" or "Yes Boy." These phrases are said among Newfoundlanders to each other all the time. A homemade apple pie is "Some good boy (bye)."

My mother approved of Jesse Owens in no uncertain terms. Her brother fought in Germany, and many Newfoundland men of her generation lost their lives in battles such as Beaumont Hamel and Dunkirk. Jesse Owens represented hope, justice, and triumph. In Newfoundland, we watched the Civil Rights of the 60's play out on our television screens from a neutral position; trying to make sense of it without being immersed in it. The words and passion of Martin Luther King shook us in our boots. We were not saints or above prejudice any more than people from anywhere in the world can be. Prejudices are developed and nurtured within historical contexts of culture. Look at the Catholic—Protestant story in Newfoundland, the indentured servant story between the Irish and the British. We were just raised in a culture where strength of character was not judged in the context of skin color.

We were all pretty white up there; the blue-white tone of skin with veins close to the surface. The bleached skin of both Catholic and Protestant Newfoundlanders had not felt the warmth of the sun's rays for much of the year across time and generations. With hair color, we were not as neutral. Freckled—faced, red heads did evoke a stereotype of a feisty temper and true grit against the image of the upper class. Money was not associated with the genetic traits of freckles and red hair, passed on from our ancestors in the Emerald Isle. I am being a little funny here, but stereotypes of class and money were linked to the history of our island home; poor Irish fishermen overcoming the burden of homage to the merchant class.

Overall, the safe, small, isolated world that we lived in allowed us to trust strangers and to reach out to people. We liked meeting people from other places and we were not threatened economically or morally by the character trait of skin color. In the context of race, the personal morals and the economy of the people of Newfoundland were not challenged by the incongruent actions of a society against the founding principles of that same society. In this one aspect, we did not have to rationalize actions that fragmented our basic morals.

Huge migrations of people were not scaling the cliffs from the freeze of the North Atlantic to share a piece of the barren land that we were born into. We had huge economic challenges, but they did not involve skin color or immigration. We were removed from the raw emotions of slavery, as rationalizations and reformations were played out in America over the course of its history. A country formed on the principles of the greatest democracy in the world wrestled within its moral conscience as a developing nation. I believe that the true strength of America is evidenced by the evolution of freedoms and rights for all of its citizens.

A college professor of mine, who had a Doctorate Degree in Demographics, lectured that individuals do not matter in the big scheme of things. I argued with him at that time from my humble, rebel position. I think about that often. I still believe that the total opposite is true. It is the combined will of individuals that sets in motion forces for growth and change. If not, we are all sheep being led to the slaughter. I believe that policy makers and leaders tend to lose sight of the thinking mind of people as individuals.

The professor really pissed me off with his lecture. Maybe that was his purpose. It did shake me up, and I think about it often. I wonder and fear if he was right. Sometimes, it does seem like we are sheep, obliviously stumbling past the hypocrisy and entitlement of politicians and leaders without the engagement of critical human questioning and thinking. I find hope and remain strong in my original position. Capitalists will tell me that I am naïve, that market forces drive everything. I maintain, that individuals come together to drive market forces and that eventually, the combined will of individual people prevails. I think a democracy is strengthened through the personal stories of individual relationships across time.

I had this experience with a patient in Florida. She was very old, over 90 at the time. She had come in with a very bad cough. She was on a stretcher because she was too weak to stand. I had to work close to her, to reach over her. I had to sit her up with the back of the stretcher to support her for an upright chest X-Ray. In the process of that rather tricky but routine work, I had to lean very close across her body. It's not as easy as it sounds to get a weak person to sit straight, to raise their arms above their head, to maneuver the stretcher an inch or so in order to line it all up, and then to have the weak patient hold the position for a few seconds. On top of that, they are required to hold their breath in at the exact second needed to shoot the picture correctly. If there is a hint of motion, or any part of the lungs are cut off, you have to go back to square one and go through it all over again. The old lady was extremely weak. I was concentrating on getting it right the first time.

Out of the blue, in the middle of reaching across her, she grabbed my arm like a vice. I looked into her face, as I wondered if I was hurting her in any way. Her eyes became very urgent and she tightened her hold. Her grip was claw like. Her long, bony fingers dug into my arm, as her eyes demanded my full attention. She hoarsely whispered the following exchange, never loosening her grip. She asked me if I knew her doctor. She said his name. I did know him. He was a black physician in the hospital. She asked me if I liked him. I told her that I did not know him very well, which was my tactful way of avoiding an answer.

He was not one of my favorite doctors to work among. From my perspective, he was distant and rude to staff members. He acted more or less like he was above saying hello or giving a friendly nod if he passed you in the hall for the hundredth time. My opinion of him was lukewarm, but I would never express that to a patient. She went on to tell me, as she squeezed deeper into my arm, that she really loved him. She said he was very good to his patients and a great doctor. That was nice to know, and provided me an insight that was different from my personal experience with him.

I will never forget what she said next to me. Remember that she was over 90 years old. She fiercely whispered, "That stuff that they taught us in church growing up was all lies. I am so glad that I found out before I die. You are young. I want you to hear this from me and to believe me. It was all lies. Blacks are not the devil. Dr.(name) is a wonderful person. I am glad that I found out the truth before I die. He is a good man, a very good man. It was all lies!" She released her death grip on my arm, laid back against the stretcher, and she calmly smiled, nodding slowly and happily that she had spoken her thoughts out loud.

Her raspy words were pretty powerful. I felt like she had an intense need to pass the evolution of her life experience on to me; to provide me the wisdom of her personal truth as the window was beginning to peacefully close on the chapters of her life. She wanted to set the record straight in her final chapter. Her story speaks of culture and teaching, and the journey we make from our childhood through the personal experiences of our lives. She grew up in the South around the 1900's. She said these words to me in the South in mid-1990. She probably lived her entire life within a 100 miles or less of where she had been born.

In America, I have observed and experienced the bi-directional effects of vulnerability, guilt, shame, and mistrust that are the outcome of America's journey with slavery and civil rights. Through the complexity of all of this, my personal experience is that the average, working, participating citizen does the best that they know how; and that their interactions across race lines on an individual basis are usually much better and healthier than the media or others would have us believe. I think this is especially so in the South. In a way, I think that people are actually more decent than they know themselves to be or that they sometimes portray themselves to be.

For example, the Don Imus fiasco is an example of my observation on race. The core can be more decent than the surface; more decent than we allow others to see, and more decent than we trust ourselves to be. In a few, brief, thoughtless words, Imus erased the substance of many conversations over the years of his broadcast that were quite reflective and probing, as he openly and honestly discussed race relations in American with a myriad of guests, both black and white. I always thought that he had great insight and compassion when he moved beyond his Archie Bunker exterior. I think an analogy for Don Imus is The Big Easy; raunchy, raw, dirty, risqué, and irreverent on the surface, but with a soul as deep as the Grand Canyon if one dared to enter. To me, both the city and the man were surrounded by a porous layer of vulgar genuineness that purposely kept the faint of heart out.

Imus' story is sort of like a Shakespearean tragedy. As my Cajun friend said, "He made his bed, now he has to lie in it." The reality is that a complex and kind citizen, who stood up for the little guy, took on perceived injustices of the powerful, honored sick children, and advocated loudly for American veterans of all races is now known for none of these things. The essence of his character is evidenced by the goodness and the sweep of his interests and life work. The dark and nasty words of his stinging speech formed a brittle shell of armor; easily cracked by peeping into the estuary of his soul, which definitely ebbed and flowed with the moods of his moments, and the back and forth of his on-air commentary and conversations. In short, Imus wore his dark side on his sleeve. His message was you accept all of me, the nonsense and the glory, or the hell with you. If you can't stomach my irreverent satire and my reactive, mean outer shell, then I choose to filter you out. I am who I am. I will scream my demons loudly. I am honest and genuine. I sting on the surface but I am a very good person if you hang around long enough to find out. I am a champion of the weakest among us. I also glory in my rebel side. I am a genuine jack ass a lot of the time. I am bad. I am good. I am complicated. I am a human being. Take me as I am, or not.

The Imus situation is such a hot potato that people don't want to touch it with a ten foot pole. I hate it when people back away from a multi-edged sword because of political correctness; or they exploit it through their own agenda. I was a regular viewer. I liked the show. I am saddened by the whole thing. I think it is America's loss. I never saw Don Imus as a racist; an idiot at times, a genius at other times, but never a racist. He has a brilliant mind. I saw him as a thinking, reflective intellectual underneath the raw exterior of his piercing person. He had a flavor that was both infuriating and intriguing. Imus was flawed and genuine; complex and yet simple. He had great taste in music. He was a quick read on human character. Like all of us, he knew others better than himself. From my perspective, he worked hard to hide his goodness and his brilliance with the nastiness of his rambling, senseless speech. I hope he is able to forgive himself, so that his future is filled with his possibility.

When I first lived in the Florida Panhandle, which is known as LA, or Lower Alabama, the usual reaction that I got from coworkers when they discovered that my husband was black was surprise. I never really took offense to that because they were not mean spirited or condescending in my presence, just genuinely sort of "caught off guard". I am sure that many of them had their own private thoughts based on the experiences of their individual lives, but the bottom line was that my husband and I hung out with and had many friends across all race lines. It was not an issue for us, so it did not become an issue for the development of our relationships with Americans, once they got over the initial reaction. This goes for both black and white Americans.

I am not saying that racism does not exist. It is just that I was able to frame negative behavior across race lines as a function of the other person's life story and the issues or demons that they had to deal with, rather than a function of me. I think it is a shame that people restrict themselves to friendships and personal relationships based on skin pigmentation rather than the traits of courage, kindness, humor, genuineness, and empathy. I choose to share my experiences and time with positive, upbeat, kindred spirits. They come in all shapes, sizes, and colors.

I think that people of all races would serve themselves better if they could step out of their box and offer a genuine expression of greeting across race lines. A fact that I have learned through the years of my jour-

ney is that people are at different levels of comfort with cross-race interactions, even something as simple as nodding at a person when you pass
in the street. I find it helpful to be aware that if a person of another race
rebuffs a genuine gesture or word from me, it is probably linked to a deep
vulnerability inside of them. This is hard to deal with because no one
likes to feel slighted or rebuffed.

The ability to frame the rebuff as a trust issue for the other party, rather
than from a reactionary, defensive response is not easy to do. However,
the high road is very effective in gradually allowing the other person to
open themselves up to you; to let their guard down, and to be themselves
around you. Sometimes, it only takes a single time to take the high road.
Other times, the person is so guarded that the door never opens. When
people are guarded, they have had prior experiences or learned knowledge to base their assumptions on. They may react to a genuine gesture
as patronizing or false. It is amazing how fast a negative give and take can
melt away if one party can move out of a defensive position.

I will try to give you this personal example. This happened to me early
in my life in the United States. I was working for a group of Radiologists
who had an outpatient clinic in Denver. I had not been working there
long, maybe a month or so. My husband and I would only be in Denver
for three months while he attended training at Lowery Air Force Base. I
had been lucky enough to fall into a summer-hire position. That is one
thing about Radiology. You can always find a job.

The Radiologists had two offices in separate buildings. The main office
employed three techs and several office personnel. The smaller office had
only a single tech over there. It was open to provide a service for doctors
who had offices in that building. The patients in the small office were all
walk-ins, no appointments. We did not schedule more involved exams.
It was very basic, a pretty simple gig in our line of work. As techs, we
would rotate between offices, one week a month at the smaller site. I was
assigned over there a few weeks into my hire. Another tech took me over
and showed me around. It was very straight forward, just a single diagnostic room, a dark room, and a small outer office.

On my first day, three patients walked into the office, more or less one
behind the other, right around 4:30 PM. They each had scripts ordering
multiple procedures. They had all come from the same Orthopedic Clinic
upstairs. The surgeon or his staff had obviously written the scripts in a
span of a couple of minutes, sending the patients down together, to get
them in before our office closed at 5:00 PM. The exams were not hard

but they were time consuming. I was not going to be able to knock these out in five or ten minutes. He had ordered an average of thirteen views per patient. With the processing of the films and the paperwork, I knew I was looking at a minimum of forty-five minutes, probably an hour; that would be with no repeats. I was very motivated to get it right the first time.

The third patient walked in a minute or two behind the person ahead of her. I was standing at the counter, working on the paperwork of the other two. She was not in a good mood when she walked in the door. She was curt with me in an agitated, condescending, and hostile way immediately. She absolutely did not want to wait as she looked around the small waiting room. I got the sense that she was used to being in control, having power, and she already had her fill of frustrations before she got to me. Many patients come in to X-Ray Departments like that. You never know what happened before they got there. Perhaps, she had already waited in the doctor's office an hour or so. Who knows? It happened a lot in our line of work, and you learn to stay calm, and keep working. We never took it personal. Medical workers are pretty good about that.

This very, well-groomed, elegantly put-together lady became more distraught; tightening the already tight muscles of her face and upper body as I answered her impatient question. I responded that it would be a minimum of thirty minutes before I could begin her exam. I needed to leave her to get started. She was livid with me, demanding better service. I told her that she could go to our other office if she did not want to wait. It was across a large parking lot, and across a street. We walked back and forth all the time. I did not think anything of it. I will admit that it was a solution for me as well. I knew that the three techs in the other office would not be slammed at that end of the day, and that she would not have to wait. She asked me how to get there. She stormed out of the office. She had stormed in, so I was not fazed when she stormed out.

The next day I came to work and my supervisor was waiting for me. She did not handle conflict very well. She was very upset and nervous. She told me that she and I needed to go talk to the Head Radiologist of the group. I had never met him. They were a rather large group of doctors. He had not rotated to the Outpatient Clinics since I was hired. Anyway, my supervisor was very hesitant to tell me that the Radiologists were all in a tizzy. The Orthopedic Surgeon had reported that his patient had accused me of sending her over to the other clinic because she was black. I had been rude and unprofessional to her.

Now, I was in a fine pickle because the Head Radiologist had never met me, and the Orthopedic Surgeon had a good relationship with this group. He sent a lot of business their way. It didn't matter intent or facts. I was going to end up eating humble pie. When I explained the incident, the first thing that the Radiologist and my supervisor told me was that I should of called for one of the techs to come over and help, rather than to send the patient to them. They were right. That was much simpler. I did not do that the day before because there was only a single X-Ray machine. The patients had to be done one at a time. However, a second tech could definitely have helped me move it along faster; overseeing the patients' changing (always time consuming), the paperwork piece, and running my films. It was an option that I had missed in the decision of the moment. It was an easy enough solution for the future.

The Radiologist listened to my side of the story. He believed me, but he was not real happy with the whole thing. How do you defend the intent of an action? I think he decided that I was my own best defense, or else he wanted the Orthopedic Surgeon to understand that he had taken this seriously. He decided that I needed to go to the surgeon's office in person to explain what had happened. He called the Orthopedic Surgeon to tell him that he was sending me up. The Radiologist did talk to him about sending patients with multiple exams down at the same time. Let's face it. We all knew that the last thing that a surgeon had to worry about was whether he was pacing his work for us. That was our problem, not his. However, it was a factor in how it all played out. The Radiologist backed me on that point. I think he felt bad for me, as he knew what I knew. I would have to assume the role of scapegoat and apologize. Beyond the race thing, there was the customer aspect. The doctors did not want the business end to be compromised. My take on the Head Radiologist was that he was trying to be pretty decent about the whole thing. He was trying to accommodate the surgeon and to defend me at the same time. I appreciated his effort on my behalf.

So, off I go. No one had bothered to mention to me that the Orthopedic Surgeon was black. He was sitting there with his arms crossed when I walked in. He was rather overweight, with a thick, black beard. His white lab coat was tight across his midriff. He was perched on a stool, sitting sideways, facing away from me as I entered his office. He did not really turn and look at me. He remained rigid, still, looking straight ahead. His affect was neutral as he waited for me to walk across the room. He was not going to make it easy for me. I had to decide to stand or sit to speak to him. I found another stool and sat across from him. He was sort of like an old owl, moody and brooding, sitting and waiting for the kill. That would be me. I explained that my motivation in sending his patient to the other office was not racist, and I apologized if it could have been perceived that way. It was the farthest thing from my mind. It was a matter of trying to accommodate her so that she would not have to wait, and to accommodate my own needs in the situation. I knew that I could manage to get the other two patients done close to the end of our scheduled hours. I was honest about the benefit in it for me.

He was still a little cool with me, nodding abstractly as I said all the politically correct things. I felt that I had to say more. It was not going well. I hesitated and then I dove in. At this point, I did not have much to lose. I told him that his patient had entered the office with an obvious chip on her shoulder. It did not matter what I did, she was going to remain angry. If she sat there and waited 45 minutes, she would have had as equal a fit as she had when I offered the services of the main office. I relayed to him that she appeared angry at the world when she walked in, and that whatever she was so angry about was prior to our incident. I felt that I was the straw that broke the camel's back for her.

All of a sudden, he started chuckling and then laughing, louder and louder. His crossed arms were rising and falling with his belly, as he really started having a good time with all of this. I realize now that he and I had just moved beyond defensive communication. I was a little confused by his reaction, but it was better than the solemn, neutral face he had shown to this point. Through his chuckles, he told me that she was really mad with me about her shoes. He was getting quite the kick out of this, laughing to himself as he thought about it. I was completely lost; her shoes? She was across the counter from me. I had not seen her feet. What did her shoes have to do with the whole mess?

Apparently, she had ruined her spike heels on the route from one clinic to the other. I had directed her to the shortest, most direct route; the way we went back and forth. We were in the basement of the building. There was a set of stairs just a few feet from our office door. They went directly to the parking lot that she had to cross. The stairs were metal, and her heels kept going through the small holes in the metal. The poor woman was already in such a mood. I am sure that she cursed me every step of the way.

The point of this tale is that it was not until I let my defenses down, and talked from my heart about what really was the issue for me that the surgeon responded to me in a real way. She was his patient. He knew her personality and her issues better than I did. He probably was enjoying the "spike heel" predicament as poetic justice or something. I am sure that he had advised her against wearing two-inch heels. Her X-Rays were related to back problems. He was having his own fun with the whole thing. So, it ended with him saying that he would try to space his patients better, and me agreeing to call for help rather than to burden his patients in the future. As I went out the door, he remained perched on his stool, laughing to himself; like the cat that swallowed the canary. I did not enjoy being the canary, but at least he was no longer angry.

From a perspective of not growing up in America, I see the race issue as a very complex, emotional web of our humanity. Feelings of guilt, shame, anger, vulnerability, fear, and mistrust have placed people in very defensive roles for dealing with each other across race lines. Americans of all races and ages are at varying places on the spectrum. There is a broad range of personal comfort levels in sharing honest feelings and thoughts with members of another race. Decent people struggle so much with saying or doing the right thing that they hold themselves back from being honest and open with members of a different race. The fear of honest communication exacerbates the problem.

My experience of living in a multi-racial family for almost a quarter of a century among Americans is that the average citizen really tries his or her best to do right by others. Some are more comfortable with themselves, which allows them to reach out more, even if they are rebuffed. I would say that for every single negative interaction, I have had about 1,000 positive ones. My personal experience is that individual Americans in the middle class make an honest effort to reach across race lines, to respect one another, and to get along in a meaningful way.

I think that the upper class bracket and the lower class segments have more problems along race lines, which is directly linked to less diverse personal experiences. If you think about it, both the upper class and the lower class tend to negotiate in smaller circles. The upper class can be compared to big fish in a small pond, and the lower class represents the bottom fish in the same small pond. The rich like their small pond so they stay in it. They have power and privilege in this pond. It is a safe place for them. The lower class barely treads water. They are unable to swim out of their small pond, sinking back as fast as they make any kind of headway. They are not as happy or safe in their confined world, but it is what they know. The paradox is that the level of comfort keeps many from finding their way out to a better place.

The middle class operates from a larger pond so to speak. They are able to at least tread water, and many can swim across and between ponds. I believe that your average, employed, middle class citizen is pretty solid in trying to do the right thing by others across race lines, even though they often screw up along the way. For me, a barometer to measure racism when behavior is stuttered or uncomfortable across race is to gage malice. If the action or comment is intended to hurt or degrade then it is racist in nature. If the perpetrator is bumbling or plain ignorant based on learned bias, but malice is not the underlying factor, then there is hope that individual experiences will evolve thinking and views.

I would like to share a dear memory of an individual connection across race lines in America. I was walking along Royal Street on a hot afternoon in July'05. I was lucky enough to attend a conference in New Orleans the summer before Katrina. I had not spent more than a single day in New Orleans for a few years, so I was very content to pass hazy time just wandering the streets. The past few days had renewed and cemented my love for the heart of that great city. The afternoon heat was very heavy; sticky and swampy, draining my energy from the weight of the atmosphere. I was strolling slowly, wandering in and out of small shops to cool off as much as anything.

I came upon an elderly black gentleman and a young man who might have been part Asian, but I am not sure about the younger musician's ethnicity. The young man accompanied the older gentleman; the young man on guitar, and the black man singing and playing the harmonica. I had seen the two of them before in the French Quarter. The old man had a grey, white beard, blue jean overalls, and a wrinkled, happy face. He had a twinkle in his eye, and at the same time, he had a humble and wise presence. He reminded me of Aunty Lucy. His voice was very soulful and powerful from deep inside of him. The young man was very quiet and reserved, and he was a wonderful musician. They were an interesting pair.

As I listlessly approached, I recognized the song that they were starting. I stopped to listen, leaning against the side of a small, open shop; staying in the shade of the buildings around me. The version was the sweetest, most beautiful rendition of *Danny Boy* that I had ever heard. The elderly man's voice created a harmony with the young man's music that perfected the song for me. As I stood there listening, my eyes watered with the whimsical memory that the soulful poetry of the moment stirred for me. At the end of the song, the old man looked at me, and very quietly he said to me, "You like my song", not as a question but as an affirming statement. I said to him, "Yes, I very much like your song."

The old, black man said nothing else, but he continued to study my response. He looked me in the eye, more or less to say, tell me more. I wonder why my song affects you so. He just patiently and gently waited for me to share my story with him, knowing that I would. I told him that it was my father's favorite song. The last time that I had heard *Danny Boy* was around my father's coffin in the Funeral Home the night before we buried him. My sister-in-law had bravely led my family to bid him a fond but sorrowful farewell through the powerful lyrics of his favorite Irish folk song.

The old man understood. He reached out and held my hand, and he nodded, smiling softly; reaching across generations, across race, and across strangers to say I understand without having to speak any words. He was about my father's age. He quietly said that he was happy to have shared his song with me. It was an emotional but sweet experience for me, and a gentle, peaceful memory to cherish. I felt that my father was standing beside me, listening intently and peacefully to the haunting and soulful beauty of the song, as he had always done. My father would have been very approving of the old man's rendition of *Danny Boy*, highlighted by the music of the younger man. I think of people who can not open their hearts along race lines. They rob themselves of so many wonderful experiences and possibilities in their short journey through life.

In the present, much is made in the media of the possibility of a black candidate for President, or at least as a front runner for the Democratic nomination. Why do the pundits keep harping away at the same old thing? If Chris Matthews has a conservative guest, he is going to ask without a fail, "Is he white enough?" Then, for the next guest, "Is he black enough?" Give me a break! Your average, thinking, engaged voter is more concerned with questions like: Is he competent enough? Is he a visionary? Can he remain his own man, and still synthesize and accommodate the counsel of his advisors? Can he lead? Can he handle national defense? Is he honest? Does he have integrity? Can he last the distance? How is his judgment? Can he transform from politician to statesman if elected? Are his policy initiatives as sound as his speaking ability? Is he a hard, strong negotiator? Does he have substance? Will he inspire us to rise to the glory, the greatness, and the possibility of America? Is he worthy of our informed vote? Basically, we're desperate to elect a competent leader. I believe that Obama appears to be worthy of a long, hard look.

If you had a heart attack, are you going to wonder if your Cardiac Surgeon is white enough or black enough? I don't think so. No, more like: How many of these have you done before? How many success stories? Where did you train? How steady, tactile, and dexterous are your hands? How is your eye sight? What is your track record? Does the head nurse of the CCU recommend you? Who is your anesthesiologist? Do you guys work well together? Are you board certified? These are the things on our mind, as we wait tentatively through the reality of our fear. We do not care much about the tone of our surgeon's skin. Other priorities come to mind.

I was in a multi-cultural class in college. I took several of these. I am always one for the rest of the story. The professor had this questionnaire for everyone to fill out. She then lined us up from highest to lowest score. She was so proud of this instrument, which would give us insight into our racial beliefs. The questions had to do with having dinner in the house of someone of another race, etcetera. I scored very high. My husband comes from a huge family, and the relatives go on forever. I had no problem rising to the head of the class on this one. A friend of mine scored the lowest. She was so distraught. This sweet, gracious lady did not appear to harbor any negative thoughts toward anyone. If I had taken the same questionnaire years earlier when I lived in Newfoundland, I would have scored the lowest. My high score or my low score were a factor of place and time, not a factor of some great racial enlightenment that I did not have in my young adulthood.

I think we have to take things with a grain of salt. There are no mind boggling answers and measurements of racial beliefs. We are better than we think we are when we follow the golden rule for everyone. Most of us behave very decently, and rise to the occasion despite our imperfect selves. I was a witness to the phenomena of our actions verses our stated beliefs my whole life growing up. As much as my father lamented about the Canadian thing and the British thing, he lived the life of a model Canadian citizen. He also had great arguments and great friendships with pro-British Newfoundlanders. They actually reveled in very spirited, loud, and genuine disagreements of the history and the current politics. Yet, they respected and cared deeply for one another through all the posturing and the temperature of their fiery, heated discussions.

This is my personal experience of race in America. Like all relationships, it is a bi-directional interaction among parties who can trust themselves enough to extend a hand. It is as simple a human interaction as it gets; and yet, it can be the most complicated human event because of the vulnerability of our human souls. It has been my experience that much of the multi-cultural literature in university classes approaches racial tension from a blame stance; white privilege and the guilt that goes along with that. Discussions can go on forever about the relativity of privilege. This slant does not get down to the guts of moving forward; things like honest communication, the dynamics of interactions, learned beliefs, and the evolution of life experiences. Overcoming the impasse of racism is a two-way street. For example, my experience in New Orleans with the older gentleman was as much a factor of him reaching out to me, as it was of me connecting with him. We connected with each other. It's a give and take, a waltz of unsure movement back and forth, until the rhythm takes over, and the dancers no longer have to think through the steps. But both parties have to take a risk with the steps to learn the dance in the first place.

Chapter 8

BECOMING A MILITARY WIFE

W<small>HEN WE WERE FIRST MARRIED</small>, I looked at my husband's military career as his job, separate from mine. At times, it seemed like a pretty cushy job, other times he worked long hours for weeks or months at a time. There was no overtime, but there was extra time off during slow periods or just "because". In the medical field, we were paid for overtime and for being on call. If we didn't work, we were not paid. There is always a give and take. We did not have Fridays off for a family day at the beach, or because we made our quota of patients earlier in the month. We wish!

My point is that I framed the military as a job, not a mandate for living our lives. I did not have a personal, patriotic, historical connection to the US Air Force or to any branch of the military. My work ethic understood the commitment aspect. I had no problem with the TDY thing. My inner sense of adventure was often jealous of a job in which one could hop on a plane, fly to another country or state, and get paid for the experience of it all. My husband and his buddies shared a special bond in their stints to Germany or to areas of the world such as the Mid-East in peace time. You could see it in their easy comrade, and hear it in their conversations and the endless jokes when they were together. Most of the Air Force guys that I knew appeared happy and easy going in the career they had chosen, especially in the 80's.

The Florida Panhandle was an easy place to be stationed as a young, military couple. I did not have that much to do with the Air Force piece of it for the initial six years of our marriage. We bought our first house. I worked in the local hospital. Most of my close friends were people I knew from work, and a few active duty friends of my husband, who socialized with us among locals. I did not go on Base for much of anything. I never liked to cook, so the Commissary was not a draw for me. I never have nor ever will go out of my way to find a grocery store. If I don't pass it on the way home, oh well! Even then, I will rationalize every reason in the world why I don't need to stop there in the moment. There must be a can of something in the cupboard that can carry us to one more day! Surely, there is. I must have rice or something to dress it up with. Surely, I do. I am telling myself all of this as I drive by. Of course, when I get home and look in the cupboard, I am lambasting myself that I really should have stopped. It's all pretty desperate. But there I am the next day, driving by again as I convince myself that we can survive one more day.

I had health insurance through my work, so I needed Champus only as a back-up to my primary insurance. The local, civilian doctors and our for profit employers loved the combination of Blue Cross and Champus cards in the wallets of their patients. That was the ultimate combination of health insurance to grease the mahogany, so to speak. I was young and content with living along the sugary, white beaches of Destin and Okaloosa Island. The bottom line was that I did not involve myself very much with the life of a military spouse other than to support the requirements and the commitments of my husband's job by not complaining or whining about the hours or the travel part. What was there to complain about anyway?

The first time that I was issued a military I.D. card, I came to know the word dependent. That was a new concept for me. I don't think that I have ever worn that hat with any glimmer of grace or surface pretense. I understand the meaning and the relationship for the purposes of benefits, security, and accountability; but I draw the line to frame myself as a dependent in any other dimension of living relative to the life of a military spouse. Dependent suggests weakness and neediness to me. The Catholic nuns did not drill us through their version of basic training without embedding character traits that inherently challenge a self portrayal of spinelessness in any sense of the word. I have met a few spouses over the years, who seemed to wallow in the literal, victim mentality of dependent. Luckily, they were few and far between.

The American military wives and mothers, who became my role models and mentors, exhibit true grit and tenacity. They do not support their husband's military commitment by sacrifice and martyrdom. Rather, they honor their spouses' service by living as largely and happily as they know how. They battle to provide a secure and full life for their children and for themselves, when many of the normal boundaries of spousal decisions are out of their control. The challenge is to accept the lack of control and to grow stronger and wiser with each new problem or setback.

I believe that the hardest duty of a military wife is to willingly tackle the unknown, and to find the positive in change. Military spouses have to look at the glass half full; to find that silver lining in every move and in every new experience.

I think military wives experience the reality of uncontrollable change in as many different ways as there are possibilities. The most stress for me, personally, was always having to leave a job on someone else's terms, not being able to stay enrolled in university classes on my terms, and having to start from scratch to find my way relative to work and friendships with each move. I could not envision myself as an unemployed, dependent spouse. That was just me. As a young adult, I had always experienced my self-worth through my ability to support myself and to contribute to the demands of making a living. So, in a way, my inner drive as a military spouse was to fight the role of dependent with every fiber of my being.

It is often the little things that drive you crazy. I had bought a new car in Florida. We received orders to move overseas the very month that I had it paid off. They would pay to ship one vehicle. We ended up selling mine at a loss (of course). I did not get to enjoy a single month of no car payments. Let's face it. As a middle class worker, I lived for the day that I would have my new car paid off. Car ownership is one of those short-term life goals that bestow great personal satisfaction on average folk. It's like you beat the system, for a brief period in the big scheme of life and getting ahead. Naturally, I had to buy something else in Germany. I ended up with an older car, car payments all over again, and no job in the mix of it. Yes, you deal with it. But it is the little things that pile up to test the waters. The silver lining was that my German car was a BMW. Granted, it was a very old BMW; but none the less, a BMW is a BMW, nothing to feel bad about for any length of time.

It was through other military wives that I came to know the essence of military service and patriotism. Many military wives have known the military lifestyle across generations. Often their fathers and their grand-fathers were in the military. They had always been connected to a sense of security and familiarity with the military community. The familiarity is not in a geographical sense. It is often just the opposite. It's more that they can go to a US Military Base or community anywhere in the world, and know that the salient principles of duty, honor, and family permeate through the community. For many military wives that I know, their sense of themselves is grounded in a somewhat spiritual connection to the loyal and patriotic values of the American Military.

I have dear friends who will drive ten or twenty miles out of their way to buy their groceries at the Commissary. Even in retirement, they factor in the distance to the nearest Base in choosing a town or neighborhood to live in. They rationalize it from a cost perspective. Groceries are cheaper at the Base Commissary. The security of any Military Base nearby provides a connection to Medical services, even though the reality of Tri-Care offers options that do not require the geographical link. I think that it is more than the access to services. I believe that at a core level, intergenerational military families find comfort and belonging in remaining physically connected to the familiarity of the military lifestyle. It reminds me of my grandfather.

I did not know him well because he died when I was a child. But, I remember that he used to wander to the harbor in St. John's. He had Alzheimer's (they did not call it that back then, just old age). Anyway, he could not find his way home. But, my uncles would know where to find him. He used to wander down there to look at whatever ships were in Port. He had sailed in his day. In his later years, they would find him standing there quiet, staring out at sea, intent and lost in the jumbled memories of his life. He was at peace in the company of the huge, merchant ships that were docked along Water Street. My uncles would report that he would get very angry and belligerent with them when they fetched him to bring him home. He wanted to just be left alone to stare out at the sea. Who knows where his mind went, as he was never able to articulate anything other than anger and resentment at being brought in out of the cold and wind. His body was frail, but his mind was deeply connected to his roots and to his life story.

I have a very good friend, who may spend her elderly years whipping up and down the aisles of the commissary, swearing and swiping at anyone who might want to slow her down or bring her home. Perhaps we will find her staring into the huge freezers at the case lot special of the week. Okay, so I am joking here! Please forgive me. But, in all seriousness, the connections to the security and honor of the military life are very real across generations for many US military families. I think that America has a unique relationship between voluntary military service and patriotism that does not exist anywhere else in the world to the same degree. It is hard to explain, but it is very real to experience.

For many of my friends, the biggest stress to deal with during military moves was to make it a positive and growth experience for their children. A parent's greatest struggle is to protect the vulnerability of their children, and to empower them at the same time. This is true for families everywhere. But the challenge is compounded ten fold across multiple military moves. Some families and children cope much better than others. Some relish in it. Others dread it. Sometimes the move is extremely positive. It can bring a family back home or to a desired area. Or it can do just the opposite.

With children, it is also the ordinary things in the big scheme of things that are the hardest, and become the most complicated to deal with. The strongest, most patriotic, loving military wife and mother that I have ever known experienced the greatest challenge of an overseas move through the trials of her son's relationship with his dog. They were going to Italy and the dog would have to be in quarantine. Also, the pet was young, very spirited, and a handful, even with the luxury of a fenced back yard. His spiritedness would be very hard to deal with in temporary housing situations, and in the unknown of the availability of family accommodations yet to be explored and found.

The most rational and sensible decision was to find a good home for the dog before they left. Emotionally, it was a nightmare for this wonderful mom and dad, and for their son. That is what I mean by true grit. The steadfast courage of military wives and mothers is exemplified in stories such as this. They make hard decisions when their choices are limited, and they model grace and honor in overcoming the challenge. Military wives ease the burden for their children and for their active duty husbands in the face of tremendous pressure and change. They do not sacrifice their lives. They live their lives hugely and honorably within the choices of their days. The qualities of humor, curiosity, anger, happiness, sadness, eagerness, and reflection carry them through the places of their journey.

I learned that the American military community expresses patriotism and commitment through a deep respect of Old Glory; the visual symbol of American citizenship, honor, and unwavering allegiance to the values of America's democracy. My husband's reaction to a Canada Day celebration brought this home for me. It was before midnight on the eve of Canada Day, July 1st. We were on George Street in St. John's, which is known for its night life. Anyway, a series of bands were performing throughout the evening. As the evening wore on, the atmosphere became merrier and louder. There was anticipation for the midnight hour as Molson Canadian was sponsoring *Joe Canadian* or something like that. I had never heard of it prior to this trip home. Anyway, it was sort of like a

New Year's Eve thing. Newfoundland is the most Eastern Time Zone in North America. The *Joe Canadian* extravaganza would travel across the country to celebrate the birth of Canada Day a minute after midnight in each time zone.

As the hour got closer to midnight on George Street, many people were starting to wave Canadian flags, swaying in groups; helped on by friendship, patriotism, alcohol, and the beat of the performing band. It was a very happy, friendly place to be. My husband was watching a group of guys in front of us. They had a huge, Canadian flag fastened to the bottom of a hockey stick. You can't get much more Canadian than that. The Maple Leaf was swaying in harmony with their group momentum. I believe the band was playing a *Melencamp* song. The beat was pounding, and the boys were having a time in front of the band stand. A bunch of friends ran up to the group, laughing and joking. They started signing their names to the Canadian Flag.

There was not a Canadian in the bunch who would think anything of that (at the time, including me). These celebrators were genuinely patriotic in the norms of their culture. My husband had to process all of this from an initial reaction of shock. He could not believe that these young people would handle the Flag in that manner. Having it taped (black tape) to the hockey stick was bad enough, but autographing it like a high school year book would be unconscionable to an American soldier. The members of the US Military show total respect for the Stars & Stripes by standing at attention, unflinching, and serious in their salute to the history of America's ongoing fight for freedom around the world.

These roots run deep and true. Children in American schools are taught to fold the flag, and to retire it at the end of the day. It is a privilege to be trusted to be on a team to raise the flag in the morning in a respectful manner in the elementary schools. Often, when I walked early in the morning in my neighborhood, I would see several older gentlemen rising at dawn, to go outside and raise a flag at the end of their driveways every morning. These elderly gentlemen would be solemn and dignified as they carried out their morning ritual alone, between themselves and their God.

Looking back at all of this, I realize that I may have appeared irreverent and rude to Americans when I first moved to the States, and especially in the company of military families. It sometimes seemed like over kill to me, and I really did not understand the historical context of the Flag to Americans. For example, the first time that I went to a movie theater on a US Base, I could not believe that they played the National Anthem before the movie began. Everyone would stand in somber attention as they juggled huge buckets of popcorn, drinks, and seats that were hard to attend to with hands full. Adults and children would have drinks and popcorn spilling as they dutifully arose, and turned towards the Flag flying in the corner of the theater. I had not yet learned how deep and meaningful the homage and respect of the Flag was to Americans. I have learned over the years to understand and to honor the earnest emotions and dedication to America's symbol of patriotism and freedom.

I have come to understand that Americans' silent reflection to the symbol of the Flag is to the respectful memory of lives lost. When I grew up in Canada, we were well aware of the might of the American Military; steady and strong along our southern border; empowering Canada's existence as an independent nation. Our potential enemies would be America's enemies. We were comforted by our relationship with America, relative to the defense of our borders and to the freedoms that we experienced in Canada. I am not sure if Canada's youth share these feelings in the present, but we were cognizant of America's protective relationship with Canada in the story of my family and in the context of our parents' values. In a way, the American Military was the silent force underlying the democracy of Canada.

My journey as a military wife became more embedded and dependent when we were stationed overseas. I did not have a work visa to allow me to carve a life away from the Base, nor did I speak the language. For the first time, my true grit would be tested against the challenges to my independence. It was probably the first time that I really got to know other military wives. Most of the women that would become my friends over there were younger than me. I was not that old, around 30, but these wives and mothers were very young. They were in their early 20's, and they had several children. They supported one another strongly.

We all know things differently. I had experiences that they did not, and they had insights that I did not. In life, it's all about stopping to listen; to learn from one another, and to enjoy the worth and the company of people in the present. I learned from these young mothers that, of course, I would have a Christening party for my baby overseas. It did not matter if grandparents and aunts were not around. You carry on and you do these types of things because it's the right thing to do, and because it matters that you celebrate life traditions when you are far from home. I learned from these young mothers the art of balancing children's needs with adult needs. I think that some of them learned from me that it's healthy and okay to reflect on self-needs; and that we grow in ourselves and for our families when we attend to that aspect, even in very small and discrete ways.

For example, it is okay to fit 30 or 60 minutes in your day to get away and work out at the gym. It is okay to work part-time if you have a need to interact with other adults; engaging your brain in a different way than in the pace of your role as wife and mother; especially, if you can work your schedule around your family's needs. It's okay to want that for yourself, to acknowledge that need, and to act on it. It was my experience that many young military mothers, who had several children, struggled to rationalize a fit for their personal needs. They wrestled with the reality of finding a niche for themselves, and caring for their husband and kids at the same time. If anything was likely to give, it was the inner, unspoken needs of these extremely, young moms. I think we learned together that sometimes fairly small and somewhat simple give and takes could ease the internal stress for us.

I had to struggle to reign in my independent streak, and the very young, military moms, who became my dear friends over there, grew in themselves over the years of their tour. I witnessed this. I smile with the memory as I think about it. It was my personal experience that many of the American girls, who I knew in Germany as young moms, had not had the opportunity to live independent lives as adults prior to marriage, kids, and deployment to another country. Most of them took it in stride, growing in themselves as much as with their families. They were a fun, energetic bunch; young and innocent; but eager to experience the possibility of their unique experiences in the foreign lands at our finger tips to explore. As our friendships grew, we explored together. We made the most of it, from the overnight shopping trips to Czech; the quick, weekend stints to Paris; or straight north, crossing the German border at Maastricht, driving the busy stretch of road through Holland to amaze ourselves with the magnificence of the tulips in bloom at Keukenhof. It was a wonder to our eyes and nourishment for our souls as we snuck in one more adventure together.

I also saw the American Military through the eyes of Europeans in the time frame of the end of the Cold War in '89 and during the Gulf War in '91. The reputation of the American Military in countries such as Germany, France, and the Netherlands was very high and respected at that time. We lived very close to the French border. The local people loved the US Military. They linked the Americans to the liberation of France, and they were always welcoming and happy to see American GIs in their small towns. That was my experience. They were eager to show us graveyards that they kept pristine in honor of the American soldiers who were buried there. These simple citizens had a need to let Americans know that they honored the graves of the soldiers who gave their lives so that France could regain its freedom as an independent nation. In the States, there is an overwhelming perception of antagonism between France and the United States. That was not my experience in the small towns of France along the German border.

In Germany, there was more of a mix of reactions to the presence of US Bases. Most Germans welcomed the Americans and felt very grateful to the economic opportunities and jobs linked to the US Forces. Other Germans expressed resentment and hostility to the presence of American Bases in their country. These were mostly young Germans. Germany was going through a lot of transitions at that time, and there was much de-bate about the future and political direction of the country. The unifica-tion of East and West Germany created a quagmire of opinions. There was great joy at the fall of the Berlin Wall and the defeat of communism in East Germany, but there was also hesitation and fear related to the economic impact on the working taxpayers from the more affluent and modern West Germany.

The situation between East and West Germany several years into re-unification reminded me of Hamdam's story as a Palestinian in Jordan. The initial open arms and welcome were challenged as the reality was felt in economic terms of one society supporting a disadvantaged group. Also, there are cultural differences that may be subtle to outsiders, but they were felt very acutely from within. West Germans would complain about the work ethic of the East Germans, a difference in expectations, motivation, and outcomes had developed over the course of the past 35-40 years. A generation of young workers in West Germany had vastly different job skills and work norms than the same generation of workers from East Germany. The friction and pains of a unified Germany seemed to overshadow any real dissatisfaction with the US Military presence in Germany in the early 90's.

Many Germans had worked with the Americans since the end of World War II. They seemed to have developed a mutual respect born over time out of necessity and reality. In Germany, I witnessed more hos-tility towards immigrants from poorer areas of Europe and Turkey than I did towards Americans. On an individual level, almost all American families that I knew got along fine with their German landlords, neighbors, and co-workers. Most Germans spoke English, especially anyone younger than about 60 years old. Some of us tried to learn German, but in my case, I butchered the language so bad that the Germans would quickly switch over to English. My German was painful to their ears.

In Europe, I witnessed the reaction to the US Military from within its embrace rather than from my former perspective of outside looking in. I can recall only a single incident in which I felt hostility towards Americans and especially the American Military. It was in the spring of '91. We were with an American group in Strassbourg, France. We came upon a small group of people from Algeria. They were protesting the Gulf War, which was winding down in Kuwait. They were burning the US Flag, and their chanting was sounding pretty ugly. The local people from the Alsace area, who are a combination of French and German descent, appeared to be upset that this demonstration was happening on their streets. For our part, we walked away from the group, as inconspicuously as we could. We had some active duty GIs in our small group, and we did not want to complicate an otherwise peaceful and lovely Saturday afternoon. The sun was shining, and Strassbourg is a beautiful, quaint city to stroll through. They had a right to protest. We moved on and all was right with our day.

I learned from other military wives how much the experience of living overseas impacted their children and themselves. We usually think of how much the American forces have impacted the foreign countries in which they have been involved. I learned from these young mothers and wives that the relationship goes both ways. Their reaction to the experience of living in Europe was very passionate and happy. They felt so grateful to have the opportunity of walking along the Champs Elysee, or of strolling through Mad King Ludwig's castles in Bavaria. They wanted their children to soak it all in; to absorb each new nuance and flavor along the way. These young mothers, from places like Kansas and New Mexico, soaked up the adventures along with their children. They loved America, but they also cherished the opportunity to live largely and happily in the present, during the brief years of their European tours.

Military wives and military families become support systems for one another. They understand their unique needs as a military community. Even in retirement, the role of military wife does not end. I think for many families, the initial retirement years are actually more stressful.

Often, the military spouse becomes the source of strength and common sense during the transition from active duty to retirement for the soldier. It is the first time in a soldier's adult life that decisions are not made for them relative to work. With all the chaos and change of military moves throughout the family's military career, the active duty member actually goes through very little personal stress from a job perspective. The move is often a step towards a promotion. Their work remains salient and intact, other than from a direction of positive growth.

The reality is that many military retirees go through a period of shock and emptiness after retirement. They live for the day, and then they don't know what to do with themselves once it comes. They may have a job lined up, but the experience of starting anew, having to work their way up from the role of "newbie" is foreign to them. Many military retirees go through several jobs, trying to find a fit for themselves. It's often not about money, as much as a need to find a job in which they feel that they are contributing; a job worthy of their experience and insight.

Most of these guys entered the military right out of college or high school. They worked through different positions and levels of management, attended schools, received degrees and specialized training; but always, they remained employed and made advances within a single career. The military wife, on the other hand, had to regroup and get on with it after each and every move. The spouse's resilience and inner strength become embedded in steel and coated in teflon. The family's armor may meet its biggest challenge ever during the transition from active duty to retirement.

Several wiser and older military wives passed this insight on to me. You don't quite get what they are talking about until it happens to you. The role of the resilient military spouse is called on to get the family through the transition; perhaps with a "kick in the pants" type of toughness mixed in with that of partial, but not total, sympathetic supporter. It's a combination of tact and tenacity that becomes the steel magnolia of the spouse's armor. The military wife wears the pin of the bold flower with grace and dignity throughout the many transitions of the family's story. Whatever it takes to carry the family through, the military spouse will do, simply because it has to be done. Isn't that the role of wives and mothers in all walks of life? It just becomes more acute because of the unique challenges of the military life. The role never really ends. The history of the military experience will remain embedded in the family story, and it will be passed on at some level to future generations.

Chapter 9

AN AMERICAN OVERSEAS

I T WAS IN THE SUMMER of 1989 that we received orders to Germany for an extended tour. We would be there for at least three years. Immediately, my thoughts went back to my friends in Canada; the many conversations hashed out ten years earlier when my two girlfriends and I were exploring the possibilities among destinations for our back-packing travel adventure. Europe was always discussed. From our "just barely" twenty-year old perspective, we viewed traveling in Europe as conservative and expected. We were rebels in our unbending enthusiasm. We yearned to explore a world that was different and unknown to us. Ten years later, and I am more than okay with the opportunity to live in Europe for several years. However, I am a little taken aback with Germany.

Of all the countries in Europe, I have no desire to live in Germany. The story of my upbringing has instilled in me an apprehension about the morals of the German people. The whole Nazi thing worries me relative to my bi-racial marriage, and to my own ability to live happily in Germany. I really did not know that much about Germany outside of what I had learned in history going back to World War I; and my parents' vivid memories and stories of World War II. The context of the Cold War, the Berlin Wall, and the TV images of East Germans being shot as they tried to cross over into West Berlin framed my thinking over the past thirty years. My overall impression of moving to Germany ebbed and flowed from anticipation to apprehension prior to our departure. My husband had been there on TDY. He had been at a Canadian Base in the Black Forest. He loved Germany. He was definitely more positive about our assignment than I was the summer before we left.

I knew that the political situation was changing rapidly in Europe. I had recently taken some college classes on international relationships and current world events. I had this wonderful professor who would stand at the black board with a piece of chalk, and draw out a map of Europe from his head. It was much more powerful than any fine tuned power point presentation that I have had to sit through over the years. Dr. Joe Mathews (with a single T) could draw the borders of the countries in Europe to accurately match the oscillating outcomes of the conflicts and wars of the 20th century. In 1987, he anticipated and lectured about the in-evitability of major ethnic confrontations in the Balkans after the fall of Tito. He discussed the common but fragile bond that tenuously brought the divided groups of that region together. He lectured that the ethnic tensions were rooted over centuries of unrest and distrust. He talked a lot about what would happen in Yugoslavia when and not if the Soviets pulled out. He explained to us that the only thing uniting the different political and ethnic groups in that part of Europe was their combined hatred of the Russians and of Communism.

Dr. Mathews shared his insight passionately with any student who was interested to listen. I was like a sponge, trying to soak up and absorb his lectures. He inspired me to understand more about world politics from a historical context relative to the present. I had one of his classes at 8:30 in the morning. I did not have to go to work on those days until the swing shift. I would wear my bathing suit under my clothes, and head to the beach from class. I would be set up before 10:30 in my rusted but favor-ite beach chair. In the off season, the beaches of Okaloosa Island would be practically deserted in the morning of a week day. I had the soothing power of the surf to cradle my brain, as I closed my eyes, and drifted through the impact of his words and their meaning for me. Dr. Mathews felt strongly that policy makers and heads of states needed to understand world history if they were to lead wisely and effectively.

I was always inspired by him; one of those rare professors who speaks profoundly to the particular wiring of your brain. We all encounter the "teacher for us" along our journey with education. I have had many won-derful professors over the years, but Dr. Mathews of Okaloosa-Walton Community College was one of the best for me. It's funny, because other students in my class were bored to death with his lectures. They would rather be anywhere but sitting in his class at 8:30 in the morning. I was just the opposite. I could handle the routine of my job, as long as I had the stimulation of his inspiring dialogue to wake me up and engage my mind. He was firm, witty, and brilliant. He was no nonsense. I would never miss one of his classes.

I was not too upset to leave my hospital job in 1989. I had my fill of

Humana. They were strictly for profit with patient needs and staff needs coming in very low on their priority scale from my employee perspective. This feeling was shared by most of my coworkers at the time. The staff was very loyal to each other and to our patients, but we did not feel any allegiance to Humana, the corporation of bean counters. Humana nickled and dimed the employees to death, as they milked the corporate bonuses and profits higher and higher. I've never understood that aspect of management in corporate run hospitals. From a strictly fiscal perspective, they shoot themselves in the foot all the time.

For example, management would under staff and under pay cleaning people, who were at the bottom of the barrel relative to working conditions and basic workers' rights. While the corporation saved a few dimes on the one hand, they risked millions in law suits, as the quality of cleanliness in the hospital operating rooms and patient rooms was compromised in the process. The cleaning staff would be given responsibilities that could not be executed within the ratio of manpower hours needed relative to work load. Their bosses would tell them that they had to stay to get it done, but they would not be paid overtime, because they were supposed to get the job done in their shift. Never mind, that one person could not realistically achieve the outcome demanded of them. Then, they would wonder why they could not keep quality cleaning staff for any length of time. People at all levels just want a fair shake.

Another specific example that technologists dealt with would make us shake our heads in frustration of the common sense factor. Workloads in any hospital can be estimated, but in reality, the volume changes from hour to hour, minute to minute; depending on what walks in or is rolled through the Emergency Room doors. At the end of the day shift, there may be a busy spurt that several technicians could clean up in a short time, but a single tech working the evening shift could not handle logistically. No, you can not be in two places at the same time. You can not finish up an added-on Cervical Myelogram and do a Stat portable in the ER at the same time. I don't care how good you are. Both of these procedures were needed in the moment, not 20-30 minutes later. Anyway, I remember many instances in which a tech or several techs were in the process of working past the exact minute that they were supposed to be off to wrap up the routine procedures of our busy days; to facilitate an acceptable work load for the one-deep, evening tech position. This was standard stuff, and medical workers all over the world will stay an extra few minutes without thinking twice about it.

In the year or so before I left that hospital, our new boss would have a cow if we stayed one minute over. Our prior Chief Technologist had walked away from the corporate nonsense of his own accord several years earlier. He was the real deal. He walked away from the corporate song and dance because he could. We were then graced with a loyal, corporate type. He was long on pleasing the bean counters, but short on what it took to run a busy X-Ray Department. From my perspective, he exemplified the cream of the crop relative to how bad it could get. You see, we were paid overtime. Our brilliant director would order us to punch out, and then he would tell the evening tech that he could call in the on call person if he needed help. Anyone who had a clue knew the tech needed help in the moment. By the time the on call person could get there, the few of us on day shift could have wrapped up the work in a calm and efficient way. Also, paying us a few minutes extra was less than kicking in the travel time and minimum pay for an on call situation. But, we were not allowed to stay even if it was obvious that we could knock it out in a very short time. We would go and clock out just to shut him up, and then return to help the evening tech before we went home. It was pure nonsense to deal with.

I am aware that people will argue that these are isolated incidents and more reflective of poor management. That is true. It was poor management. But, at the same time, these types of business practices are systemic in corporate run hospitals. Managers are pressured to stay within the budgets, and to out perform each other for a bonus at whatever level of management they may achieve. You see, our director would explain that the on call pay came out of a different pot than regular pay; so from his perspective, the configuration of the figures on the budget spread sheet over ruled the common sense approach to professional health care. In a way, he was right. He got bonuses and we did not. Capitalists would take their hats off to him and scoff at our ethical souls.

Around that time, the CEO of Humana or someone high in the company was indicted related to a stock thing. The value of the employees' stocks was suppressed. I don't remember all the details. I do remember that the guy still got a huge bonus, even after he was indicted, when employees were negatively impacted with the losses to their hospital retirement savings plans. It was a good time to be walking away from Humana, from my perspective. As I crossed the parking lot on my last day of work in the fall of 1989, I remember distinctly thinking that I would never again work in a for profit hospital. I am all about not operating in the red, and I understand the expectation of profit relative to business and capitalism. I totally support supply and demand and market forces. But there is a difference between acceptable profit and greed. I was well versed on the range of sins, and gluttony was on the list taught to us over and over again during my school days.

Humana was a business to the Big Whigs, but it was a hospital to us. I had some wonderful friends there. We really had a great friendship and respect among the young staff at the hospital. We put in honest, hard, and busy shifts at work, and we socialized a lot together outside of work. We worked hard and we played hard. The young Americans that I worked among were from everywhere in the States. For the most part, they were not stationed there with the military, as would be expected in that area. They had just migrated to the sugary, white beaches from places like Upstate New York, Oklahoma, Ohio, Texas, Alabama, and the list goes on. We were all in our 20's and 30's. We loved the Florida Gulf Coast, the sunshine, and the beach lifestyle. The easy momentum of the area inspired us to live largely and happily in the simple but abundant pleasures of the coast. My husband and I were sad to leave our friends, but we were open to the adventures of Europe (if only it was Italy and not Germany).

It is October. I have been in Germany just a few days. I am watching the Berlin Wall crumbling down, disappearing from history, as individual people frantically and exuberantly claw away at the cement and mortar. The monstrosity quickly dissolved into rubble on the TV screen in my hotel room. The literally concrete symbol of the Cold War was torn down in days, not weeks. I understand that the fall of the Berlin Wall, and the defeat of communism in Eastern Europe is huge in the scale of world events. I am trying to find a place to live in the small scheme of things. At the same time, world relationships are transforming so rapidly that it will take years before countries truly digest what happened during those few days in October, 1989. It was an exciting time to be in the middle of it, once we found a place to live. I consciously have these thought as I am sitting on the edge of my bed watching the activity in Berlin. My husband has reported to work already. I will go outside in a few minutes to find a bakery with some strong, black coffee, and to find a direction for my day.

It would be the following fall, at Oktoberfest 1990, that I would witness the sheer joy and unchecked emotional outpouring of the average German citizen from both the West and the East to the country's heartfelt reaction to the long-awaited unification. It was the first time that East

Germans could attend the world renowned, weekend long party. For me, personally, Oktoberfest was like Mardi Gras; way too crowded, too over the top, been there, done that, and I would never go back. Just like I enjoy New Orleans in the ordinary, I enjoy a routine, week-day afternoon in a Beer Garden in downtown Munich much more than the crazy drama of the hectic rivalry of the annual event. But, the level of unchecked happiness that the German people felt at that moment of their history as a nation was a sight to behold and to appreciate. I know that there have been major growing pains since then, but at that time and place, the feeling was one of future and possibility. I sensed that the Germans were finally able to look ahead together, East and West, young and old. Their future looked and felt brighter than their recent past. They expressed exuberance that Germany was united and free.

It took less than a month for my initial hesitation and concerns of living in Germany to be totally dismissed. The Germans, who I would come to know, were very open and reflective about Germany's role and history in the 20th century. They would often bring it up, and discuss it. They were not overly defensive. I always thought they were still trying to figure it out, to process the extent of what had happened, and how their parents and grandparents had gotten to the point of the horror of World War II. I think the following example sums up my understanding of the complexity of the issue for the average German citizen.

We lived in a small, rural village, about twenty miles from the Belgium / Luxembourg border. It was a very beautiful, peaceful area. You could drive to Paris, Amsterdam, and Brugge within five hours; and to many other cities in France and the Bene-Lux in less than a few hours. I was talking to a German national, a gentleman who I worked with and knew fairly well. He was quirky and proper at the same time. He was well educated, and he had a great flair for conversation, and intellectual exploration. He was telling me that his mother's home was one village over from my village, about five miles down the road. She had died many years before. He had casually brought up the topic of his mother, but he quickly started to go to a deeper place in his head and in his soul.

He was explaining to me what a wonderful woman his mother was. You could tell that he was very touched by her memory. He spoke of her with an awed, sort of reverent tenderness to his voice; hushed and warm in his tone and body language. He smiled gently as he started to say more, and as he tried to articulate his words and his feelings about her. He slowly went on to say that his mother was always a good Christian, and that she had not accepted the Nazi propaganda in the 30's and 40's. After he said that, he stopped talking. You could see his brain working as he hesitated with his thoughts before he said more.

He then said to me in a very deliberate manner, "If you listen to the Germans of my generation, there were no Nazis because none of us was ever related to one. But then you walk through the grave yards of our villages, and the head stones show one Nazi soldier after another." He smiled sort of tentatively and hesitantly at me. He stood there for a brief moment, said no more; then he turned towards the door. He started to slowly walk away, shaking his head to himself as he walked, looking down. He got a few steps and he stopped and glanced back at me. He then stated, "But I am telling the truth about My mother. She was never like that. She was a very good person. What could the decent people do? What choices did they have? They, too, would have been killed if they spoke out...But then again, we all have free will and choices."

He said these words, and then he turned away to walk outside to smoke his cigarette. I did not follow him outside. I left him alone in the deep, dark place of his thoughts. When he came back in, we carried on with work. We always had easy, genuine conversations, lots of laughter and comrade, as we both loved the work that we were doing over there. The topic of his mother never came up again. The conversation cemented my understanding of the dilemma for him and for many of his fellow German citizens. He was older than me, probably in his late 50's or early 60's at that time. You could tell that he had wrestled internally with his rationalizations and counter arguments for many, many years. He knew that there were no answers, just reflections.

We worked together in the ITT (Information, Ticket, & Tours) office on Bitburg Air Base. It was a NAF (non-appropriated funds) job, which is another word for minimum wage, bottom of the barrel job in the hierarchy of US government service jobs. But, any job is what you make it. I worked with some very smart Europeans and Americans in my humble, NAF job. We all had a passion for travel and for providing information to our customers that would be useful to them. We researched cities and countries to update our services and to expand our Tour Program. Eastern Europe had opened up. It was great fun to put together the first tours for American service members into Hungary, Poland, Eastern Germany, Czech, and Slovak (yes, the country of Czechoslovakia had separated into two distinct countries).

We put together 10-day tours to destinations like Italy, London, The

Loire Valley, Warsaw & Cracow, and numerous shorter tours to Paris, Munich, Salzburg, Vienna, Amsterdam, Bavaria, the Rhine Valley, the Mosel, Lucerne, and many more. It was the lowest pay that I had ever earned since my stint as a cashier at K-Mart when I was in high school; and, yet, it became a very stimulating job for me. I collaborated with my boss to convince our superiors to let us expand the Tour Program. They agreed, and the world was at our feet to research and explore. A lot of DOD (Department of Defense) teachers traveled on our tours, and they were a picky bunch. They expected a standard, and we worked hard not to disappoint.

We wanted to maximize the potential for the average American families who came to us. If it was the family's "once in a lifetime" week in a destination such as the Tyrol area of Austria and Switzerland, we strived to cover a broad and deep introduction to the area, without ruining the adventure and the fun with too much driving, and on and off buses. It was a tricky balance. The central ingredients to a successful tour were doing your homework in advance, quality accommodations centrally located, a bountiful breakfast in the mornings (everyone enjoyed that, especially if it was in a locally run, family establishment rather than a chain hotel), experienced and knowledgeable tour guides, and the combination of weather and luck to be on your side. We worked to take our customers to a few outstanding areas, rather than to throw in so much that you could not absorb or enjoy any of it. Sometimes, we arranged trips with train travel. Rail travel in Europe presents wonderful options and the service is precise, dependable, and comfortable.

We were trail blazers in working with travel agents in Eastern Europe who had not fully transitioned from communism to capitalism. They were partially there, but not quite. In some areas, the quality of the available accommodations had to be weighed against the desire to go there. In the early 90's, cities like Bratislava were still struggling to break into a standard that would be acceptable to the Western market. It doesn't matter how cheap it is, Americans do expect clean sheets, and not just blankets. It was very difficult to pay some establishments; juggling US currency, payment methods, and government paperwork against a "state mindset" that had little to no experience with the concept of private, paper trail, invoices prior to payment for services. They were used to verbal commitments. They trusted us to pay. They saw no need to send us an invoice. I think they saw it as an honor thing, and they did not want to insult us. On the flip side, we had government accountants breathing down our necks, demanding detailed invoices, preferably in English. It was interesting to break it all down, and to address the multitude of issues.

We were proud to upgrade our tours to provide comfortable, clean, quality accommodations that were centrally located. I felt that the location of the hotel or pension was key in offering patrons flexibility and choice. The great cities of Europe could be explored independently, or in the company of tour guides, or a combination of both; depending on the comfort level and the travel experience of the customer. The point was that travelers would not be locked into staying with the large group for the duration of the tour unless they wanted to. When I started working in the ITT office, the overnight tours to Paris always stayed outside of the city near the airport. It made no sense to me. All of our customers had no choice but to return back and forth from the hotel to the city, tied to the schedule of the bus. What was the fun in that, especially for repeat customers who desired to experience the ambience of Paris on their own? The Paris Metro is very easy to use, and the city is great for walking. It was a simple, logistical change, but it made such a difference for our customers. It's always the little things that make or break a service business.

In Poland, we could get doctors and college professors to do city tours quite reasonably. Medical providers and professional educators were still employed as state workers with state wages. A college professor told me that he could make more money working as a desk clerk at the new Marriott in downtown Warsaw than he would earn as a professor of history at the state university. These highly educated men and women were supplementing their sparse wages by giving city tours to American tourists. Many Poles did not speak English, so the services of the professional segment were greatly needed. The capitalist market in Poland was expanding exponentially. The reality created an ethical dilemma and a level of resentment for the doctors and the educators. I have recently read that many professional Polish workers have migrated to other cities in Europe over the last 10 years or so. This had not yet happened in the early 90's.

The Polish people were very eager to talk to Americans about anything. They had this great appreciation for personal freedoms. Small things that we take for granted were new for them, and they were bursting to engage our conversations and our thoughts. I felt very grateful to experience the wonders of personal freedom and democracy through the eyes of the average Polish citizen. It was refreshing and grounding to my own sense of things. The Polish people had a most extreme reverence for democracy and for Pope John Paul. They linked the two together fervently.

They blessed themselves and some kneeled down if they even walked in front of a Catholic Church. Many females carried a little lace veil in their purses or pockets to put on their head when they entered a church, which they would do regularly; just pop in on their lunch break, or on their way home from work. I had not seen this intense and heartfelt level of reverence since I had been around the Catholic nuns in my childhood. It was like stepping back in time, witnessing an outward demonstration of faith that was not the norm in the everyday lifestyle of Western democracies.

The Poles credited the Pope with both the inspiration and the execution of the Solidarity movement and the long awaited fall of Communism in Poland. The Polish people have a very, strong faith in God, who was represented to them through the iron will of the People's Pope. There was no doubt in their minds of the role of faith and His leadership in the fall of Communism across Eastern Europe. They acknowledged the other world events that played out to include the Russians bogged down in Afghanistan and the hand of Reagan's America in all of this. For them, the world events were linked to the influence of the Pope, and to the work of God in the liberation of their beloved Poland. My thinking and my response to my own identity with America enabled me to easily relate to the Polish people. They questioned and they pondered, and they questioned more to find a deeper level of personal truth and understanding.

I was also deeply affected by Auschwitz. I had been to Dachau in Munich, which is dreadful, but Auschwitz-Birkeneau is beyond human comprehension. I would like to try and put into words the feel of that place, even 50 years later. We were there in April. The Camp sits on a barren plain with no trees in sight to block the wind, which howls and roars across the emptiness. I was wearing heavy socks, leather boots, jeans, layered thermal shirt and fleece, and a heavy duty, water proof, wind resistant Timberland jacket. I had gloves and a wool scarf wrapped around my neck. I was chilled to the bone at Auschwitz in the spring time.

It was raining sideways. The sting of the wetness sliced through my skeleton with the bite of the wind. I had a lot of adipose tissue around my bones to supplement the insulation of my heavy clothing. The Jews were starving, rib cages busting through their emaciated, stretched skin; clothed in tattered, cotton garments, or naked. I could not get over the coldness and the dampness of this Polish waste land in the spring. What about the brutality of the bitter winter sojourn, day after day, night after night, hour after hour, minute after minute, second after second? I can only imagine the peace they must have longed for; the basic human need for an existence in this hell on earth to finally end.

The Germans kept meticulous records that are on display at Auschwitz. They documented the train numbers, times of arrival, departure cities, names, birth dates, and dates of death. Most of the internees survived within a range of weeks to an average of two months from arrival to death, if they were not immediately selected for elimination. The train tracks were built right up to the door of the gas showers. Auschwitz-Birkeneau was built for one purpose only. It's all there to see and to feel: the ovens, the gas showers, the pony tails, the glasses, the suitcases, the sleeping stalls, the experimental buildings, and the mass grave sites. For me, it was not the sights of Auschwitz, but the sheer weight of Auschwitz pressing on my shoulders and engulfing my humanity. I did not see Auschwitz. I felt Auschwitz. I shuddered under the enormity of Auschwitz.

How could human beings do this to one another? I remember a black and white picture on one of the walls that is frozen in my mind. The guards took pictures, like trophies or souvenir shots on vacation. There is a close up picture of a well dressed, healthy, strong, young German officer who is caught in mid stride a frame before his boot connects with a skeleton of a human being who is curled up in the fetal position in the mud, waiting for the slam of the soldier's black, shiny boot against the fragile frame of what was left of his or her human body. The handsome SS Officer is smiling widely and happily for the photo. The cold horror of the dynamics of that singular, person to person interaction permeated my being at Auschwitz, and has been imprinted on my brain ever since.

The soldier might as well have been going for the winning goal of a soccer match for the expression of sheer glee on his young, scrubbed face. He was strutting for the camera like a peacock in heat; his plumage colored in the sheer strength of his black boot aiming for the emaciated rib cage of his powerless victim. This photo visually represented *The Third Reich* for me. The rest of the camp I felt in the bitter cold and the heavy weight of the place, but the image of the soldier's smile; his carefree action frozen by the camera in mid-stride will forever haunt my memory and my understanding of Hitler's "Final Solution". For me, the young soldier had reached a self-rationalization that the form in the mud under his feet was not a human being. How this happened and why underlay the unanswered questions and the guilt that my German friend and co-worker dealt with on a daily basis in the murky estuary of his soul.

I became very embarrassed and irritated to be associated with an American in our group during this somber day at Auschwitz. She was a DOD school teacher. She had her camera out, and she was flashing pictures wherever we went. She appeared to have no consideration of the setting of Auschwitz as a dignified, reflective, spiritual place. A camp survivor, wrist tattooed with his number, was speaking to us. He was over 80 years old. He was an official guide of Auschwitz. The old man had tears in his eyes as he told us his story. He was expressing his fear that the story of the Holocaust would die with his generation, the last of the survivors. This was prior to Spielberg's release of *Schindler's List* and prior to the opening of the Holocaust Museum in Washington, D.C. I hope that our elderly, elegant, anxious guide is finally at peace with the scope and outcome of the Memorial, dedicated to passing on his personal story to future generations.

His words were strong, focused, and determined despite the frailty of his age. As I listened to him, I felt so sad and humbled by him. Not only had he lived through the hell of Auschwitz and Nazi Europe, but he had never been able to leave this place, either mentally or physically. He had dedicated the rest of his life to making sure that future generations would know what happened here. He expressed passionately, "They must know what happened here, and they must never forget. That is what I ask of you. That you tell people what you saw here. Please do that for me." So, I am telling it, as best as I can with mere words and ink. It does not seem enough.

This teacher was snapping pictures from all angles as the Auschwitz camp survivor spoke to us; crossing in front of him, walking over lighted candles in an area that was obviously a shrine to the bodies burned in the ovens there. She was not taking pictures of him. She was taking pictures around him, oblivious of him, as he stood there, pouring his heart and his soul out to us. This adult, educated, school teacher was shamefully and utterly disrespectful to the experience of the story of Auschwitz, and to the quiet but powerful dignity of the old man. It was obvious that she was not listening or attending to anything other than her camera. It was like she was on a photo shoot in a mock setting that was arranged totally for her wants. He was just another prop to her. Her arrogance and her ignorance were irritating me to no end. She reminded me of why I hate traveling in groups. I set tours up, but I am mostly uncomfortable with "group think" and of being associated with the behavior of others in a group situation.

Basically, this teacher didn't have a clue. The camp survivor sensed my growing irritation and that of other Americans in our group. He came over and quietly told us to leave it be, to let it go, and to leave her to her picture taking. He said it did not matter if she was rude. It was more important to him that she go ahead and take the pictures. He frankly noted that she would not be able to pass on the message and the story of Auschwitz in any other way. He did not want the world to forget. I was humbled by him. I guess in the context of his life, an obnoxious tourist was the least of his worries.

To this day, her behavior bothers me. She exhibited the "ugly American" image that those of us who grow up outside of America can not stand. I know that she is the exception. I know this because by then, 1994, I had lived and worked with Americans for over ten years. I had become an American citizen a few years prior. Her behavior especially bothered me from the perspective of a fellow American. I felt angry that our group would be tarnished by the mindless actions of just one of us. But, there were other visitors at Auschwitz besides us. We were the only Americans. I could see the silent eyes of people from other countries as they followed her. You could not help but notice her arrogant, inconsiderate behavior. The silent grimaces of visitors from across Europe and elsewhere spoke volumes to me across the room. I could no longer observe all of this as an outsider. Instead, I had to wince and swallow my pride as an American, who was being loudly and blatantly represented in a personally, uncomfortable manner.

My husband and I extended our tour in Europe to almost five years. There were so many places to go and so much to see. We would spend lazy weekends touring the Mosel River Valley and the small, charming towns that wound through there. Many German families owned wineries along the Mosel. The fields of grapes would stretch up steep cliffs from the river for miles and miles. We would explore one wine cellar after another, as the owners entertained us with great stories and even greater wine probes. We learned to taste from dry to sweet, to wash our palates with water in between, to sip not gulp (that part was harder for some of us, especially in our groups of young GIs), and to acquire a basic understanding of the subtleties of wine making and wine drinking. Unfortunately, we did not become wine connoisseurs, but it was fun in the process.

Like most American military families in Europe, we traveled through France, Belgium, The Netherlands, Germany, Austria, Italy, and

Switzerland. They are your standard, "must do" destinations. There is nothing standard about the wonderful cities and countryside to be explored in Europe. Train travel is worlds apart from the service we know in America and Canada. My favorite memories are not of the big cities, though I did love Paris, Vienna, and Prague the most. But they are of the smaller places that you would never know about without finding them yourself in the wandering of your days.

Utrecht in Holland is one of those places. I had never heard of Utrecht before I found my way there. It is an old canal city like Amsterdam, only quainter and cleaner than Amsterdam. My parents were visiting us. My husband had to work for a few days at a US Air Base in The Netherlands. My father and I set out to explore on our own on a beautiful, sunny day. We took the local train into Utrecht. We really had no idea where we were going. I had not been there to get the lay of the land or to plan what I would show him. Well, we had a great time walking through this city of canals and bridges, old churches, shops, and a huge open air market. By mid-afternoon, we sat at an outside table in a café along the canal. Many local people were sitting outside soaking up the sun. In Europe, the norm for workers on a Friday is to break free mid-afternoon if the sun is shining and the day is bright.

My father was facing the canal, sitting back, really enjoying his day. He was expressing that he never thought he would have the opportunity to visit Europe and see as much as he had. He was amazed that the story of his life had brought him here. The day before, we had traveled through Belgium and the Ardennes. Some of the most famous battles of World War II were fought there. My father had studied and lived through the history of all of this from the perspective of an ocean removed, but linked emotionally in the experience of his generation. He really was quite awed and respectful of the opportunity of seeing the places that he had read and heard so much about.

That was the positive thing of living in distant places, being able to share the experience with friends and family members. Anyway, my father had been gazing at the canal behind me. He spoke in the soft Irish brogue of the Avalon Peninsula, nodding for me to look behind as he noted in a hushed, conspiratorial sort of way, "Them young fellows over there must be some hard up." Now, being raised in Newfoundland in the time of my father's upbringing, he had an intimate and thorough understanding of "being hard up." I looked behind me to see two young, healthy looking guys in a small boat, just hanging out, laughing and talking, looking and sounding very much like they did not have a care in the world. They did not look at all "hard up" to me. So, I answered him, "What do you mean?" Dad acknowledged, "Well the poor bastards are having to share a smoke. They've been passing the same cigarette back and forth for the last five minutes. It's a roll your own." You have to know my father. He had always been very observant. He loved people and their stories. He was 70 years old, and he was sincere as all get out.

Well, that became one of those father and daughter moments where you move from a "child" to a "fellow adult" even though you have been living on your own for the past fifteen years or so. I looked back and "of course." I hesitated for a brief moment before I answered him. I took the plunge. "Dad, that's not a cigarette. It's a joint." He said, "What? What are you talking about? You mean drugs?" I had to spell it out. "Dad, that's marijuana. They're smoking a marijuana joint. It's legal here." He answered, "Well, I'll be God damned! I thought I had seen it all." Again, you have to know my father. He always probed new things and new experiences very deeply and fervently. He was not one to let an opportunity like this pass him by in a nonchalant way. He was a great story teller, expounding his Irish wit to find the humor in the mundane, and to share it with others. I knew that this event would provide him great fodder for future yarns with his friends in Newfoundland when he returned home.

My father stands up, walks over to the side of the canal, right above the two young gentlemen, hands on his hips, and stares down at them, really checking it out. He is so blatantly staring that one of the young guys looks up, and without missing a beat, he holds up the joint and said, "Hey Pops, do you want a toke?" Well, I thought I would die. My dad just shakes his head, smiling, and jokes down to them. They talked back and forth for a few minutes. Dad even asks them about smoking it without a filter. He was amazed at that. He was exploring all the details. Dad was laughing. They were laughing. They were enjoying each other. When dad sat back down, he had the biggest grin on his face. He said, "I think I'm going to have another beer on this one." The waiter brought him his brew. He raised his glass in the air and said his favorite Irish toast, "Long may your big jib draw." He took a swallow, laid his glass down, and sat back in his chair. He said, "It really is legal here, all drugs? How do they do that?" Our happy conversation continued. All was right with our sunny afternoon in Utrecht. I guess that day, and the fun that we shared is one of my fondest memories of exploring in Europe.

Another great memory of a "nowhere" place was in the forest area near the border between Luxembourg and Germany. We lived very close to there, and we would often spend a lazy few hours strolling through the cobbled streets of Echternacht. It is a small but classically beautiful European town that sits around the banks of the Elbe River. The river forms the border between Germany and Luxembourg. Half of the town is in Germany, and half is in Luxembourg. On this particular day, a friend of mine was visiting me from the States. She wanted to hike through the marked trails that are around there. When I say hike, I really mean upright movement in the outdoors. This was pleasure walking only, an excuse to enjoy the blessings of a blue sky and the warm breeze of the day.

We were probably a few miles into the woods, when we rounded a bend to see a tavern sitting along the trail, more or less in the middle of nowhere. The humble establishment provided a respite for hikers. My friend and I could not believe our find; a pub with bar stools and all. She describes this experience as the most memorable event of her two-week visit, during which time we covered by train many of the highlights of Europe. Of course, everyone who came to visit me over there thought they could see it all in a few weeks. For Anita, the tavern in the woods, sporting a *Bitte ein Bit* sign was Europe. It felt so unique to the civilized flavor, which simple folk like us associate with the essence of Europe. Forget the art masterpieces of *Le Louvre* in Paris and the *Academia* in Florence, Anita remembers fondly our afternoon in the woods along the German / Luxembourg border; and the simple pleasure of sitting down to enjoy a fresh brew for her and a mineral water for me (I was pregnant); served in cold glasses by a local character, in the middle of the woods. We always set our standards pretty high.

I believe that these small experiences form the core of our life stories. It does not matter where we are or what we see; it is the little, sometimes quirky, life connections and conversations that stay with us, and revolve the lens of our prism. We stagnate our thinking by not opening ourselves to listen to others and to be at peace in the present. We restrict our possibilities in the security of our status quo, even when things are amiss. If we can't connect with the people of our journey, then we are not able to connect the dots, to make sense of our story. Who comes home from a great vacation talking about the architecture of the buildings? The tangible treasures of various cities form the backdrop, but the smaller tidbits that affect us emotionally are what we remember, and what we grow from.

It's the same in our every day life. It's not the travel to other places that is as important as how we relate to the people and events in the passing of each and every day. Insight is gained from daring to explore the world that we are exposed to, to seek new knowledge from our interactions with people from all walks of life. It's when we think that we have the answers that we have to step back. For it is then, that we don't even know the questions, let alone the answers. I guess I always knew this instinctively, but sometimes you have to walk ten miles to see, to feel, to hear, to smell, and to find what has been in front of your face all along. The important thing is that you dare to walk in the first place. The walking is the living.

I would return to the States after living in Europe for almost five years. I am now an American citizen. I find myself back in a place that I am familiar with. We were lucky enough to get orders back to Eglin Air Force Base. It is more or less our home in the States. It's the only place that I had lived in for any length of time. I love the climate, the beaches, and the people there. But, I am uneasy and I do not feel grounded in the present. I am a mother to my daughter and a wife to my husband. But who am I to me? What do I want to do with my life?

I only know what I do not want to do, which is to go back to working in a hospital. I had gotten much more out of my X-Ray career than I had ever dreamed possible back in 1974 when I started (a full 20 years earlier). I just knew in my heart that I had walked away from it finally. What were my options at this stage of my life? How many military wives dealt with the very same dilemma? Up until this time, the pieces had fallen in place for me. But, in my late-thirties, I felt like time was slipping away. I did not feel like a victim, as in "Woe is me, I've wasted my life." It was not that. I felt more like time was passing too fast, and I had not figured out my fit yet. This was my mood when I returned to the States in the spring of "94.

Chapter 10

THE POLITICS OF ME

T HE GOOD NEWS WAS THAT we were going back to the same town and the same friends that we had left almost five years earlier. But, I would learn that you can never go back. You can return to the same area, but in reality, you have to go forward. You can not go back. If you remain in one place, you never think about these things. You are naturally going forward in the familiarity of your life. But, if you leave somewhere that you like or somewhere that is known to you, you often yearn to go back, even if you are enjoying the present. Your memory is of the place and the people that you knew when you left. As time passes, the same people and places change in subtle ways while you are also changing from the experiences of your own journey. For me, it was more than subtle. Several of our really good friends had moved. They were no longer there. Other couples had gotten divorced or were no longer together, which altered the dynamics of the entire social circle. I was now a mother. I would have to balance the demands of raising my child with a strong, personal desire to get back to the university thing. I had not taken any classes in Europe. The cost per credit hour was triple the amount that I paid in Florida. Finally, there was the job dilemma.

From a pragmatic perspective, after a year of resisting the inevitable, I ended up back in Radiology; a full six years after I had crossed that parking lot in 1989, swearing to myself that I would never work in a hospital again. There was not a whole lot of opportunity for someone with great experience setting up European Tours around the Panhandle of Florida. There are only so many ways you could go to Disney. We all know that travel is different in the States and in Canada. People of all ages don't take tours. In Europe, many people would book a tour, especially if they had never been to the city or the country before. There is the whole language thing. The tour was a great way to get the lay of the land, to get an overview, so that you could go back on your own with your family and friends, and explore from that baseline of at least having a clue where to begin.

I swallowed my pride and went back to my fate. In the end, I was able to accept the inevitable because I had a plan. As long as I had my agenda; to see light at the end of the tunnel, I could handle the short term load to get there. I went back full-time, but locked my commitment into 32 hrs/wk, and not 40 hours. It doesn't sound like much but it was huge for me. Ownership of my daily schedule was my carrot. First of all, I left for work after my daughter's bus arrived in the morning, and I got off in time to get home ahead of her. The hours of 8:00—2:30 are great for working moms. I don't know why more companies don't look at full-time benefits for working mothers based on a 32 hr/ wk, pro-rated salary. It's a win for everyone. That's just my 2-cents worth. I had a boss and a personnel director who would work with me. They valued my prior work experience. I have learned through the years that working females should advocate for themselves more. We sometimes create our own nightmares with our silence and our martyrdom. Some of my friends along the way have not worked at all to stay home and raise their children. This is fine if your own personal needs are being met. If not, it is hard to find balance when many employers are still not flexible with the needs of working moms. With the shortened day and with a steady pay check, I could continue as a full-time college student. I had a plan.

I can honestly say that my X-Ray career always gave me the flexibility to find a job anywhere, and to work whatever shifts I requested. It is a great job if it suits you. The money is not bad. Medical people are wonderful to work with. One of the main problems for me in Radiology was that the direction of personal growth in the field had become very technical over the last 20 years. CAT scanners, MRI scanners, and Cath Labs are highly computerized. The direction of advancement in the job was not an interest for me. I enjoyed the people aspect; the variety, the intensity, and sometimes the comedy of the Emergency Room work. I enjoyed the challenge of getting really good, diagnostic views of trauma victims, the more difficult and critical, the more I engaged whatever I had to give. But sitting behind the control booth of a CAT scanner would bore me to tears. I totally resisted engaging myself in or learning the intricacies of the computerized scanners. Most techs who move forward in that field know about as much about the images as the doctors who order them. As the jobs with the bigger pay checks and promotions became more technical, the more I distanced myself from a career focus in Radiology, like I ever had one in the first place

I was focused to stay in college and to graduate with some kind of degree. I did not know it at the time, but my journey with education would take me to an entirely different career field than I had ever anticipated for myself. I will always be grateful for the advice of my old friend from New Jersey—to just go back and take classes, to start somewhere. The rest will work its way out. It's all about the process. I would like to pass this on to young people. Don't wait to start if you're not sure of what the end result will be. The learning will take you somewhere and empower you along the way. The choices become greater and broader the more you dare to query. It all comes down to giving yourself the power to maximize your choices in life.

In the context of time and place, the security of everyday living was shaken to the core in the fall of '94 in the Florida Panhandle. Hurricane Opel had blown through there to rock our world. People who had lived in places like Navarre, Fort Walton Beach, Destin, and Pensacola for years and years had gotten comfortable with the threat of hurricanes. Every year, several would come into the Gulf of Mexico, skirting around, but the catastrophic impact of a direct hit from a major hurricane had not been felt for decades. People had become complacent. Even the Military Bases did not see fit to order a mandatory evacuation until about four hours before the Eye of Opel was passing over. The key word here is mandatory. We had to pack up "whatever" and get in our cars to head north when the storm was already upon us. We were not given a choice.

Many of us have memories of sitting in cars on Highway 85, unable to move in traffic, as the radio was directing people to go into the ditches on the side of the road if a tornado was sighted. Comforting! Our cinder block Base houses had been around for over fifty years. We would of rather taken our chances from inside those cement blocks, than to be stuck in traffic on a highway going nowhere. Everyone learned from the experience of Opel. People would evacuate days earlier in the future as hurricanes with names such as Dennis and Ivan were projected to visit our shores. It was a good lesson as the decade since Opel has seen one hurricane after another along the Gulf Coast from Texas to Florida.

Opel was our Katrina. It takes years for an area to get over the shock of the immense destruction of a natural disaster. My heart goes out to the people of New Orleans and the Mississippi Gulf Coast. The impact was so wide spread, and the population centers so much more dense than what we had to deal with in '94. For many people caught up in the reality of a natural disaster, the experience alters their sense of the safe world that they had spent a life time creating for themselves and their children. I have a friend who told me that she had panic attacks after Opel. She had been stuck in traffic for hours and hours, unable to move, with her three young sons in her van as the storm raged around them. Her home was flooded out. She always had built a secure and controlled life for her family. It was life altering for her to deal with the slamming power of Opel's direct hit. I had another good friend who literally packed up and moved. She had lived in paradise on the white sand beaches of Okaloosa Island for almost twenty years. She could not bear to stay and rebuild.

Many Floridians are bitter because they have learned their lesson of where to build and where to live. A moving sand bar is not too stable in a hurricane. At other times, it is paradise. The take of your average, working class, tax paying citizen in Florida is that if you choose to soak up the view and the luxury of living in the middle of Destin Harbor or some other high risk area, then you should do so at your own expense. The reality has become that if your insurance does not bail you out then FEMA will. Either way, it's the average working Joe, who is affected the most. The insurance rates for everyone in Florida have gone through the roof, no matter how humble the home, or how many miles the property is from the Gulf. And developers keep building high rises and private homes, costing millions; knowing full well that it is only a matter of time before another hurricane blows through there. The rich and the entitled will be bailed out by the government to rebuild again, always bigger and better, and only available to the privileged few. This is America, right? Those who take risks get further ahead. What about when the far reaching costs of the risk are at everyone else's expense?

At the same time that we were dealing with the Opel mess, I would vote for the first time in my adult life. I was now a citizen. Being true to the roots of my parents, I would take my right to vote seriously. Politics is in my blood. My genetic code is wired to delve into the informed aspect of my vote. Without possessing a knowledge base to discriminate, what really is the point of voting? I began to question, to pay attention, to listen, and to probe for clarity. The task of an educated vote was not that easy for me. I had spent so much of my adult life out of North America, and my knowledge of American politics was grounded in the responses of my father to all forms and levels of government during my childhood. I knew more about Kennedy, Johnson, Nixon, Ford, and Carter than I did about Clinton, Newt Who?; and the rest of the players of the mid-term elections in the fall of '94.

First of all, I did not know if I should register as a Democrat or a Republican. I chose Independent, which is really where I was in my head and in my heart. My parents had been extremely vocal and strong Conservatives in Canadian politics. I know that many Americans will say that there is no such thing as a Conservative Canadian. Maybe that's true in the frame work of the Christian Right agenda in the States. But, in the context of conservative values and life styles, Canada is split down the middle between Liberal and Conservative. I agree that the average Liberal in Canada is far to the left. That is why my parents adamantly opposed those beliefs their entire life. I think that the difference between Canadian Conservatives and American Conservatives is in the area of tolerance. Many Canadians actually live much more conservatively in their personal lives and within the boundaries of their conservative values than many Americans who loudly and adamantly describe themselves as Conservative.

For example, Canadians are much more hesitant to accumulate vast amounts of personal debt than Americans are. They can not claim the interest paid on home mortgages as a tax deduction, so they are very cognizant of how much interest they have to pay over the life of the loan. They tend to take out their home mortgage loans with shorter terms. The higher payments of the shorter terms keep your average home buyer within a more humble range of home purchase costs. Their comfort level with debt is more aligned to the realities of their take home pay. In essence, middle class Canadians tend to be more frugal in their daily living. The value system of the average, working parent is that their child will go on to some level of secondary education before they would purchase their first car. If they could afford both, great! But, if they were to go into debt for one or the other, the education would take precedence over the car.

This was the value system when I graduated in the mid-70's, and it has not changed that much in the present. For example, my nephew, who just graduated with an Engineering Degree after six years of university, bought his first car at the age of 24. He has worked many part-time jobs since his teen years, but he balanced his income with a little play and a little savings. He understood that he could not take on the long-term expense of a car, insurance, and upkeep until he was done with college. This is a pretty standard, common sense, type of mind set for your every day, Joe Blow, Newfoundlander. The expectation of instant gratification has not evolved to the extent that it has with the average middle class American kid. I remember when I first moved to the States in '83, I was shocked that high school students owned their own cars. It's a difference in cultural values. Now, I have a 15 year old, who is counting the days until she has some level of car to drive to school. Her cousins in Canada will not go there at the same age. The cultural norms support different expectations in the teenage years. Newfoundland teens will most likely share the family car until they possess the ability to support themselves.

I have heard politicians and analysts use the term fiscal conservative. I guess that is what I am talking about here. Then, there is the morals piece. Are Canadians less moral or more moral if they are more tolerant and less judgmental? My point is that there is a lively and real debate in Canada between Liberals and Conservatives. My parents would be shocked and a little angry to find themselves described as Liberals by American Conservatives. On the morals aspect, my personal experience is that the average Canadian is very private and internal with matters of the heart and matters of the soul, as are many Americans. Most people are more concerned with keeping their own house in order. They don't spend a lot of time fretting about other people's choices and style of living. They have enough trouble keeping up with their kids, their work, paying the bills, fitting in some fun, and just plain living. I don't think individual citizens of either country can claim the high road on morals.

For me, these are the fundamental differences between self-described Conservatives in the States and self-described Conservatives in Canada. I tend to be a little defensive when my Republican friends describe me as a Liberal, based on the fact that I grew up in Canada. Liberal was a dirty word in my household growing up. My father and mother very vocally and rationally challenged the values of the Liberal Party at the provincial level in Newfoundland, and at the federal level in Ottawa. We lived through the antics of Joey Smallwood and Pierre Elliott Trudeau with loud disgust, frustration, and protestations in my home on a daily basis. My father would debate anyone and everyone on the perils of the Liberal Party. My father was a working class conservative, Catholic, Irish politician to the core. He could articulate a position and defend it with the best of them. And he always did: loudly, adamantly, and often.

My own journey towards my role as a voter and a citizen in the United States has given me the opportunity to really explore and reflect on my personal ideology and value system. I know that if I had remained in Canada, I would have voted as a staunch and card carrying member of the Progressive Conservative Party my entire life. I was born into this. I would not have given it much thought, other than to rationalize and debate my point of view with anyone who was up to the challenge. After all, I was programmed to think of myself as a conservative. I am very comfortable with a conservative perception of me, as linked to the family and educational values of my upbringing. Within this framework, I should be very comfortable politically to find myself in the middle of the Florida Panhandle in 1994; 75% die-hard Republican, Clinton haters to the extreme.

I should be very content with the local and federal politics in this time and place. The Panhandle was Joe Scarborough territory in 1995 when I returned to Radiology and the medical field. The hospital staff that I worked with worshiped him. So, why am I so hesitant, so profoundly unsure of my identity as a Conservative in the context of American politics? Why can I not demonize Clinton, like everyone else around me? The politics were very nasty, and very personal. It crossed the line for me when the heartless comments were publicly directed at Chelsea Clinton. She was just a kid. Outspoken members of the Christian Right attacked her appearance of all things. I was a little confounded at the intensity of the hate. I did not understand how a political party that bragged about family values and morals could attack a child. Politicians are fair game, but their kids? That was new for me.

Over the past twelve years since then, I have had many discussions with anyone who will talk politics with me. I am still probing, trying to find my way. I changed my registration from an Independent to a Democrat after the 2004 elections, but I am not locked into either party as a definite vote. Around that time, I even stopped going to church for about six months or so. It seemed like patriotism, blind allegiance to the President, and attending church on Sundays were one and the same in the culture of the Catholic Church that I was attending. I had to back away from it for a while, to put some distance between my thoughts and my faith. I am okay with all of that now. I have come to see myself as a Conservative Democrat. My own sense of right and wrong, of trying to live within the golden rule have prevented me from aligning myself with the Christian Right, which has represented the voice of the Republican Party to me since the early 90's. The less vocal but even more forceful power of influence in the Republican Party appears to be corporate America, advocating for the interests of the wealthiest of the wealthy. Those multi-million dollar bonuses on the backs of workers' rights and wages don't sit well with me.

When I grew up in Newfoundland, the interest of the wealthy was seen to be tied to the agenda of the Liberal Party. The alignment with the elite and the entitled cemented my parents' disgust with the agenda of the Liberal Party. In America, it seems to me that neither party has a clear distinction relative to the interests of the few verses the interests of the many. But when it comes to degrees of influence, I believe that the interests of corporations are more heavily represented in the Republican Party, to the detriment of the interests of the middle class base of the country.

I have involved myself in listening and probing for deeper understanding and clarity. The Catholic values of my upbringing seem to be in conflict with the judgmental rhetoric of the Christian Right Wing of the Republican Party. I can not get beyond that. The mean intonations and indignant righteousness of the outspoken Christian Right grate against my internalized concept of right and wrong, of basic decency, of a minimal standard of fairness and kindness. I visualize Jesus in the temple; swiping his arm in anger, lashing out against the hypocrisy and the arrogant entitlement of the Pharisees and the tax collectors. When a popular author of the Christian Right attacked the widows of 9/11 with cruel and careless words, I knew that my own Christian values could not align myself with the mean spirited, hurtful, lashing perspective; targeted at anyone who had a different opinion or an opposing view.

I have little tolerance with external excuses; blaming others for the choices we make. I believe in self-discipline and hard work. A very good friend of mine told me that I am more Republican than Democrat. That may be true relative to the ideals of the Republican Party, but a party of true conservative values is not the outcome that I have seen in American politics with the Republican Party since I have explored the direction of my vote.

I think this started to become driven home for me when I watched the Gore—Bush debates leading up to the 2000 elections. I can honestly say that neither Gore nor Bush appealed to me. One seemed pompous and boring, and the other seemed to stumble through an articulation of anything that spoke leader or critical thinker to me. I was really struggling with the direction and the value of my vote in the 2000 election. I watched all of the debates, which did not do much to make me feel better about either of the Presidential candidates. At one point, the issue of taxes was raised. I don't remember what Gore said. It was not inspiring nor memorable to me. On the other hand, I do remember the essence of what Bush said.

At the time, it really struck me. Bush was defending a tax incentive for the wealthy. He said that he believed that people who worked harder should be rewarded more. I thought to myself. He actually believes that those who are wealthy work harder than those who are middle class. Gore did not respond to Bush's point, as I am sure that he thought the same thing. Bush's words and their meaning stayed with me ever since. I think that the powerful and the rich are so out of touch with the struggles and the work ethic of your average citizen across the range of the middle class; that they actually believe that they deserve to be rewarded more because they work harder. I don't know enough about the American tax system to have an informed opinion on whether the wealthy pay their fair share of taxes. I have Republican friends, who have assured me that the wealthy pay their fair share. The tax burden is not shared fairly by corporations. The corporate tax loop holes and incentives are huge and greatly benefit a very privileged, very miniscule percent of the population.

Of course, some of the wealthy work very hard. However, there are many who have never known a hard day's work in their life. Bush's framing of the entitlement of the wealthy linked to hard work spoke volumes to me across the TV screen. The Republican Party lost my vote in that moment, and the more that I reflected on it, the more it resonated as outside of my own thinking. I came to realize that the ideology of the wealthy as entitled more than that of the middle class was a clear distinction for me. This ideology was linked to the Liberal Party in Canada in the experience of my upbringing. My search to be an informed voter has led me to weigh my personal values, my sense of right and wrong against what I determine to be the principles of each candidate. If neither candidate inspires me, then I have to look at the ideology of the party. I struggle with my understanding of the American political system to this day. I think this is because of my own sense of frustration and despair with the events of the past six years.

As I move forward in my quest to become a full, participating American citizen, I have many discussions with co-workers and friends, probing their beliefs and their thinking. From 1995 to 2000, I am working in a small hospital in Niceville, Fl, a very tiny town, heavily Republican and proud of it. In the second term of the Clinton Presidency, the average citizen in the Panhandle of Florida was angry and vehement in their disgust of Clinton and the Democratic Party in general. It was not an overall friendly environment for spirited debates and questioning. The active duty military and medical workers were two groups who loudly opposed

the incumbents. I wanted to know more, to understand the rational be-
hind their strong views. I did have a male co-worker, who was a staunch
Republican, and who liked to discuss issues. We had great conversations.
I know that he enjoyed them as much as I did.

One of our topics was abortion. He always brought it up. It was sort
of like he was gleeful to draw the controversy of abortion into our range
of conversation; often when he had someone else around, sort of two
against one to get me on this particular issue. My pro-life view for myself was a given. I understood what I knew to be my truth on the issue
of abortion. I just had a harder time with a perspective that told other
women what to do. My reflections of my own mother's life muddied the
water for me relative to choice. In my mother's day in Newfoundland,
young women were required to leave their jobs if they worked in government service after they were married. My mother fell into this category.
She never complained about it later on. It was the normal thing in that
time and place. However, I was always aware of how happy her voice
was, and how much she enjoyed her memories of her working days. She
loved it. Her eyes would light up. She would laugh. She would tell us
over and over again her favorite stories and escapades. My parents did
not marry until the early 50's, when they were both close to thirty. So, she
had worked for a decade or so, before she had to resign. The only other
option was to stay single. Her choices were very limited.

Throughout our childhood, mom did not work. She was always home.
I really liked coming home from school, and she was there. We struggled financially. Most of the families in Newfoundland were large. Our
Catholic mothers did not have an option of birth control. I think by
the mid to late 60's, this was changing. I remember my mother talking
about the priests advising that personal decisions would have to be made
against one's conscience. I think this type of advice was given in private
and not in public. It was a little late for my mother's generation in any
case. For the most part, the reality of large families and a single parent
working was grave, financial hardship. Families were stretched to make it
from paycheck to paycheck; to make the groceries last within the budget.
I know that Americans think of Canada as being very socialistic relative
to America. The main difference is in health care. The only other social
program is welfare. The families that I am talking about were the working
middle class. They were too proud for welfare. There were no programs
like WIC with free dairy products for low income families. We just had
to make do within our budgets. Many families could not afford fresh

milk. Block cheese was very expensive, a treat to get a piece. The standard was canned milk, Carnation. To this day, I don't drink milk. It was hard to acquire a taste for Carnations out of the can. My mother would warm it up for cereal and hot chocolate. It was better like that.

I remember that my mother went back to work for a short time when I was in high school. Her job was a temporary slot. The position was only open for a year or maybe even less. I can honestly say that my mother appeared the most satisfied and happy that I had ever seen her during that brief time. She genuinely reveled in the whole work experience. I think that she was very effective and competent in an administrative role, and she really enjoyed the adult piece of it. She would talk of her friendships and interactions at work with great joy for years after her employment ended. These are my personal memories, but they speak of choice and roles. My mother never complained of staying home. It was just that she lit up and became a different person when she worked for that short time, or when she spoke of her working adventures as a young adult. Most women juggle work and family through the relationship of choice and birth control. In my generation, we could not imagine a world without choice in these matters.

Outside of my memories of my mother's life relative to choice, I had my experience in Saudi Arabia. How could I not see choice differently after witnessing the reality for women in that country? I just think that many of the people who loudly oppose women's choice take it for granted. I made a conscious, adult decision to control my body through birth control until I was ready to explore the option of having a child. That was my choice. From a strictly, conservative Catholic perspective, some would say that my choice was sinful. I guess that will be decided between me and my God.

Where do you draw the line between birth control, the morning after pill, and abortion? If you break it down far enough at the cell level, what about condoms? We are talking about half the cell here. Ah, but that would be addressing male choices and lifestyles. I have never heard the most fundamental pro-life advocates taking on the composition of the cell. If people on the far right have broken the physicality of the miracle of life down to the attachment of the cell to the wall of the uterus, then what about the formation of the cell in the first place. These are all things to ponder as individuals wrestle within their conscience, and their sometimes self-righteous views of what others should do.

Personally, abortion crosses the line for me. However, if a young girl is raped and she becomes pregnant, would it be wrong for her parents to want her to have an abortion? Where do you draw the line? What if this was your daughter, and she was 14 years old? I don't know the answers. Emmanuel Kant is a famous German philosopher. One of his moral doctrines is called *The Categorical Imperative*. I am always drawn to the complexity of issues such as abortion with his posit. He states that if something isn't right for everyone then it is right for no one. So, there can be no exceptions ever for abortion, unless it is right for everyone. I think that most people would agree that abortion is not right for everyone in any circumstance. Hence, that will make it right for no one, ever, in any circumstance. Kant's *Categorical Imperative* has become the barometer for my own personal view. However, I feel the issue is so multi-faceted and personal that health decisions, privacy, and choice play hand in hand between an individual, their health provider, their partner, their own moral code, and their God.

For the most part, my Republican friend and I walked hand in hand on the abortion debate. We reached a consensus. I know Republican women who support abortion relative to a woman's choice. I don't see abortion as a Democrat / Republican position because there are such diverse views across the range of possibilities in both parties. It is a moral dilemma. I don't see it as having meaning in a political sense, other than its power as a wedge issue. But, what really is the truth behind the wedge when both parties have diverse views on the subject? If all Republicans were pro-life and all Democrats were pro-choice then it matters. But, there is no true consensus in either party on the issue of abortion. The key note speakers of the 2004 Republican Convention, Giuliani and Schwarzenegger, have both supported a pro-choice agenda across the span of their political careers. Yet, the Party runs on a pro-life stance. It doesn't add up in my books.

The other major domestic issue of our time is the immigration debacle. I am totally opposed to illegal immigration. The main reason behind my view is the long range effect of an illegal labor force on the evolution of a class system in this country. Block visas also bring down wages and workers' rights. If I am not mistaken, a rejection of the ruling class in England was the underlying current of the Revolutionary War in America. If you travel to any third world country, you are knocked off your feet by the wretched conditions of the poor relative to the obnoxious wealth of the ruling class. A work force of illegal workers has no means to advance. They do not pay taxes to support the country in which they are living. The outcome of a growing, illegal work force creates a gap in the labor market that draws down the salaries of legal workers. This creates a no win for everyone except the entitled, the rich, and the powerful. Corporate profits go up as salaries go down. Is that what America has become? Is that what We The People want?

Having stated my opinion, I am not about looking down my nose on hard working people. Who can look with disdain at the maids who clean about every hotel room in this country, or at the roofer who sweats in the dead heat of the summer from his manual labor? Your heart goes out to them. It is more troublesome to think that they have no means to make a better life for themselves from the stance of an illegal, or under a block visa situation. I do not harbor any bad feeling for churches and religious groups who lend a willing hand of charity to those who have less among us. What else should they do? Illegal immigration is a legislative and enforcement debacle. The political will of the policy makers seems to waffle all over the place on the illegal immigration issue. Just about every country in the world enforces its borders. In the wake of 9/11, how can America not protect its borders? It doesn't pass the common sense test, let alone the decency test. I think this is another political issue where Democrats and Republicans are all over the political spectrum. It depends on whether you are an average Joe or an elitist. There are powerful, influential, and wealthy Americans who have an expectation and a desire for a servant class. That is the heart of the matter for me.

I think that the average citizen is moderate and fair. Whether you are a Democrat or a Republican, you want common sense government and a stable future for your children. Most people tend to vote with the political party of their parents; within the comfortable boundaries of their own personal history. This is true all over the world. I believe that the extreme polarities of the political right and the political left advocate ideologies that do not align with the vast majority of citizens. The outspoken leaders tend to seek out information that supports their view, while dismissing and demonizing alternate views. This is okay if you are running the Junior League or the local church sponsored Garden Party. It is scary as hell if you are running the government of the most powerful nation on earth. I can honestly say in all of the discussions that I have had with many Republican friends over the course of the last decade that I have gotten very few answers beyond a deep hatred for Clinton and Carter. The standard response is that the Democrats are no better, and it's better than the Clinton years. Is it? I think that voters across both parties need to delve deeper into issues.

For me, the answer has to be found in the electorate. It is easy to blame the government when things go wrong. But, what about *We The People?* Voters have a duty to be informed and to ask hard questions in hard times. The present is a very hard time for American voters. I believe that citizens must rise to the occasion. Leaders will march as high as the standard that we impose on them. If we are satisfied with the status quo, then it will remain so. This is not a Democratic or a Republican issue. This is the reality for the voters of America. The direction of the future for our children is determined by us in the present. I think that no vote should be taken for granted. The young soldiers of America deserve better than that. They will continue to do their duty, but *We The People* must honor their service by the power of our informed vote.

I am no closer to finding answers in 2007 than I was in 1994. If anything, I have more questions. As I move forward, I am wary of falling into the trap of a sheep or an avoidant mentality displayed by the *Desperate Housewives* and the *American Idol* circuit. There are other things to talk about. I thrive on shaking out the cobwebs, stirring it up a little. I think I irritate others around me with my quest. But that's who I am. I've had to live with my nomadic mind my whole life. I have no choice but to bother my friends a little or a lot every now and then. It's good for them. It's good for me. It's healthy in our advancing age to stretch the dendrites and the axons; to slow down the calcification of our pituitary gland; to challenge the shrinkage of our ventricles; to exercise the pons and the medulla; to keep our thinking and our conversation engaged in the present; empowering ourselves to remain sharp and ornery in the mystery of our future.

The engagement and the critical thinking is the part that we must hang onto; the part that we must not let slip away without an honorable and hard fight. I want to hang on to my awareness and to sharpen it as long as I can in the physicality of my being. My girl friends and I struggle to overcome the sagging of our muscles and the wrinkling of our skin daily, as we become lazy in the pleasant distractions of our bountiful existence. I remind my dear friends of the dangers of our combined complacent minds, when they would rather talk about anything other than politics or the Iraq War, and I would rather talk about anything other than the latest episode of Desperate Housewives. They humor me as I try my best to humor them. We just pour another glass of fine wine as we smile at each other and gently placate whoever has the greatest need in the mood of the moment.

Chapter 11

80% FREE & REDUCED

A YOUNG MOTHER IS STANDING ACROSS the counter to register her son in December of the school year. When the registrar asks her what school he has been in, the mom hesitates, and goes on to say that he has not been in school since the fall of the previous year. She is not sure what grade to enroll him in. I come out of my office as my friend in the outer office is coming to get me. I have very good hearing and I am already on my way. Say that again? He's 9 years old. The mom told us that he had been expelled from attending public school for two years at the age of seven. My mouth fell open. We were having *No Child Left Behind* rammed down our throats in the public schools. The same system that would tolerate **no excuses** from educators in getting this child to a grade level standard had expelled a seven year old child from attending any level or type of public school program for two years. My point is that there are stories in the lives of children that the average person does not have a clue about. I was one of those people, until I became the Guidance Counselor in an elementary school with an extremely high-risk demographic base. You name it, we had it. About 90% of our students came from single parent households. Many of them did not have permanent addresses. They had a lot of learning, emotional, and behavioral needs. They had no medical insurance and no preventive dental care. We were 80% free & reduced, and a full Title 1 school. When I began, I did not know what that meant. I would soon find out.

Yes, that is where my journey with higher education and my role as a mother had taken me. I say my role as a mother, because raising my child was a big factor in my choice to work in the public school system. I have always been very pragmatic. It's the "get on with it" Newfoundlander in me. By the end of the 90's, I had to make a decision regarding internships with post-graduate study. I had done my first internship in a mental health setting. I decided that I was too old and too cynical for that line of work. My years with emergency room work over the course of many night shifts had already acquainted me with the world of addiction and crazy. If throwing up charcoal around an NG tube doesn't cure you, no amount of counseling is going to help. My degree was in Psychology and Counseling. I was always drawn to university classes in the social sciences, philosophy, political science, and current world events. No wonder I had been a little restless in Radiology. But, in the end, my mother's choice for me with X-Ray Technology had allowed me to travel, and to have experiences in international relationships that I never could have known from a purely text book exposure. It's funny where our journey takes us, and how it's all somehow connected in the big scheme of things.

The person who had the most influence in my decision to work in the school system had no idea that she impacted me in this matter. It was the summer before my daughter started school. My husband was TDY that entire summer. Anyway, I was still working in the small hospital in the Panhandle of Florida. This girl, who I worked with, had a daughter who was about twelve years old. I would drop my five year old off at the YMCA on my way to work. The Y had a summer program. My daughter was not all that fussy about going, but she was happy in the afternoon when I would pick her up. They included swimming lessons in the Y-program, which was a real draw for me. Anyway, my colleague at work was the same age as me. She was always giving me a hard time about taking university classes and considering a career change at our age. She would say things like, "People don't do this at our age. In the end, you're going to keep doing what you're doing. You're wasting your time." She wasn't being mean. She just really thought that I was spinning my wheels. I would let her go on. My thoughts were that whatever I did, I was going to age. I could age doing what I was doing, or I could age exploring new options. Either way, the getting older thing was still going to happen.

At about 11:00 AM every day, she would call her daughter at home to wake her up, and to remind her to get out of bed. The little girl was home alone. My friend only worked until 1:00 PM. I talked to her about getting her daughter in a summer program in the mornings. She told me that her daughter had already been there and done that over and over again. She explained that about the time children get to the pre-teen years, they have outgrown the range of summer programs for the most part. She would discuss how the adolescent years were the hardest for her, as a working mom, relative to summer vacation. Her daughter was too old for most programs and too young to work. She had cut her hours back to part-time because of that. I really reflected on her insight. I couldn't stand the thought of leaving my daughter home by herself in the future, as those hard decisions would fall upon me.

That was a real factor for me. As women and mothers, it is nice to have choices when it comes to raising children. The role of mother reframes the priorities for working women. Fathers change also, but in a completely different way. I believe that most men see themselves as a provider and a protector. Even though many families have both parents working, it is usually mom who juggles the dental appointments, the allergy shots, the soccer practices, the Boy Scout fund raisers, the read-a-thon at school, and the list goes on. Even as dad shares some of these responsibilities, it is still more than likely mom who sets the appointments up; and then has to remind her significant other for the hundredth time of his commitment. Just about every mother that I know struggles to stay on top of the million and one little things that it takes to run a household and to raise children. Never mind throwing laundry into the mix.

I will be very honest and say that I did not have a great, spiritual calling to go into public education. It appealed to me from the calendar perspective. The older I got, the more I liked the idea of working to a school schedule, aligning my time off with my child's school breaks. That was it for me. I had no preconceived notions and no prior experience with the American Public School System. My only desire was to find a match that would work for my family. I was a little selfish as I prayed in church on Sunday for help in finding a job that would bring me personal satisfaction, and in which I could be effective. I had gone to university for the last six years, juggling my life to grow within myself. I was now ready to put theory to practice. I had no idea that the public school system in the nation was embarking on major changes, grounded more in politics than in effective practice. For many experienced teachers, it was a time of frustration and despair. For me, it was a job to learn so that I didn't embarrass myself too much.

I think that most people hear *No Child Left Behind* on the news and through school reports without having any real notion of what the law actually mandates. The words, themselves, ring justly and make good press. The intent behind the federal law appears to be heartfelt and sincere. The problem for me is the basic assumption of *No Child Left Behind*, and the method used to measure accountability. It's sort of like the Iraq War. If the basic assumptions are flawed, the rest sort of falls apart! The first basic assumption of *No Child Left Behind* is that achievement gaps exist because of failing schools and failing teachers. If this were true, then it would take a blink of an eye to hire in better teachers and to equip failing schools with the newest and the best; and the troops shall come marching home, so to speak. The government could recruit all the smart people from the business world and corporate America; the ones who are so smart that they deserve multi-million dollar bonuses for showing up to work. These brilliant minds can go on sabbatical for a year or two, and fix the problems of children's learning with a flick of their magic wands.

The following is what I have encountered in the public school system of America as a parent, and from the position of inside the system. First of all, many public schools are not failing. I want to say that again. Many, if not most, public schools are not failing. If the mission is to reform the areas with massive problems, it would be helpful to identify these specific schools or the specific districts without tarring everyone with the same brush. From a purely diagnostic and fiscal model, a more targeted awareness would be helpful in matching resources to need. Supposedly, the present system of accountability does that. That might be true if the government is spending millions of tax payers' dollars measuring what it claims to be measuring. This is the fundamental consideration of the next basic assumption of accountability; the validity of the measure.

Do standardized test scores measure the performance of schools and teachers, or do they measure the performance of individual children? From a purely objective stance, as soon as you get into standardized testing, you are measuring very narrow things. You are either measuring where an individual child scores against the average child of her or his same age on the same measure at that point in time (population norms); or you are measuring where the individual child scores against an academic standard for that grade. But once again, the standards are determined over the course of a few years against where the average child will score in the content area. Either way, you are measuring each child against the performance of the average child. By the very definition of average, half of the children will come in above this cut-off, and half will come in below it. So what is the point? Even if you succeed in raising the standards, the norms will also go up, and you will still have the population of kids spread across the spectrum. That's how standardized tests work.

I think it is helpful to look back. From my personal story, the history of the Catholic nuns and education is well documented. But, within that very rigid and very high standard of excellence, students were never held accountable based on standardized tests. The current system of accountability is very different for today's children relative to the system of accountability that was in place in the public school system for our generation and during our parents' generation. Did we turn out so bad? We were accountable for paying attention in class, doing our homework, attendance, studying, taking tests linked to instruction, and showing respect for our teachers (developing as good citizens). We were taught, and then we were tested on what we were taught. We endured rote learning and developed self-discipline during our younger years, so that we had the baseline skills for critical thinking in our middle and high school years.

In the present, where is the product of the failing public school system nation wide? There is a lot of rhetoric, but is there a lot of actual data to support the total failure of our public schools? Has the nation produced less-capable doctors, fewer engineers, not enough lawyers (God forbid), too few computer analysts, less critical thinkers (other than an over-represented sample in our elected officials), and less public servants than in generations past? Where is the outcome that supports the collapse of the public school system? Statistical numbers are meaningless, if they represent an irrelevant measure in the first place. Data can be manipulated to support any agenda. For example, a perception of a failing public school system supports a rational for the outsourcing of American jobs or the practice of hiring workers from third world countries through block visas. The premise is generated that American workers are not as highly qualified. This takes the looking glass away from a deeper look at corporate greed and irrational profit. Or, we usually hear the argument that our children can not compete with students from China and India in math and science. If this is true, it is more than likely linked to cultural values than failing public schools in America. If you go to any awards ceremony in the universities or public schools of America, in which the very top percentile of students are being recognized on merit, you will see an over-represented sample of Asian and Indian students. These same children are the product of the American public school system.

My first year on the job in an elementary school was a steep learning curve for me. I have total respect and admiration for the fine educators in the public schools that I have encountered and worked with. Just as in any line of work, some are better and more dedicated than others. But, isn't that life and the human condition? How can we negate that with standardized tests? Do we even want to? I can tell so many wonderful stories of teachers, office staff, nurses, aides, and administrators who grace the hallways of our public schools. It is a tragic injustice to hear the media and legislators degrade public education when there are so many skilled professionals getting thrown into the mix. The result has been that teachers and administrators have become very defensive. It is very hard to grow and reflect from a defensive perch.

I think God did answer my prayers and match me to the right job, in the right place, and at the right time. I was hired into the poorest and lowest performing school in our district. However, I was to work with the finest staff of educators that anyone could hope to find in the best schools in the country. The teachers at my school were there because they were dedicated and because they loved teaching. Most of all, they loved children. These teachers felt needed and they responded to it. I always think a medical comparison is so fitting for education. The workers are the same. They are not there for the glory or for the fast money. They are there because they thrive from affecting others who need whatever it is that they have to give. If a doctor is seeing patients with repetitive, minor complaints, he is less personally satisfied than when he successfully treats a very sick patient. Teachers are the same. They have their own personal needs met by teaching children who need them and who appreciate them. Poor children do both.

If there is a single factor driving effective teachers out of high-risk schools, it is that they are being blamed for everything that has gone wrong in the child's life outside of school. Our philosophy at our very challenging school became "it is what it is". We would give 110% in the course of our day, every single day, and at the end of each and every day, we could look at ourselves proudly and honestly in the mirror, and know that we did everything that we could. A guidance counselor's role is more or less defined by the principal of the school. I was hired by a wonderful principal who gave me a lot of autonomy in my job. Her only directives for me were to focus on early identification, and to form a relationship with the teachers. I had no idea how valuable and needed these two things were in this particular school at the time of my hire.

I worked in the school next to the smelly sewer plant for six years, from 2000-2006. First of all, I had to find the school. Anyone who has ever driven along Racetrack Road in Ft. Walton Beach has been rudely affronted with the strong aroma from the out-dated sewer plant on most days over the course of many, many years. Most people smell rather than see the beast, which sits a block off of the main road. I had no idea that this concrete and chemical insult to natural breathing sat atop of an elementary school, until I was hired to work there. My prayers had been answered with a job in which very few experienced educators from other schools were beating down the doors to transfer into in August of 2000. The poorest and lowest performing school was not a draw in a district that was embarking on a stated agenda of 'eating educators alive' relative to comparison ratings of standardized test scores. Why else would someone with no experience and no contacts get hired in any school district?

On the other hand, the teachers who worked there were committed, highly qualified, and had stayed at this school from a perspective of personal choice. Their main stress and frustration were not with the needs of the children, which were many and huge; but with the total lack of empathy and understanding on the part of policy makers in supporting the specific needs of a high poverty school. The only response was "no excuses." It's a matter of semantics to change facts into excuses. When facts are dismissed so that pre-conceived agendas can be pushed forward, then a skewed premise becomes the barometer for a baseline of relative truth. A tilted playing field is the underlying premise of *No Child Left Behind*, and schools such as ours were on the drainage end of the field. We were up to our necks in the muck, and no one was sending us a life line.

By the fall of 2006, our needy school had become a poster child for policy makers who want to brag that there are no excuses from high poverty schools. The reality is that the students, the teachers, and the entire staff work their butts off day in and day out to succeed, not because of *No Child Left Behind*, but in spite of it. The one good thing about working in the poorest school in the district in the fall of 2000 was that we were pretty well left on our own. I think this is the experience of any public school. There are a lot of directives to comply with, but individual school sites have to take the bull by the horn, and figure it out. We decided to focus on the intent and the spirit of *No Child Left Behind*. The intent is simple. It is the hope and the drive that pulls the most exhausted of teachers out of bed every morning, and puts a smile on their face as they cross the parking lot to enter the building for yet another grueling day. Unfortunately, the intent gets lost in the details; the mandated outcome of trying to measure abstract concepts with a data base of loose numbers. We are talking apples and oranges. The problem for hard working, dedicated teachers is that the measure of accountability is so riddled with uncontrollable variables, that nothing makes sense. They can not link the toils of their job to individual student's standardized test scores.

In essence, teachers and administrators feel overwhelmed with theoretical mandates that lack common sense.

So, what did come together for the staff and the students of the lonely school by the sewer plant? I believe what happened is that we became a staff who moved beyond defensiveness and territorial issues. We put our efforts into reflection, introspection, collaboration, and best practices. The spirit of the staff mandated that we keep laughter and sound, common sense in our days. We would find the humor in the ridiculous and put it all in perspective. We had an awareness that we were on our own. There can be comfort in that knowledge, once you accept it and move forward with it. It was almost like put it out there, deal with it, find peace with it, and move beyond it. I can not say what will work for every school, but I can offer some insight as to what has worked and continues to work in an 80% free and reduced, high-risk population of students.

As an outsider coming in, not just to this particular school but to the profession of public education, the most obvious thing to me was how beaten down the teachers were. They loved teaching and their students, but their overall moral was pretty low. The outspoken critics in the media and in the government did not value or honor their skill and their professional service. Teachers are not in it for the glory, but it becomes despairing when they are kicked in the face every time they turn around from a public policy perspective. In 2000, the political and legislative forces in Florida were promoting charter schools and parental choice. A painting of the public school system as failing was needed to validate the transfer of tax dollars to fund charter and private schools.

A system of assessment was put in place to prove the point. The crime was that the charter schools and private schools, which were receiving tax payer funding, were not accountable for the same assessments or for any assessment for that matter. The decks were stacked against the public schools. I have never really bought into the concept of charter schools relative to a democracy and access to quality education for all. If tax dollars fund charter schools, and they replace failing public schools, then it seems that the charter schools become the public schools. They will encounter the same problems. The difference is that their "charter" allows them to pass the problems on to someone else (back to the public schools). The issues remain. It's like a dog chasing his tail.

Relative to my personal story, what did I have to offer this staff of seasoned educators? Not much in the very beginning. Believe me; the teachers at my school were seasoned, wise, and wary. They had been around the block a few times. The notion of a guidance counselor, who had never spent a day in the class room, was a concept that they would have little tolerance for. They were quite capable of eating me alive. It took me about two conversations with a couple of hard core, bad-ass teachers for me to realize that I needed to keep my mouth shut and to learn from these veterans. I did not need to enlighten them with my college educated, psychological theory and insight. I think I was the one who needed my head examined. My saving grace was that I, too, had been around the block a few times relative to working with people, and integrating myself into new situations. I knew that I was going to have to earn their respect and their trust. I could do this by keeping my mouth shut, finding allies among strong teachers, building on those relationships, and learning, learning, learning.

At the same time, our district was taking on the mission and the mandates of *No Child Left Behind* in a literal way. This meant that many standard practices were being challenged and discarded. As in any organization, there is much resistance to a perception of irrational change from experienced staff when they were never given a voice in the process. The timing was ripe for me. When the district personnel gathered administrators for training, the guidance counselors were always included as an integral part of the administrative team. So, I was hired on the salary of a first year teacher (pittance), and found myself sitting in the company of the big guns, as they were being challenged on accepted practices and given new standards for accountability that did not make educational sense to them. For me, it was invaluable insight. I could view it all from a non-defensive, non-threatened perspective. At the same time, I was receiving the newest training coming down the pipe relative to practices in the public schools of the nation, and in particular, our school district. All politics is local. *No Child Left Behind* is as much about politics as it is about education. Our district was no exception. I think that it became very hard for veteran staff to discriminate between political agendas and sound policy decisions; to tease out the growth areas from the blame areas. The process would be very hard for any organization, business, or government agency.

I could compare what was happening there with other professions. I often heard enlisted guys in the military talking about how the Maintenance Officers would change every time they turned around. The young officers would be rotated through different Squadrons in an organization on a regular basis. For the seasoned and experienced guys in the Squadron, they always knew that the officer would make his mark by changing whatever he encountered on his arrival. The pattern was to take something that was not broken, but to change it anyway. I guess if you are "in charge" then you feel that you have to do something. Then, the next Maintenance Officer would rotate through, and change it back, and it would go back and forth with every staff change. Through this, the views and the input of the experienced, airmen were often dismissed. I guess the inexperienced Maintenance Officers had drafted the federal law that would control funding in poor schools for the next decade.

You see, the funding consequences of *No Child Left Behind* only apply to Title 1 public schools, or to schools of poverty. What that means is that many schools in the nation do not meet the provisions of *No Child Left Behind*. However, the law mandates that only Title 1 schools (high poverty schools) have to publicly identify themselves as failing or in need of improvement. The schools with higher income populations often do not meet the cut-off scores for all of their sub-categories either, but these schools have no requirement to meet standards for improvement. Only Title 1 schools are affected in a real way. The higher income schools usually bury their achievement gaps by focusing on their other accomplishments, which are very real. The poor schools are not given the same luxury.

This is the slippery slope of the federal legislation. Schools with the highest risk students are accountable to a more rigid standard than the non-poverty schools.

Over the years, the layers of the onion have begun to be peeled open, but in early 2000, the educators in my district did not even have a paring knife. They were told to put up and to shut up, or they could find the door. When people have put in their years; the blood and the toil towards full retirement, they put up quietly and dejectedly. And they pray for the courage to make it through for a few more years. The system is broken when surviving becomes the motivation for dedicated and experienced professionals to sustain their dignity and their sense of purpose. I hope the nation finds its way back to honor teachers in the public education system, rather than to continue to demonize them and to blame them for the multiple failures of the human condition in our culture.

The relationship that I gradually built with my teachers was to gently guide them to recognize and to own their power and dignity of self; to value their skill and to be proud of their craft. At a time when the whole world was telling them what they were doing wrong, they needed to reflect on what they were doing right, and to internalize that knowledge. They did not need to expend energy in defense of their teaching. If that was the case, then they needed to get out of the profession. My small role was often as simple as becoming an available and an empathic listener. At times, finding viable solutions to their myriad of problems was not as important as the listening.

For the most part, the teachers' problems reflected the problems of their students. Many of the teachers had not reached a place in their heart for objectivity and self-reflection. They had used up every minis-cule cell in their pulsing organ of life to deal with the needs of their stu-dents. They weren't even aware that their tired muscles and circulatory vessels were craving rich, oxygenated, bright- red blood cells. I like to think that I helped them to lighten up a little bit; to take undue pressure off themselves. What I began to see was that teachers in our high needs school had taken ownership of issues in the children's lives that they had no control over. The burden of the ownership of external problems had weighed them down, deeper and deeper into the muck.

Working in a high needs school is like working shift work in a busy trauma hospital. The needs are so massive that sorting through it is a lot like triage. You quickly sift through the bullshit to deal with the more substantive issues. In a busy ER, that means that the sprained thumb from the softball game on Saturday afternoon will wait until the real traumas are dealt with in the middle of the night. In our school, that meant showing up was enough. The back pack and school supplies would be passed out without a blink of an eye. That was small potatoes in our day. You also learn what you can effect a change with, what you can con-trol, and what you have to move on from. At the end of the shift, hospital workers walk out the door, passing the caseload off to the next shift. In effect, medical workers compartmentalize. They cross the parking lot and they carry on with the rest of their life until they walk in the next day, and give it their all for another eight hours.

What I saw in a lot of teachers was that they had no one to pass it on to. They hung on to external problems, dwelled on them, and owned stu-dent issues that they had no control of. Teachers tend to be strong in the feeling domain of personality types, so they take on the burdens of their students' lives, and stress themselves over trying to fix issues that are not theirs to fix. The burdens multiply exponentially with each child and ev-ery story. The ownership of all of these external issues makes teachers less effective in the delivery of their craft. The one aspect in which the teacher can make a significant impact on the child's outcome becomes entrapped within layers of compassion and distress for the perceived hardships of the child's life. In my relationship with these experienced teachers, I looked for a way to articulate my observations and to take them to a place of self-reflection and personal growth. If they could compartmentalize the things that they could control from the things that they could not control, they could put more energy and focus into areas in which they could effect a change for the child.

I believe that the ultimate gift from a teacher to a student of any age is to empower children to own their learning; to be able to link engagement and effort to incremental success; and to become aware of this power of self at a young age. It is easy to say the same thing with catchy phrases like *Be All That You Can Be, Let Your Star Shine*, etcetera. It is quite another thing to provide high-risk students with the skills needed to obtain the product or the desired outcome. I think the Catholic nuns had it right with the discipline of learning piece and their no nonsense approach. Learning is hard work, much harder for some than for others. It's like riding a bike or kicking a soccer ball. Balance and athleticism are very natural for some children and a nightmare for others. It's all about brain systems, how the circuitry in our head is wired, what current it runs on, how the organ systems overlap, and how it's all glued together electrically and neuro-chemically. Learning is pretty amazing stuff for some of us, and scary as hell for others. It depends on what we are learning. Are our skills being tapped or are our deficits being highlighted? We all tend to avoid our deficit areas and to excel in our strength areas. Then, we add on the cultural layer of values, work ethic, motivation and trust. Human beings work harder at something that they trust that they have a stake in.

I believe that the piece missing in the nun's model was early identification. In the 60's and in the early 70's, no one (not even the medical profession) knew much about learning as a function of brain systems. It was 1975 or '76. I will always remember the first and only time that I saw a medial procedure called a Pneumo-Encephalogram. This particular diagnostic nightmare became obsolete after the invention of the CAT Scanner. Prior to the slice and dice of computerized tomography, doctors had very limited diagnostic tools to assess brain function and brain abnormalities. Skull X-Rays did not tell you much about the miraculous grey matter inside of the cranium.

The actual procedure of a Pneumo-Encephalogrm was a form of torture to watch. The patient was prepped and then strapped into an electric chair-looking type of contraption. The techs would check and recheck the tightness and the integrity of the straps over and over. This was because the patient would be flipped upside down in the chair, and then suspended in mid-air, as the Radiologist injected air into (I assume) his spinal canal. I only saw one of these and I was about eighteen at the time. I was so shocked by the whole thing, that I will never forget the event. I remember that all the doctors, the nurses, and the techs were extremely cautious and nervous. They were very concerned about the patient's welfare, his discomfort level, and the risks of the procedure. They did not like having to put the patient through the exam. It was critical to his diagnosis and treatment. As the air was injected, the upside down patient screamed out in pain. The point of the exam was to use gravity to fill the ventricles of the brain with air, so that the size and the shape of the ventricles could be seen on X-Rays of the head. The primitive and scary Pneumo-Encephalogram provided a very basic assessment of brain function.

This was only about thirty years ago. The medical world and the field of education have come a long way with research and knowledge of brain functioning since then. However, there is still a huge gap among educators, the medical profession, and parents regarding how brain systems overlap to impact learning in children. Teachers and parents deal with the symptoms. Sometimes, we discover pieces of the etiology in collaboration with parents and medical providers; or, we suspect that we have a handle on a part of it. We are never certain. The same diagnosis does not manifest in the same way for each child. The brain remains such a mystery; so complex, so wonderful; an entity onto itself. We synthesize the pieces that we have with best practices, research-based strategies; a multi-pronged approach. It is sometimes a trial and error method. If a certain strategy is not working, then stop beating a dead horse. Try something else. The key for the child, the parent, and the teacher is to keep trying; to give it your all, and then some.

Growing up, the nuns and our parents did acknowledge common sense things. They would say things like, "Johnny is not book smart. But he can do wonderful things with his hands. He can build anything." Or, "He will make a fine mechanic. He knows motors inside out." There was an awareness of different types of ability. Genuine honor was bestowed on the professions of carpentry, auto mechanics, construction, plumbing, and technical work. Dignity and pride were linked to making an honest living and a strong work ethic. I think about construction jobs. In Edmonton, there was a lot of high-rise construction going on when I lived there. I often changed buses downtown around the same time that the hard hats were calling it a day. The streets were busy with people walking to and fro. The young guys always seemed happy and proud of their work. There was good money in construction in those days. I saw the same pride in the faces of the burly working class in Australia and Germany. I worry sometimes when our children, in the present, link construction and trade work with illegal immigration. They are told by their President that there are jobs that Americans will not do. What does that mean? The only other country that I have lived in that had jobs that its citizens would not do was in Saudi Arabia. Believe me; we do not want to become a nation in which certain workers are categorized and separated from the values and the respect of the country.

Early identification in the field of education is a valuable tool to use with young children who struggle with the fundamentals of reading, writing, and math. It is purely a diagnostic model. For example, a little girl who is struggling with basic reading skills is exhibiting a symptom of a learning problem. The root of the problem may be located in the temporal lobe of her brain or the occipital lobe, or somewhere in between in the spider web of connections and pathways that crisscross and activate one another in the mystery of our ability to read fluently and with comprehension. For some children, fluency is the issue, but their comprehension is fine. For others, it's just the opposite. For someone else, it's neither of these. Things like word recall, short term memory, word and letter discrimination, or an emotional piece linked to the anxiety of failure are identified. The etiology of the same symptom may be found in many places. More than likely, an overlap between several different systems of the brain is involved.

This is very complicated stuff when you break it down. However, breaking it down is helpful and often necessary to empower the child to bypass or work around the deficit area. A teacher can't reinforce the individual strength areas of their students if they do not know what they are. For example, if the problem is auditory processing then it's pretty futile to keep pounding away at phonics as the sole teaching tool for reading. It works wonderful for many of us, but if your brain can not channel the auditory signal for interpretation, then more of the same will only frustrate the child and eventually shut them down. Behavior problems become manifested, especially in boys, as they do not want to show their vulnerability with the learning process. There are no magic pills, but basic knowledge and awareness of the child's area of struggle does empower effective teachers in their skill. Would a doctor treat the symptoms of an infection without trying to identify the source of the infection? Early identification in education is not about discriminating against children at an early age. It does just the opposite.

It has been my experience that there is a lot of resistance to early identification from administrators and parents. Administrators link early identification to numbers and budget issues. Parents don't want to pigeon hole or stereotype children with labels at an early age. The accepted practice is to wait it out; to give children time to mature and to develop. Well, children are going to mature and develop whether they are evaluated or not. I have always seen early identification as a purely diagnostic tool. If a child has low insulin, do we want to wait it out; to give the pancreas a few more years to mature, to balance out its production? The brain is no different. It is an organ system, the most complicated and the most amazing organ system in the creation of man. The field of medicine is just beginning to unfold the wonders and the complexities of the brain. And yet teachers are expected to walk on water, to bring every child to the same level of learning in a standard time frame. I hope that I helped teachers to put the ideology into perspective, so that they could move forward with the possible and the pragmatic.

In my high-risk school, we accepted state mandates from a platform of working within the system of accountability. We really had no choice. We decided to tackle *No Child Left Behind* in our school one child at a time. If we gave it our all for each and every child, the standardized test scores could fall out as they may. We would let state and district bean counters worry about all that. Our job was to educate children to the best of our human ability. Our teachers could sleep at night knowing that they had put in an honest and proud day's work each and every day. We got down to the basics. We dug in hard, and we kept going. The teachers and the staff had been doing this for years, but they were beaten down with the ongoing burden of comparison to higher income schools.

I hope that I helped them to redefine the basics through honest reflection and analysis. I worked to support them through the struggles of their very hard work. What did I have to give them? They gave me a lot. They knew how to teach. I had no background to make them better teachers from the perspective of the skill of their craft. They had the power to do that for themselves through collaboration and peer mentoring; in conjunction with sound instructional leadership at the school and district level. For me, the challenge was to help them to reframe the mandates of standardized assessments away from a defensive perch towards self-growth and reflection. It was more like "shag them" (the bean counters). How can we make this work for us? How do we make it work for the kids? What does all of this really mean in the big scheme of things?

Our school philosophy evolved towards intimately knowing each student's reading and math level at the beginning of the school year; and continuing to track their academic progress all year from an analytic model. If a child was showing no gains, what could we tweak? What could we do differently in the eight or often ten hours of the day that they were in our care? Sometimes, we were doing too much; offering too many resources so that the continuity of the child's schedule became too disjointed with our good intentions. Other times, we needed to add access to more specialized interventions. There was no single answer. I think that too many people outside of education believe that there is a silver bullet. Everyone was involved in the process. If there were areas of deficit in either subject for any child, we picked the academic indicators apart with a fine tooth comb. We had no mandate to over identify or to under identify specific learning disabilities. We were not out to medicate our problems away. That doesn't work anyway, unless neurochemistry is the primary issue. Then, it has the possibility to work very well with careful and diligent medical and parental monitoring. The pros and cons need to be weighed heavily by parents and medical practitioners in collaboration with educators and school psychologists in an ideal situation.

We worked hard to perfect an open model incorporating professionals, family members, the students, and educators; keeping our focus on academic outcomes. The barometer that we used for a harder look was level of academic achievement in core subject areas. It was not demographic factors such as race, sex, homelessness, or socio-economic status. It was strictly academic achievement. If they were below grade level, even to a miniscule degree, our mission was to give them extra help; to empower them to keep treading water and to learn to swim before they sank too low to reach. We did not want our children to experience failure. Developmentally, the best gift that we could give them was ownership of success, developing skills of industry, trust, and self-confidence with the process of learning at a very, young age. We did not want to beat them down with retention in the early grades, which was becoming the mandate of our district and our state relative to *No Child Left Behind*.

It is common sense, that if children experience any degree of success at an early age, they will be more motivated and confident in their journey with education. Teachers are in the profession to maximize the level of success for every student. These are not new concepts in education. What has changed for teachers the paradigm of public education from a national perspective. The nation's value system has shifted. Public school teachers are blamed for the long-reaching effects of poverty, unstable home environments, homelessness, mental health problems and addiction problems of caregivers, negative environmental influences, and weakened family structure. Teacher's grading practices are compared to standardized test scores. The paradigm for public school teachers is qualitatively different than the model of past generations. I think the jury is still out on whether the system of standardized accountability is raising the bar in education for all.

I believe that the hope for success with extremely at-risk groups in the current system is through early identification; targeting supplemental instruction to specific deficit areas at a very early age. A lengthened school day and an extended school year provide children extra time as needed, if needed. I am not advocating an extended school year for all. The model is effective for some, and the benefits gained from early, incremental success are enormous for young students who are in danger of failure. Parents are big players in decisions regarding what is best for their child, relative to academic need. I can honestly say that in our school, many of our parents trusted us to make the hard decisions for them. Our single mothers experienced huge struggles in everyday living. They passed the hat to us regarding their child's needs with education. It was my experience that the more the child began to feel success verses defeat, the more some parents engaged in their child's journey. The success of their child seemed to give them hope and eased the burden of their days. All parents have the same dreams for their children. Overwhelmed parents do not have the personal resources (time, money, skills of self) to deal with any more problems. However, they become very responsive to hope. They relish in the wide smile of their child, as pride of learning eradicates the scowls and the frowns of failure.

It was also our experience, that the most impoverished of students did not mind attending half-day summer school. They actually asked for it and were excited to come. They were pampered and tended to; usually small group instruction with dedicated professionals, who also enjoyed the less hectic pace of the summer schedule, but who still gave it their all to work with children who wanted to be there. There is merit and hope in the spirit of *No Child Left Behind*, which is to close achievement gaps for at-risk subgroups. The achievement gaps do exist. The issue has become that we don't need to destroy the foundation to raise the ceiling. We need to support and to attend to strong, veteran teachers so that they can feel validated to carry on with the trials of their days. The strongest reformers and leaders of effective change already grace the hallways of our public schools. The key is to identify the strong teachers and natural leaders, and to empower them to move forward, rather than to blame them for things that are out of their control.

For example, I believe that we need to take some burdens away from teachers and away from public schools altogether. I am going to be a rebel here, and let my conservative thinking shine through. Public schools are in the business of educating children. They should not be in the business of educating parents. I believe that school funding should not be channeled in any way into parent training classes. The norm for many models of education reform is to involve parents in a global outreach effort. Yes, the obvious thing in a high-risk population is the parent piece. But, what is the role for the public school system?

First of all, we live in a democracy of free will and responsibility of choices. Parents make choices each and every day. We all made choices in our young adult years and our teenage years that impacted us for the rest of our lives. Every day of our adult life, we make decisions. Our choices are all different. But, they are ours to make. Adults do not respond well to judgmental views of how they ought to live, how they ought to parent. It is easy to pass judgment on others from the circumstance of our personal lives. Anyone who works with a high-risk population of children is acutely aware of the hardships of their home lives. The bottom line is that we have no power to effect a change in the lives of children outside of school unless we come across a situation of mandatory reporting. Even then, our power is to report only.

The reality is that emotional neglect is very seldom prosecuted through the court system. Only, the most blatant of cases are pursued. In my experience, the children of crystal meth addicts were eventually removed, as the neglect became so blatant, that even social services could no longer find a reason to keep the child with the parent. Even in those circumstances, some of the children were more despondent. For some, a bad parent is better than no parent. For others, the removal appeared to empower the child. There are no easy answers. The problems are massive. Most of what goes through the court system is the tip of the iceberg. The

Pandora's Box of neglect frustrates everyone, but the power to change a child's home life is in the hands of the adults in the home, in the decisions of their days, in the relationships of their lives. For the most part, the life-style choices of families are very resistant to outside influences. Would that be different for any of us? We make our choices and we live with them, or we live to change them. Either way, we live as we know how.

Having said my piece here, I do believe that public schools of high-risk populations have better access to family needs than agencies, which are funded to deal with the very same needs. I am a strong advocate of greater collaboration between government agencies and the public school system. If a parent needs help with social services, such as housing or ac-cess to medical care, schools are ideal referral sources. But, where is the help for schools to turn to? One of the greatest frustrations that we dealt with was the bureaucracy of government agencies. As professionals, we could not even beat through the layers of paperwork and recorded phone messages to access a live, thinking human being, who could help parents in need in the moment. Our local Department of Health had every rea-son in the world why they could not treat sick children. We wrote letters to legislators; not a single representative responded to our appeal for help relative to medical services for children of poverty. We worked with many dedicated case workers from the Department of Children & Families. It became obvious that they were as overwhelmed as we were. They would pick our brain for answers as much as we picked theirs.

It became easier for us to work with local medical doctors, optom-etrists, and dentists to access services for poor children by setting up a billing system in which a school fund directly paid the bills for medical services. We were saddled to deal with issues outside of education, be-cause of the collapse of a competent government system relative to the welfare of children. There is a great need for better collaboration, but the burden of parenting classes and social services should not be laid at the steps of the public schools. Teachers, as natural caregivers, become entrapped in the spider web of need. Other agencies are funded to ad-dress these issues. They need to step up to the plate more in a real way. An actual person rather than an endless trail of 1-800 numbers would be a start.

Our school fund was not paid with tax dollars. Rather, local churches and organizations, at the grass roots level, kept the small fund afloat. The biggest contributor was the "Toys for Tots" annual fundraiser. It was or-ganized and supported by leather-clad, Harley Davidson Motorcycle riders; guys with grey ponytails and gals with tight jeans, who were proud and free to fund public school charity accounts, without layers of bureaucracy and red tape. They gave us money for poor kids at our school, and only asked that we spend it judiciously. We did. We worked hard to get the biggest bang for the buck for these kids and their parents. In my six years there, our balance never went in the red. We came close, but we managed to stay afloat. We had a wonderful book keeper. She had a great working relationship with Albertsons and K-Mart. The local shop keepers guarded the school account as much as we did. No one was going to get alcohol or cigarettes on those accounts. Instead, they bought things like diapers, shoes, socks, under wear, jackets, and groceries. Power bills and water bills were paid so services could be turned back on. It's a little hard to read your twenty minutes a night with no power in the house. Medical services and dental appointments were paid on the backs of the local Harley- riding heroes.

Parents make choices in how they live. Children do not. For me, that is a fundamental difference to consider in working with high-risk children. Often, they have not been taught the skill of owning their choices in things that they can control. They are so overwhelmed by everyday life things. They worry about their parents. They tend to take on adult issues without fully understanding the intricacies of the crisis. Several years ago I was sitting on my bedroom floor, sorting through papers in my closet, which had piled up from college classes. Anyway, the TV was on in the background, as I mindlessly shifted piles of chaos into more organized piles of chaos. Oprah Winfrey was being interviewed by someone, Diane Sawyer, maybe? Anyway, Oprah had just returned from Africa. She was discussing poverty in Africa relative to poverty in America. She was talking about choices; how the poor in Africa did not have the same choices as the poor in America. At the time, I remember thinking that her observations were valid except in the case of children. Children of poverty in America are born into hard lives. They have no power to choose the reality of their lot in life.

They do have the power to make a change for themselves as they grow up. The key is to make them aware of the potential, and to tap into the child's learning zone of success at a young age. It all sounds so easy and such common sense. What about when the child has changed schools six to eight times by February of the first grade? The Bush administration's push for parental choice relative to mandatory school attendance actually feeds the beast of neglect in low functioning families. That is the reality for many high mobility kids. Usually, they live with a single parent who can not make rent. They move from pillar to post, staying with a mix of acquaintances for days, weeks, or months at a time; until the stress of the living arrangement inevitably falls apart. The parents often pull the kids out of school without notice, and allow large gaps between enrollments. Parental choice is its own can of worms.

So, how do teachers save them all? The reality is that they don't. You do the best with every student while they are in your care. You teach them hard, and you hope; and you move on to the next one, one child at a time, one class at a time. In high risk populations, the class dynamics are always changing with the steady rotation of students. Teachers often told me by the end of the first grading period that it did not matter how many challenging students they had in their class room; that, it would be such a simple joy to be able to keep each of their delightful cherubs for the rest of the school year. By mid- semester, the teachers had a handle on their students' academic needs. The teachers did not mind being in the trenches with teaching. The good ones actually thrive on it. In our school, we knew through experience, that our teachers would lose and gain several students a month throughout the school year. By the end of the year, we were lucky if we had half the students that we started out with. This was the reality of our Title 1 School, year in, year out.

Our students judged wealth by whether you lived in a house or a trailer. The littlest one, five and six years old, would often walk up and out of the blue ask, "Do you live in a house or a trailer?" We managed to come up with an answer that validated all living circumstances, as we sighed inwardly at the weight of the question for us. The older elementary students stopped asking that question by about third grade. They would get annoyed when a younger sibling asked it in their presence. Children are insightful and proud. I think that we tend to forget the perception of what matters from the world view of a small child. They tend to remind us all the time if we step back and listen. Shame adds layers of distress for many children of poverty, as they juggle their personal reality against the reality of the average child in America. How do you acknowledge their vulnerability and empower them to be strong at the same time? You deny neither and you deal with both.

For us, it did not matter how much baggage a child had. If only the child would stay enrolled in our school for even a couple of years at a time. Can you imagine having your child change schools three to four times a year, as you were struggling to survive in crisis mode? There is not a whole lot left over to deal with your child's personal problems under the demands of working about sixty hours a week between two minimum wage jobs. You still can't scrape enough together to make rent and pay water, electric, and gas deposits; keep the car running at the same time, and keep your baby in diapers. Single moms find other single moms or relationships to ease the financial and emotional burdens of just surviving. Often, the situations are unstable and do not last long, resulting in deeper layers of despair and stress for the parent.

School can be a constant in the child's everyday life if the family is not always on the move. From a systems perspective, more affordable housing and better enforcement of child support laws would do more to close achievement gaps for low income subgroups than standardized test scores will ever do. There will always be children along the spectrum because they are the product of our human condition and our human struggles. The facts and the stories of children's lives demand that we honor and support the teachers in high risk public schools. Policy makers have shifted the blame on class room teachers for multiple system failures starting with the family system, the nation's health care debacle, and the housing—wage gap for low income workers.

My story with 80% free & reduced took me to a new place of insight and self-reflection. The veteran teachers did not need me to help them teach. Give me a break! Anyone who is loudly lamenting the shortcomings of public school teachers needs to walk a day in their shoes. Those who think they know better will be running for the hills as fast as their condescending legs will carry them. Our students did not need me or anyone else to feel bad for their hard lot in life. Sympathy is the last thing that they needed from their guidance counselor or from their teachers. I believe that the validity of my little piece of the puzzle was in helping teachers to reframe *No Child Left Behind* away from accountability of the teacher towards an understanding of and a reflection on achievement gaps of sub-groups of students. We were sort of rebels, but not rebels without a cause; rather rebels with a cause. Our rebel part was to say the hell with the accountability piece. The cause piece was to figure out a way to integrate data from multiple sources to understand more about the learning needs of our students, one child at a time.

It was my experience that the teachers were very open to this model. Classroom teachers will do anything to help a struggling student in their classroom. It eased the burden for teachers to have a team of professionals hashing through the pieces together. That is what early identification is all about; diagnostics, information gathering, and synthesis. There are no silver bullets, no easy answers. The facts are that some children have to work much harder than others to learn the same thing. The beginnings of hope for all children are to tap into incremental success early, to link the success to the control of the child, and to empower the discipline of the child's effort through his awareness and pride of his success. After all of that, we have to accept children where they are along the spectrum of God's creation.

What did I learn about myself through my journey next to the sewer plant? I know that somehow my life experiences with different cultures, my training in diagnostics and psychology, my medical model of thinking, pragmatics, flying by the seat of my pants, an Irish sense of humor, and an adult beverage when all else failed were key to my survival. I was honored and grateful to work with and to learn from the best of the best; from our front office staff to our school psychologist all the way down the hall to our very kind and competent nurse. The bubbly and brilliant smile of our mental health therapist kept both the students and the staff from falling into the abyss, except when she fell with us. Veteran teachers as mentors and two wonderful principals showed me the way from bus duty to lunch counts. Volunteers from all walks of life quietly, anonymously, and willingly mentored our students. It took all of us to come together for the students and with the students. This is the story in the public schools of the nation. I believe that those who demonize public schools undermine the fundamental liberty of a democracy. I also believe that they have never spent a day in the public schools, or they would not be so harsh and ill informed in their criticism.

During the years of working in this honorable school, I was privileged to be able to continue in a doctoral program of study. It was a good marriage for that time and place in my life. As I worked in the trenches in the day time, my professors and fellow learners helped each other to put it all in perspective in our evening discussions and research analysis. It was very calming to take a wider look at a myriad of frustrating, daily issues; not the least of which involved legislative mandates that made no educational sense to the reality of our days. The pendulum swings. We were experiencing the knock out punch in the public schools around 2001 to 2005 time frame. I think the pendulum is gradually swinging back towards a more common sense awareness of the needs of low income school populations.

I can honestly say that I also learned a lot from the parents of some of the hardest cases at our school. There are people who lead very unstable lives; mostly linked to choices that they made in their teenage and young adult years, but who are insightful, intuitive, and honest. I learned that these wise and wary parents do not respond well to patronizing or conditional responses. Without realizing it, we all place conditions on our interactions with others. We will give so much, but we shut down when we don't get the response that we need. So, when a parent does not show for several scheduled meetings, or does not respond to multiple phone messages, we judge and we begin to disengage from the process. With enough rebuffs, we often give up. The problem is that when we give up on the parent, we are also giving up on the child. We are not even aware of it. We have sympathy and empathy for the child, but we alter our expectations. We behave in a natural, human way to disappointment.

I want to give this example. We had a child who demanded a parent meeting in no uncertain terms. There were layers of issues and multiple attempts to have an honest, open, and informed conversation with the parent. After several missed meetings, the mom proposed a time that would work for her. We verbally confirmed the meeting with her the day before. Well,…as it went so often in our days, no show again. We did not react too strongly, but we were disappointed. Several days later, out of the blue, the mom is standing at the counter asking for whatever paperwork she needed to sign. I called her in my office. It was not as simple as signing paperwork. This could be compared to giving consent for major surgery without listening to the risks and long term outcomes. The meeting was to decide some very real and some very hard educational choices for her child. We did not want to just hand her papers to sign. Her understanding and her voice in the matter were critical to the serious decisions that had to be made.

The mom understood this. She was extremely intuitive, bright, and brutally honest. She looked me in the eye, and she said, "I know that I screwed up again. I don't mean to, but that is what always happens with me. I miss appointments. Things happen and I can't commit ahead of time. That's how it is with me. I try to do better but it never works for me. That's how I live. But, I am here now. I care. I want to do the right thing. I care for my son. What do you need? I am here now." She held her head high, she stood strong and tall, and she did not flinch as she waited for me to respond. She was very proud and very strong as she forthrightly and honestly put in on the line for me. Well, what I needed was for her to come back when I could gather all the players for a scheduled meeting. It is hard to pull multiple teachers and professionals out of class rooms and other meetings in the moment. A few of them were not in the building. She didn't need a lecture from me. She was well aware of the big picture. She was telling me that the big picture did not work for her. She lived in crisis mode, and right now, she was here to take care of business. Could I step up to the plate? Could I work with her through the lens of her life?

Well, we gathered who we could. We scrambled. We had the meeting, and we had a very positive outcome for the child and for our relationship with the parent. I knew that if I gave her the standard line and expectation of parental behavior that it would be over between us, and for the child. She was giving me a choice in the way that she knew how. Over the years, she continued to have trouble with appointments, but we learned to work with each other. We actually dealt with it from a place of humor. She was able to laugh at herself. She helped me to see things outside of the lens of my own life experience. She had one of the hardest personal stories that I dealt with in that school. Her life was somewhat of a mess. But she and I respected each other. I think she understood me more than half the professionals I dealt with. She was a force to be reckoned with on an individual level. She could cut it to the chase with five words or less, and she grasped issues intuitively. Her cognitive side was out of sync with her functional side.

How many of us feel out of sync with our lives; perhaps more at some stages and times of our lives than others? It's a lot harder when the financial piece is stacked against you. I learned from all of this that the most important thing for educators is not to give up on the child. If you stay with the child and help the child to carve a sense of success with learning, then you have fought half the battle with the parent. This is true of parents across all levels of the economic spectrum. We all want our children to be happy and successful in school. Public schools should be empowered to focus on the learning needs of all children.

Relative to my personal story, I learned that I tend to challenge assumptions of policy initiatives; and at the same time to find a way to connect the dots, to make the system work in the present, despite the nonsense. I get very frustrated by people who have roles in the decision making process, but who do not step up to the plate. I have little tolerance for professionals who shrug their shoulders helplessly, when they are the ones holding positions that warrant them a voice in the process. This comes down to leadership. If you surround yourself with people who are hesitant to explore for deeper clarity, and to challenge ambiguity, then the result is that many workers in the trenches are left holding the bag. I learned that sometimes you have to kick the bag out of the way to address the real issues. I learned this through the tears and the laughter of our days in the poor school by the smelly sewer plant. I have moved away from the area, but I think of my friends who remain in the trenches. I continue to tip my hat to the staff as they carry on with the courage and the conviction of their days. I hope that I played a little part in standing shoulder by shoulder with them; to empower them to toss the heavy weight of the accountability bag out of their hands, out of the school's playground, over the fence, and into the waste of the sewer plant where it belonged.

Chapter 12

TRYING TO UNDERSTAND

I KNOW EXACTLY WHERE I WAS at 9:30 central time on the morning of September 11, 2001. I was sitting in a room in our district office, attending a half-day training on what else; *No Child Left Behind* mandates and district expectations for compliance. The attacks on the Twin Towers and the Pentagon have become the defining, emotional event of my life in the big scheme of things. I am not sure why I have been so impacted. I did not personally know anyone killed that day. The sense of unease and foreboding that I felt on the escarpment in Saudi Arabia in 1982 came flooding back to me when I learned that the majority of the terrorists were Saudi citizens. These guys were not raised in a vacuum. I realize that it was almost twenty years earlier that I had sat on the curb in the square of Khamis Mushayt, and listened to the speakers from the local mosque spew vengeful words of hatred and non-tolerance of infidels. The worst of the worst were targeted by the Imams as the allies of Israel, the followers of Christianity and Judaism, and as the non-believers among Muslims of the Wahabi version of Islam. Yet, our policy makers continue to convince us that our major allies in the Mid-East are certain nation states and not other nation states.

Sometimes, I think the administration is like the jury trial of the O J Simpson case. If you want to believe something bad enough, then you align the facts that validate your need, and you continue to see things through the lens of your prism and your personal life story. It's what you know, and the objective truth is too unbearable to accept. The black jurists in the O J trial needed to believe that he was innocent. They needed to believe that one of their own, a hero, was once again being given a raw deal. The facts were that OJ was a hero to them and a role model to their children. It was critical to protect this belief, if not at a conscious then at a sub-conscious level. They did not trust the American Judicial System. I think that we are in such a deep hole, that our government leaders need to believe that the values of our Western culture are supported by the oil producing Gulf States. The whirling estuary of our mutual dependency has diluted an honest assessment of our role in the Mid-East, and especially with Saudi Arabia. I think that the Saudis also have needed to reframe the facts and the history of the 20th century, as the present has spun out of everyone's control.

I pray that the actual hope is that all countries are being forced to reflect on and to understand more deeply what has happened, how it happened, how it continues to happen, and what are the possibilities for the future; both in the immediate and in the long range. This all comes down to trust and relative truths. These are the fundamental issues between Western Democracies and the Mid-East. I stand firm that the major weapon against terrorism is rooted in the noble and free lives of hard working people, who are protected and represented by a government of the people. However, the people of a place have to trust themselves to find their own way. The founding principles of America and the implementation of those principles have made America stand tall and strong in the world over the course of the 20th century. Other democracies were born from similar principles. The American Constitution was framed within the ideals of a combination of the best from our elderly neighbors across the Big Pond. The difference has been that as America gained world dominance since World War II, the might and the power of America were viewed as a sign of hope for the citizens of many oppressed countries in the world. There is a reason why Poland has remained firm and loyal, supporting the American effort in Iraq, when many other allies have extricated themselves.

The exception to this view during the same time in history has been through the lens of the average citizen in the Mid-East. In the context of the same part of the world, fanatics have enflamed the embers of mistrust, fear, and personal experiences to create an entire world region of people who know truth very differently. This is what I understood from my many conversations with my Palestinian and my Saudi co-workers and friends. They had been exposed to a different set of facts than we had in the Western world relative to the same world events. This was over the course of their life-time, their parents' life-time, and now their children's life-time. The outcome became sort of a self-fulfilling prophecy between Western democracies and the Mid-East. As they lashed out with guerilla type warfare against Israeli citizens, the Western world allied itself more with Israel. The more that we legitimized Israel's reality (from our perspective and from our TV screens), the more the citizens of the Mid-East felt isolated and ignored, so they fought more fiercely and more violently to be heard. The gap got wider and wider between us.

When anyone of my generation anywhere in the world hears the word Palestine, we have a visual of a very volatile and hopeless place. The citizens of the Mid-East visualize young boys, between the ages of seven to fourteen years old, who are futilely throwing stones at tanks with a look of despair and hatred in their eyes; or of crying mothers and grandmothers, who have their bodies slung helplessly and hopelessly over their dead sons, fathers, and small children. In the Western world, we see the same anger and the tormented grief wrinkled into the mothers' faces. We also see the same images of the young, skinny boys defiantly standing erect with deep, black anger in their eyes. But, we see guns or rocket launchers in addition to the stones in their hands. We also see the despair and the fear of Israeli citizens as they watch their dead and bleeding being carried off buses and out of market squares. The same look of hopelessness and anger is in their eyes.

We see the same things, but we understand the facts very differently. All across the world, we have felt helpless to stop it. In the Western world, we turned away from the TV, and we carried on with our lives. In the Mid-East, the anger and the bitterness have fermented to create a deep distrust of us. Since World War II, the seeds of the distrust and anger at the Western world have become thick and gnarled roots, deep and impenetrable to the many futile attempts of world leaders to pull them apart through negotiation and mediation. At the same time, the average citizen in the West has felt more helpless to even understand the layers of the problems and the violence. As the combined will of the leaders of the free world put the Palestinian issue more on the back burner, the more the hatred and distrust of the West grew. Then, across the same span of years, the Russians, the British, and the Americans played out their own power grab in the Mid-East; juggling for control and market shares of the black, liquid gold that spewed angrily and abundantly from beneath the desert soil.

When the Bush administration sent Karen Hughes on a tour through the Mid-East around 2004 to enlighten the citizens of the Mid-East on her personal knowledge of the President, I could not contain my rage at how out of touch our leaders appeared to be with the reality of the Mid-East. This was not about Bush on a personal level, that he really is a nice guy if you get to know him. Karen Hughes would have a hard sell with your average citizen in Europe, let alone with the viewers of Al Jazeera. Whenever, I see our political leaders holding hands with the Royals of the Gulf States, I clench up inside. I'm afraid that we are putting all our eggs in one basket; and that the basket is even more fragile than the eggs that it holds. I believe that the basket should incorporate moderate leaders, intellectuals, and clergy from all countries of the region, all sects, and all political parties. If we try to align ourselves with any single group in a system of nations that were formed on tribal alliances, fundamental beliefs, and conquering weaker groups; then our alliances will always oscillate with the politics and the power of the moment. But, if we work honestly and openly with a cross-section of leaders from across the region then at least there is a hope, that perhaps a door can be cracked open, even a millimeter at a time. We owe our soldiers and the decent people of the Mid-East that millimeter of hope. And, we gain legitimacy when we stand true to the morals of our democracy; the same standard for everyone.

To me, the Western world, and America in particular, appear to be dangling like a puppet on a string since 2003. In Prague, street vendors sell these wonderful minarets. They are always working them as you walk by, enticing tourists to stop with their dexterious manipulation of the multiple strings. I always have a visual of these puppeteers as America has been drawn more and more into the multi-directional layers of Mid-East politics and regional disputes. I see Al Qaeda controlling one handle, and the other players in the Mid-East collectively manipulating the other handle; as Western policy makers dangle loosely above the ground, unable to find a rock or any type of stable surface beneath their feet. Our troops have found the ground, and they are holding it with blood, life, and limb; as their leaders flail loosely in the wind. That is the image for me. I can't get it out of my mind. It scares the hell out of me, as I see the strings getting more twisted and more entwined until the puppet has to be discarded and restrung. The knots of the original strings have become too tight and too tangled to salvage. I think that it's time to restring the puppet and to change the puppeteer. The terrorists appear to be two steps ahead of us. It's like we are in this master chess game, and our side is the novice. I don't know a thing about chess, but I do know that it's time for the novice to become the master. We have to regain control of the chess board.

I think we had done that in Afghanistan after 9/11 and prior to the fiasco of Iraq. For the most part, we were not bombing civilian populations. We were fighting the bad guys in the mountains and we appeared to be winning in the moment. The world was behind us; perhaps not all of the Arab world, but a good portion of it. There remained, even then, a level of satisfaction that someone had taken on the West. Moderate leaders of the Mid-East will probably deny my premise. However, I believe that the average citizens of the Mid-East, who have felt oppressed for generations, wrestle with mixed feelings within their conscience. It's like the Irish—Protestant struggle in Northern Ireland. On the one hand, the violence is not condoned by moderate people on either side. However, inside ourselves, we struggle to balance out our understanding of the whole mess, feeling an allegiance to the historical context of our personal truths.

I have read book after book, trying to learn more about the historical story of the 20th century in areas such as the Pakistan / Afghanistan border region; trying to link the history of the rugged, mountain terrain to some hope for the present and the future. The more I read of the history of the region, back to the British involvement in the 19th century, the less hopeful I become. I believe that Western interests have never been trusted nor tolerated among the tribes and the fundamentalists, who have always controlled the territory deep in the mountains of Pakistan, along the Afghanistan border. I search for current articles out of the Mid-East. I think it's critical that we listen to what the citizens and the leaders of the Mid-East are saying in the present; to hear, to reflect on, and to be informed. I believe that there is a glimmer of hope encircling the overwhelming fear of a regional war. It's a glimmer, but a glimmer can open wider and wider, one molecule, one sun beam at a time.

The glimmer is directly linked to a resolution of the Palestinian conflict. The terrorists will continue, no matter what. However, I believe that they will become more and more marginalized if the combined will of all participating countries can find its way towards the dual-state solution for Palestine and Israel. It is the critical issue that can ground the entire region to a more solid footing. Every article that I read coming out of the Arab press addresses the Palestinian issue over and over again. But where is the hope? The two-state solution has been around for at least a decade. I believe that the sliver of hope is linked to the sense of urgency and to the combined will of the moderate leaders in the region to participate in and to facilitate the process. The leverage for the Mid-East is that Western countries need respected leaders and influential forces across the region to engage in the sectarian strife in Iraq as a moderating influence.

The leverage for Western countries is as a moderating force for Israel. The win for everyone, everywhere is for the region to settle down; for decent people to believe that there is a future for their children; and that the future will be brighter and more prosperous than the present.

There is a lot out there to read from experts in the field, from historians, and from journalists. My words and my thinking are framed by my personal experience with Saudi Arabia in the early 80's. Based on this short but critical piece of my journey, I believe that Abu Graib set American diplomacy and a chance for a positive outcome further back than we have realized in the framework of Western thinking. This is because we saw Abu Graib as an anomaly. The citizens in the Western World, who have interacted with the American Military across several generations, know for a fact that the behavior exhibited in the Abu Graib documentation are not in any way typical of the morals and behavior of the average American soldier at any level of engagement or rank. We know this for a fact over several generations. The average citizen of the Mid-East has been taught just the opposite across the same generations. They have had extremely limited access to multiple media and written material.

American and Western women have been described as immoral whores and prostitutes by fundamental Imans across the Mid-East, ever since world regions became more global. In the West, we believe that the behavior of the American guards in Abu Graib exhibited a shocking exception to the rule. In contrast, the citizens of the Mid-East view these images as the rule of Western behavior. Their perception of the truth is validated every time one of those photos is aired or viewed. It does not matter where the truth lies along the spectrum. Through Abu Graib, the hard copy images cemented the relative truth for the average citizen of the Mid-East. I think that many of us are still grappling with how Abu Graib really happened in the context of the American Military Command, and the documented rules of conduct going all the way up the chain of Military Command and Control. How high up did the strict discipline of the US Military break down and fracture? We will never know, but we will live with the outcome of those images forever.

In essence, Abu Graib provided tangible proof for the repeated warnings over the drum beat of the 20th century across the Mid-East. People of the region were taught a singular, judgmental view of the moral behavior of citizens from the Western world. From personal experience, I can tell you how deeply those descriptions pierced into the perplexed minds of female, medical workers in Saudi Arabia. The fundamentalists were handed, on a silver platter, their recruiting tool for the foreseeable future by the frozen and undeniable images of Abu Graib. The actions of the female American guards, displayed and imprinted forever in those photos, are especially harmful and long reaching. A picture speaks a thousand words.

Just as I have the face of the handsome SS soldier cemented in my brain from the walls of Auschwitz, so will the citizens of the Mid-East remember the vulgar and immoral actions of the female American soldiers in those pictures. The validation to protect and to hide their own women behind the veil will be harder to overcome because of the effect of those images. The cry for more freedom for women in countries such as Saudi Arabia will be undermined and exploited by the fundamentalists through Abu Graib. The long-range, social outcome has not been discussed very much in the American media. I am not sure if this is denial or ignorance on our part. I think that the intelligence community is aware of the damage. The response to bull-doze Abu Graib is a futile attempt to erase the reality from my perspective.

I have thought about all of this, what it means to me, what it means relative to the complex progression of world events. You know, when I was in Saudi Arabia, working with women from just about every democratic country in the world in the early 80's, it was the American females among us who spoke up loudly and fiercely to challenge the treatment of Saudi women. The rest of us from Canada, Ireland, Scotland, Australia, Norway, Denmark, Sweden, Jamaica, and Germany sort of more quietly processed the whole thing. I engaged in many conversations with my co-workers. In reflection, it was usually after one of my female American workers verbally challenged the lifestyle and the teachings of that time and place. I would be drawn in to either back up the American challenge, or to articulate a balance between the American and Mid-Eastern views. Both sides were less likely to accommodate the other's perspective.

In a way, the American women saw it more as a personal fight. It was like the rest of us understood that the reality was out of our control; that it wasn't our fight. I don't know that any of us were more right or more wrong. In a bigger scheme of things, the women of the other Western countries were more likely to look away, to not engage directly and self-righteously to the injustice of it all. The American women could not process the treatment of Saudi women in as detached a manner as the rest of us did. This is my personal observation on reflection. They were braver and bolder; much more inclined to outwardly stand up for what they believed. We were more likely to observe the culture from the position of the background. My perception is that the American women and the Mid-Easterners saw things more black and white. I think the rest of us saw more grey.

Also, there is something to be said, that we were more programmed to sit back, and to let our American co-workers fight the fight; to articulate democratic views for us. We usually agreed with them. We were just less likely to express our impressions in so direct and challenging a manner. I can extrapolate this reflection to the present and within the bigger picture. Many Western democracies are more or less content to sit on the sidelines, to let America fight the fight, to expend its blood. The question becomes whose fight is it. I think that there is no question that fighting Al Qaeda and extreme, terrorists groups is the fight of the free world. There will be no negotiation or accommodation with trained and irrational terrorists. The terrorists will not engage in any way towards a peaceful resolution and they will continue to attack in many areas of the world.

On the other hand, the issue of Iraq is greyer for many Western democracies. If invading Iraq was about spreading democracy and basic human freedoms, then why Iraq and not Saudi Arabia? Most of the terrorists were funded with Saudi riyahls and through the teachings of the State controlled educational system. The terrorists may have left Saudi Arabia to train in camps in Afghanistan as young adults, but their cultural beliefs and values were formed as they grew up in Saudi Arabia. American policy makers seem to split hairs with their engagement in the Mid-East relative to human rights and the spread of democracy. The reality is that democracy will actually empower fundamentalist factions in many countries including Saudi Arabia. In a way, I think Osama Bin Laden is hated as much by the Saudis for exposing their dirty laundry as he is for his actions against America and other Western countries. The attacks have also spread inside the Kingdom, which has caused the Saudis to step back and to begin to readjust their thinking and their teachings. To what degree and across what domains of culture are yet to be known in the West.

Based on my quest to find articles out of the Mid-East in the present, I believe that there is still a lot of denial in the Mid-East, and especially within the Gulf States. At the same time, I see incremental indices of hope in other readings. For example, there was an article in the *New York Times Magazine*, Jan 2006, titled *Big Iman on Campus*. It was a short interview with a Saudi Royal. He had just donated $20 million to Harvard and $20 million to Georgetown to advance the study of Islam. I had a visceral reaction that probably raised my blood pressure to his curt responses in the article. The question was posed to him regarding investing in Judeo-Christian studies in Saudi Arabia to bridge the gap between Christianity and Islam and Judaism. His exact words as quoted in the article sent chills down my spine, as I had hoped for a more honest and reflective response five years after 9/11. Instead, he snapped, "Look. You have to understand that the population of Saudi Arabia has zero Christians."

Well, that's like Hitler saying in 1944 that Nazi Germany was not anti-Semitic because there were zero Jews in Germany. Actually, there has been throughout the 20th century, thousands and thousands of Christians employed in Saudi Arabia for years at a time. The facts are that it is illegal to practice Christianity in Saudi Arabia. Bibles are forbidden and confiscated at the airport if they are found in luggage. That is where the denial comes in for me. I am not saying that the Kingdom needs to change its laws. That's for them to decide and to deal with. I am just saying that to twist the truth to suit the needs of the American readers is not helpful to an understanding of the facts, and to a deeper and honest understanding of our cultural differences.

I believe that the actions of the 9/11 terrorists and Al Qaeda were emboldened by the Islamic reaction across the region in the summer of 2001. Israel's measures to squelch the Intifada in the Palestinian territories were viewed to be given a green light by the US. There was a sense of outrage and anger that permeated throughout the Mid-East. I think an awareness of the historical context is helpful to the big picture. These brief excerpts from published articles give a sense of the dialogue in the Mid-East in the months leading up to 9/11. A statement by The Palestinian Leadership, posted August 31, 2001 on Ain-Al-Yaqeen: " *This morning at 10:15 our great brother Abu Ali Mustafa **martyred as US made apache gunship helicopter** of the Israeli occupying forces, launched from a short distance two missiles at the office of the **martyr** in his house killing him instantly, and wounding ten other **civilians**. This attack was planned and approved by **the criminal Israeli Government…, covered by the USA Administration granted Green Light** by **supporting Israel blindly and absolutely** thus approving its measures against the **defenseless** Palestinian people.*" These words and similar sentiments were repeated over and over again across the region that spring and summer.

In June, 2001, The Organization of Islamic Conference (OIC) Foreign Ministers requested the UN to set up an international criminal tribunal to try Israeli officials as war criminals. In the same conference, the Secretary General of the Gulf Cooperation Council said that the Intifada is a **legal revolution** against the worst aspects of military occupation. The Intifada began almost a year earlier. By the spring of 2001, the outrage and the anger against the West, symbolized by the power of the American Military, was overwhelming across the region. From the perspective of the countries across the region, Palestine had been abandoned by the leaders of America and Europe. Dr. Madani, the Assistant Foreign Minister of Saudi Arabia at the OCI Conference is quoted, "What happens in the Palestinian occupied territories and what happens in the Holy Al Quds is an **Islamic issue** as much as it is an Arab and Palestinian issue." (Ain-Al-Yaqeen, June, 2001).

Bin Laden's fatwa, issued several years earlier, manipulated the plight of the Palestinian people to legitimize an Islamic religious edict against the United States; that Muslims should kill civilians and military personnel from the United States and allied countries until they withdraw support for Israel and military forces from Islamic countries. Even though Bin Laden had been publicly shunned and criminalized by the leaders of the Mid-East prior to the summer of 2001, there was a very real connection between the sentiments of the region and the terrorists' perceived legitimacy of complete Jihad against the United States and its allies. In the summer of 2001, Iraq does not appear to have been a major player in the dialogue across the region. I believe that Saddam Hussein was marginalized in the context of Mid-Eastern leadership at that time.

Ain-Al-Yaqeen published an article that appeared in a Lebanese magazine, *Al Sayad*, dated October 5, 2001, less than a month after 9/11. In this article Prince Naif, the Saudi Minister of the Interior held a news conference at the Ministry of Interior in Riyadh. The article reports that he called on leaders to not only study ways of combating terrorism, but to also look at the reasons for terrorism and its roots in order to reach fundamental solutions. Prince Naïf called on the international community, especially the United States of America and Europe, to take seriously the Palestinian cause; and the international community should side with what is right and just: and that the Palestinian should regain their homeland. Three weeks after 9/11, Prince Naif is quoted, "*This should be carried out if we want to eliminate the motivations that originate in the Arab countries...A difference should be made between terrorism, killing of the innocent and children and attacking their property and those who are defending their cause like our Palestinian brothers, which is their right. If we want to fight terrorism correctly, we should look at such basic matters and deal with them so that they will not be a cause for anger by some people as they are causes infringing on the faith and feelings of people in the Arab world."*

So, we move forward to the present. Ain-Al-Yaqeen summarizes the following in an article dated December, 2006: "*The Gulf Cooperation Council advocates firm stances that renounce terrorism in all its forms and sources. The regional leaders note that terrorism is a world crime which demands regional and international coordination and collaboration. The Council members conclude that terrorism is an extremist intellectual phenomenon which has nothing to do with a religion and identity.*" For me, personally, I am still hearing denial in these words. I would propose that as much as the Western world needs to be committed more totally to the Palestinian situation; that the Arab world and especially the Gulf States need to delve deeper into the formation of fundamentalist beliefs within the teachings of the time and place across generations. You can not separate intergenerational teachings from outcomes.

I find a sense of reflection and hope in the following excerpt, taken from a speech given by Prince Turki Al-Faisal at New York University, delivered Nov 16, 2006:

"One reason is a matter of demographics. The oil boom years of the 1970s created wealth, and the wealth was used to develop our nation. Infant mortality rates dropped significantly, and life-expectancy increased among Saudis. As a way to help its people, the government put in place a **social welfare system.** *This was designed to take care of our citizens from the cradle to the grave: free education, free health care, interest-free mortgages for first-time home buyers, interest-free loans for small businesses, and subsidies for farmers. As a consequence, many Saudis began large families. And their children are now a part of the generation coming into the workforce. Another reason is a matter of* **generational interplay.** *Like you, your Saudi peers have grown up in a different world than their elders. Unlike you, the difference is actually quite dramatic. Some fifty years ago, Saudi Arabia was still primarily a nomadic society, with few large cities. For most people in the Kingdom,* **tribal association remained stronger than national identity.** *About thirty years ago, as I mentioned, many changes began to take place. The Kingdom opened to telecommunications. We began to build modern hospitals and schools, skyscrapers and malls, highways and airports; where a few decades*

earlier only desert existed. For Saudi youth, the amount of political, cultural, and societal change their parents and grandparents have seen in such a short period of time is difficult to grasp. My generation saw modern Saudi Arabia built. This generation was born into it. As the Kingdom continues to grow and modernize, and as young Saudis today face their own set of challenges; the online revolution and satellite TV, globalization and the new economy; we want to be sure they are sufficiently grounded in their heritage and culture... **The governing of our nation has been grounded in the Islamic Shariah and Arab tribal custom,** *and we have remained a pillar of stability in the face of a tumultuous region. We have worked diligently to strike a balance between providing for the modern welfare of our people and obtaining a consensus form our citizens about what type of change they can manage. We have been successful. Saudis are being prepared.* **They are being educated, and they are being protected form deviant and corruptive influences.** *We are making sure of this, ladies and gentlemen, because our children truly are the keys to the Kingdom... The Kingdom is in the process of reviewing all of its education practices and materials, and is removing any element that is inconsistent with the needs of a modern education. Not only are we eliminating what might be perceived as intolerance form old text books that were in our system, we have implemented a comprehensive internal revision and modernization plan. New curricula emphasize critical thinking, math, and science, and these curricula also emphasize the teaching of true Islamic values and the positive skills necessary for good citizenship and productivity, as well as how to safeguard community in peace, the environment, health and human rights. In every level of education, from grade school to high school to college,* **the government has gone so far as to sponsor lectures that promote moderation and tolerance.** *Even kindergarteners are made aware of the importance of tolerance and peace. Saudis can not deny that terrorism and extremism pose a serious threat and can be a corruptive influence to youth. So we are making sure our young citizens learn about its evils and understand the true nature of our Islamic faith."*

It should be noted that this speech was given to an American audience, but it never the less is indicative of a deep reflection and a historical analysis of the internal struggle inside the Kingdom of Saudi Arabia over the course of the past fifty years or so. Reading between the lines, and based on my experience in Saudi Arabia, I take note of his words referencing Shariah Law, Arab tribal custom, and the ongoing need to protect the youth from deviant and corruptive influences. I understand the deviant influences to be our Western lifestyle, and especially in regards to the role of women. Abu Graib will have cemented the comparison of the purity of Saudi women against the vulgar behavior of Western prostitutes. Women are viewed as either one or the other in the teachings and intergenerational beliefs of the Kingdom. The Shariah Law reference implies continued restriction of religion freedom. The Arab tribal custom translates for me that allegiances and deals across power players in the Kingdom will continue to walk a tight rope; balancing the modern world against the historical traditions of desert alliances, fundamental beliefs, and blood ties.

I think that Prince Turki's recent speech at New York University reveals the essence of the struggle within Saudi Arabia; the need to remain true to a very fundamental version of Islam, and to modernize at the same time. The reality has created opposing forces, and the Kingdom is struggling internally to find a balance with both. The lifestyle of Osama Bin Laden, renouncing everything modern to include electricity and running water, represents the extreme and isolated under currents of the fundamentalist, tribal piece. The development of Saudi Arabia as a world force and a viable member of the global community is the opposing faction. The ruling class is divided between both factions. I believe that this internal struggle spilled onto the world stage with 9/11, and the struggle continues; to balance the tribal, fundamentalist forces with the development of the Mid-East into the 21st century. Many other countries are also struggling internally to come to terms with the tribal and sectarian foundations of individual nation states across the region.

Some of the moderate countries have had more success with accommodating different factions than other countries in the region. Saudi Arabia has not accommodated non-believers (Shias) and people of the book (Christians and Jews) within its borders in the 20th century. It's a fact that needs to be honestly addressed in the context of terrorism and fundamental belief systems. Around all of this, the Palestinian—Israeli dilemma permeates. The ongoing conflict is deeply interwoven to ignite and intensify the underlying currents of the region. When it comes to oppression, it is easier to blame outside interests than to look within. I think that the world crisis has evolved to force all countries to look within. Pointing the finger needs to be replaced by folding hands, finding commonalties, and leaving alone what is not each others to interfere in. Leaving it alone is not the same as denying it. The situation is too urgent to maintain the status quo of the 20th century.

This is where I have come to with my understanding of the intersection of the West and the Mid-East in the present. My generation grew up in the same time span as the leaders of Al Qaeda. I am just a simple person, trying to put some level of context on the outcome of the past six years. Our nightmare in fighting terrorism has been the reality in many countries of the Mid-East over the life story of the same generation. In the West, we knee jerk react to nation states such as Iran or Iraq in isolation. The average person and our political leaders do not seem to see the strife and the bitterness in the context of the region. Our understanding is in contrast to the connective glue that seeps through and cracks across the fault lines in the sand of overlapping issues for the people of the region.

I believe that the mess in Iraq will not be resolved until the leaders of the countries through out the region engage in a very committed and serious way to dialogue, to compromise, to honest reflection, to mediation, and to accommodation of each other. The process requires the collaboration of skillful negotiators and visionary thinkers from Iraq, Iran, Syria, Egypt, Jordan, the Gulf States, Lebanon, and the Palestinian Territories. From the Western side, a serious and intense involvement as a broker with Israel in the Palestinian conflict is acutely needed. Moderate, decent, ordinary people across the region literally see the lifeless bodies and dismembered limbs of their Muslim children, brothers, and sisters on their TV screens every night. They understand the sectarian reality, but they also see US soldiers and American policy igniting the chaos. When people die day after day, the truth is relative and becomes irrelevant at some point. Thinkers and diplomats from the region are needed to facilitate the diplomacy of a cease fire in Iraq among sectarian groups. The fight has to be refocused so that honorable soldiers can target and defeat the terrorists from tactical positions of strength, making a move on the chess board to address terrorism on our terms.

By that, I mean fighting them outside of civilian populations. They can only hide behind the skirts of women and children for so long. As long as they are hiding, they are not a threat to us. They can wait us out in the caves of the remote, mountain locations. We need to be just as disciplined to wait them out in densely, populated areas. The terrorists have the advantage in cities where they speak the language. They have the knowledge and the ability to manipulate the fears of civilian populations. They hide and melt into the population to draw us in. Every time that a civilian is killed in the cross-fire of the mouse trap, we lose. We become the bad guys in the eyes of the citizens, who we are supposed to be liberating.

Fundamental terrorists are programmed and brain washed to attack and kill. For them, killing us is the only value of their life. They will follow our soldiers wherever we lead them. We need to become the masters of the chess game, and to relocate the board away from the roof tops of the masses. I visualize the puppeteer of Al Qaeda yanking our strings and dangling us limply in the wind every time a civilian death is blamed on the US Military in Iraq. They can sit quietly and invisibly in the black abyss of the mountain cavities, smiling smugly, as they draw us deeper and deeper into the bowels of the sectarian strife; a playing field that we do not fully understand, but which they have manipulated to their extreme advantage. The argument is heard every day from US leaders that to leave Iraq is going to empower Al Qaeda; to provide them a win. Well from where I sit, we are once again allowing them to jerk our chain. Will we stay there forever so that they won't distort the facts to validate their relative truth? Give me a break! We need to get back to having them react to us, rather than discussing military options relative to what Osama is going to interpret and translate. We all know what the terrorist leaders will say, no matter what we do. I am more interested in silencing their voices for ever, rather than wincing weakly over the irrationality of Al Qaeda's words and responses.

The other argument is to fight them over there and not over here. Just who are we fighting over there? The uneducated, angry, poor Arab fighters who are humping it across the border of some country to fight Americans in Iraq are not the trained, polished, sophisticated, educated, English- speaking terrorists, who pose a very real threat to us in North America and Europe. These are two separate groups. Make no mistake about that. I believe that we did some very serious harm to the leadership of Al Qaeda in Afghanistan in 2002. Also, the funding has been drastically impacted as the Gulf State countries of the Mid-East have worked with international intelligence sources to track and eliminate the money component. I hope that the same agencies are tackling the formation of new and existent fundamentalist schools as they pop up in various regions of the world to include Sudan, Asia, and the lesser known countries of the old Soviet Union. It is critical that the breeding grounds for future recruits are identified and wiped out, at the same time as the tentacles of the present threat are dismantled and destroyed. Our own vigilance has increased exponentially since 2001. International awareness and cooperation has also intensified exponentially. It is too simple to say that we have not been attacked over here because we are in Iraq. And, we have lost more lives in Iraq than we imagined possible several years ago.

My point is that our policy makers and leaders need to think and act more proactively and less reactively. They must listen to the intelligence analysts whom they employ. Your average Joe Blow citizen wants the sleazy side of politics to be separated from sound and informed policy. At the present time, it makes little difference how we got into Iraq for the soldiers on the ground. The Republican voters would like to forget about it, and the Democratic voters are more interested in bringing our soldiers home. The bottom line is that we all want to move forward. I believe that every thinking adult in the country has an awareness of the ideology piece and the minimization of any intelligence that deterred from the ideology in the lead up to the war in Iraq. It's done! It's out there for anyone who wants to examine the objective facts. The 2006 mid-term election brought some accountability into the picture. We want to move forward from here. The wary populace are more interested in how we get out effectively and intelligently than how we got in. We want to liberate our soldiers to fight terrorists without being bogged down in the middle of a sectarian nightmare. If we want to be worried of what Osama might say if we withdraw from the alleyways of Baghdad, we should pay more attention to how the Russians were defeated in Afghanistan. They seem to be bleeding us slowly and deliberately in Iraq in the same manner. Osama has had a lot to say about that.

Louis de Corancez was the French Commissary of Commercial Relations in Aleppo, Syria in the early 19th century. Napoleon was interested in developing Franco-Persian alliances at the time. Aleppo was located on a major trade route connecting the Ottoman Empire to the desert tribes of the Arab world. Corancez wrote a book, *The History of the Wahabis up to 1809.* His book was translated into English much later. A brief excerpt is worthy of our contemplation in the present: *They are wary of engaging the enemy before he is weak enough to have lost the will to defend himself. Thus they pillage rather than wage war. They waver at the first sign of resistance, and are as speedy in fleeing from the enemy's range as in pursuing him beyond it. They cling to this course of action tenaciously, fleeing the enemy when he faces them and following in his steps when he in turn takes flight. Thus they spy on him for days on end, awaiting the opportunity to surprise and slaughter him without great danger, convinced that the finest victory lies in destroying everything without incurring any loses themselves* (found in *God's Terrorists* by Charles Allen). I believe that the Western world has been purposely drawn into the desert terrain of generations of tribal warfare and primitive tactics, which are deliberately chewing up our military might patiently, meticulously, mercilessly, and tenaciously.

I have given my voice here for what it is worth. I understand that I am a female. What do I know about battle and war? I am also a voter, a synthesizer. I am listening very closely for a competent leader of either party who can step outside of a narrow, political agenda to provide sound, objective judgment and honest leadership; worthy of the price of our soldiers' blood; worthy of the direction of our children's future. Partisan issues continue to divide our law makers into whining, reactive puppies on both sides of the aisle. I would like to challenge the citizenry to step up to the plate for the sake of our country and for the sake of the young soldiers who are expending life and limb on our behalf. We need to demand more through a conditional vote. Too many of our votes are taken for granted because we can not step outside of our comfortable lifestyles and our complacent thinking to demand vision and informed, balanced leadership in our elected officials. There is no point in sending US soldiers to die in Iraq for democracy when we are making a mockery of it with our dismissal of critical thought and our uneasy but silent compliance.

I had been in a book club with an amazing group of women in the South for about five years or so. We read a range of books, a lot of nonsense, a lot of literature, and a lot of fun. But, there was always avoidance to read anything with a political or a real world twist to it. An intelligent, educated, vocal, spirited, and passionate group of women resisted any mention of a current best seller from an investigative journalist or a policy person. I realize that there is a cultural component here. My politically feisty, Irish Newfoundland upbringing took me to a different place with dialogue and real world discussions in social circles. Or perhaps, it was my formative years with the Catholic nuns. They hammered us hard to probe for clarity, to take the issue a little deeper, to challenge assumptions, to think it through, to break it down, and to apply abstract concepts to real world issues; only girls in our classes to comply and hash it out; no holding back with our comments or our insight based on what the boys might think of us. Our book club gatherings were vocal, insightful, and intellectual in a fun, female kind of way. However, there was a very polite but consistent resistance towards a political or critical discussion about current affairs. It always perplexed me. My personal solution was to refill my glass of red wine. The Iraq War and the present weigh heavily on my mind. I don't know why, but I have a need to engage in a dialogue on the subject. It is so complicated and so messy, but dismissing the topic as "taboo" in social conversations appears to me to be less patriotic than hashing through the layers.

How else can we refine our informed vote for the sake of the troops, for the sake of our children? As women, we have half the vote. We need to challenge ourselves with our responsibility. I always feel like I'm preaching, needling, pushing the envelope, annoying others. But my mind ticks away and I have a need to push; to voice my thoughts; to engage my friends. I don't want to sound self-righteous or condescending with these remarks. I am just very perplexed at the apparent need to disengage from any level of critical debate and conversation regarding the pieces of the puzzle from a political perspective. In a way, it's a bit of a paradox. These same strong American women will openly and directly challenge perceived injustices or political situations in other regions of the world. They had no problem reading *Kite Runner*, and discussing Afghanistan from the perspective of a relationship story; no messy American politics to contemplate and discuss in the narrative; no threat to the comfort of our social evening.

It was my American friends and co-workers who loudly and clearly spoke up in Saudi Arabia. They were much more comfortable with expressing their opposing views than those of us from other Western democracies. However, it is my observation that American women are very resistant to discuss American policy or American politics from within, at least in broad social circles where there is the probability of debate and opposing points of view. From my experience growing up in Newfoundland, it was just the opposite. My parents and their friends would heatedly discuss local politics in social circles. They were less inclined to vocally criticize other nations directly. I ponder my sense of an outsider with my thoughts. I have a conscious awareness that my life story has instilled in me a curiosity of political thinking and verbal interaction that seems to be out of sync with that of many of my female friends.

I have a very good friend who supports my writing. But, she is always telling me to write something fun, that people do not want to read serious things. She is one of the people who I annoy with my political quest. I had a recent conversation with Chris, my back-packing soul mate and my life long friend. We both feel somewhat old and a little more genteel now, relative to "the day". She also told me to write something fun about her. I always smile when I think of her and our adventures together; like the time that we almost fell into the glacier in New Zealand, trying to help an elderly gentleman who was too old for the dangers of the icy ledge. Or the time that Laurie, Chris, and I spent a day laughing over Chris' state of bloating as only a traveler can get with a long and unforgiving bout of constipation. We could laugh over anything in the responses of our odyssey to the rhythm of our days, even when the blues were drowning out the reggae in the pulse of our moments.

My point with my rambling is that just about every female that I know around the age of 50 (ish) has a passion for continuing the fun; seeking to explore the adventure; finding wisdom, grace, and happiness in both the memories and the forward march; fighting the age thing with every bit of estrogen and elasticity that we have left. The estuary of my soul demands that we also continue to stretch the axons and the dendrites through the ebb and flow of our moods, our quests, and our thoughts. Strong and active minds will support and intensify our desired endorphins. A thinking and colorful prism of self will enhance and impassion the needed fun of our living. Our world demands the complexity of our clear and intuitive female minds as mightily as it relies on our compassionate strength of spirit and *joi de vie.*

Chapter 13

A BLINK OF AN EYE

IT'S AN EARLY SUMMER EVENING, warm and gentle, around 1969. I am soaking up the last bit of the day, anticipating the long, lazy hours of day light saving in the North Atlantic. It does not get dark in Newfoundland in the summer months until around 10 PM. I do not mind the routine activity of the moment, as long as I am outside, and the evening is serene; no rain, no wind. I am hanging out in the front yard of our white, two-story house in Corner Brook. A car pulls over to the curb. There are two passengers in the front seat, a man and a woman (no kids in the back seat). I remember this mundane fact because it was not that common in our culture to see two older adults without kids in tow. I have never seen these people before. That fact alone is also not that common. Corner Brook is a very, small town. I would recognize just about anyone that my parents knew or spoke of. The man asks me if the Rossiters live in this house. I nod and smile, yes. They ask me if I am one of the children. I answer yes. They tell me that they know my parents. Are they home? I go inside and get my dad. He comes out, soon followed by my mother. Immediately, this couple and my parents act like best friends. They are so excited to see each other. They talk non- stop for an hour or so at the side of the road. They don't come into our house because they have a reservation later that night on the ferry to North Sydney. It's a big deal and a major hassle to miss your reserved spot on the car ferry. The six-hour crossing sells out months in advance for July and August. It is the only way to drive off the island. They had just a few minutes to say hey. They stay longer than they plan. They have so much to say to each other; laughing, talking fast and furious to catch up on the years.

Later that evening and even into the next day, my parents continue to talk about this couple in a very spirited way. They were thrilled to see each other. I hear my parents trying to figure out how long it has been since they saw each other. My mother thinks maybe it's been 14 years, at least 13 years. My father thinks no, it can't be that long—seems like yesterday. I remember experiencing a conscious awareness, as I listened to them, that my parents had a life prior to me; a life that I knew little about. This was different than hearing stories and reflective memories, or of visiting old friends or distant relatives. This was more like I was given a glimpse into a world that I had no knowledge of, or that I had never thought about. My parents seemed to be connected in a very passionate, fun, and intense way to a time in their life that they relished in the present, but that did not include me or my sister and brothers. These strangers knew my parents as adults prior to children. My parents were engaged in a very intense and emotional way to the couple; to a degree that really surprised me, and gave me something to reflect on. As I listened to the happiness and the excitement in the voices of my parents and their long lost friends, I remember thinking how could they be such good friends when they had not even spoken to each other in 14 years or so (longer than my entire life). It was very unreal to me at the time.

It is 1985 or '86. Laurie has come to visit me in the States. We spend a wonderful weekend in New Orleans. I remember the silly things. We accidentally end up in a gay bar on Bourbon Street at two in the morning. We look around. We laugh largely as we figure it out. We blame it on the music. It drew us in. We are remembering Australia. We're older now. It's not so shocking to our sensibilities, the myriad of plights and passions of the human experience. We laugh at ourselves. We dance. We don't linger long, but we enjoy our fun in the moment. Laurie gets sunburned on Okaloosa Island. It was cloudy. We walked a long way along the white, sugary beach. Laurie has always been so aware of skin issues. She was the Sun Screen Queen in the South Pacific when Chris and I were too foolish and too young to care that much. Laurie is shaking her head. She knows better. Of all people, she knows better.

At the airport, when she is leaving, she begins to cry. I am very perplexed. Why are you crying? We have never gone there before. We both traveled a lot at that point in our lives. Someone was always flying somewhere. Laurie was the mature one; visionary, intuitive, seeing things further ahead than me; contemplating the future while I navigated in the present. Why the tears? Laurie said to me, "This time it's going to be different. We are going opposite directions geographically. We're going to get more settled; careers, family, husband, and children. It will happen. We're not going to see each other for a long time. I don't know when I will see you again. It's true. It makes me sad." She smiled at me through her tears, elegant and proud, gracefully bearing her soul, and bravely forcing a sincere, gentle smile to settle her insight and her tears.

"Nonsense", my response is total dismissal; denial of an unknown future that neither of us had any control of in the moment. Her smile widens as the large, wet drops continue to roll down her aristocratic cheek. She looks down at me like I'm a young child. She is wiser. She hesitates in her smile. She knows better. She leaves it be. She leans down; a long, hard, clinging hug; one more, deep, eye-locked, smile at each other. Laurie pulls away. She starts to say something. She shakes her head; one more, brief, fleeting, all-knowing smile. She turns to walk away. I watch her back. She is off. I watch her until she is out of sight. I watch a moment or two longer, thinking, perplexed at the intensity of the exchange. I did not expect her to be sad. I ponder her words. I drive home slowly, thinking, wondering...

It is the blink of an eye. I am now my parents. Time has passed. I have not seen her since our farewell in Okaloosa Terminal. Was it 1985 or 1986? No, can't be that long, seems like yesterday. We have kept in touch over the years. I have pictures of her daughters. Has it really been more than twenty years? Where does the time go? No. It can't be that long—seems like yesterday. When I see her again, we will talk and talk, and laugh, and probably cry. It will take the blink of an eye, and we will be one again. It seems like yesterday. I have remembered her words from the airport many times since then. Laurie was always so wise, so kind, such a deep soul. At an intuitive level, destiny and fate somehow connect the people and the places of our journey. Laurie's father and my father, who never met one another, both died of Parkinson's. The connections are real; a little scary and a little wonderful at the same time. They surround our stories. They are a part of us; who we are and who we become.

It is the spring of 2007. My daughter is going away on her first overnight band trip, on her own, no parents as volunteer chaperones. She did not want us to chaperone, and likewise, so all is good. She is 15. As I am saying good-bye in the school parking lot, we are double checking. Yes, she has money. Yes, she packed her ID. Yes, she has her cell phone and her charger. She is asking me what time of day should she call me. Then, she quickly recovers from this question with, "Oh never mind. It doesn't matter. I forgot. You don't have a life. You'll be home any time in the evening. I don't need to worry." She laughs in the way that implies I'm teasing, but then again, not really. In a way, she is sharing an intimate awareness with me in a smart-ass, joking, teenager sort of way. She is aware that I am in a lull with the whole life thing; my spirit of adventure, my fit, choices, a sort of mental cross roads of competing inputs. I need to hook myself up to a satellite tracking system; just punch in my final destination and it can tell me how to get there. I am definitely lost in the fog of my present. She knows this, but she does not know how to fix it anymore than I do. So we joke about it.

As I am driving home, I remember that evening with my parents, almost forty years ago. How much of our lives do our children really know about us? A blink of an eye, and here I am. I have no life in the eyes of my child. I remember thinking that my parents were ancient when they were younger than I am now. I thought their lives were very boring and mundane, especially my mother's life. The life of housewife and mother was not that appealing to me in my teen years, or even in the years of my young adulthood. I knew very early on that I needed something different for me. I would not be described as an outwardly selfish person, but in that aspect of self, I was very directed at a very young age. The first inkling that I had into a world of my parents as adults, apart from their role as parents of their five children, was that warm, summer evening in 1969.

I contemplate on the response that I want to give my daughter in the hectic coming and going of the school parking lot. I say nothing. We laugh together, hug, and she spots a friend. She hurriedly walks away, turns to wave one time, and she's off. I drive away. It's a beautiful, hushed evening, no traffic on the road. My car radio is on. I like the music. My thoughts are not something that I can easily put into words for a quick, fitting retort to her rather tactless but somewhat accurate observation of me in the present. She has her future ahead of her, to fill in, and to color as she passes through the experience of her life. I smile to myself as I drive along the windy, country road. I smile as I think that she really doesn't have a clue. She doesn't know that she doesn't know. That's the beauty of it all; the innocence of a teenager thinking they have all the answers up against the grace of a parent who lets it be. I think of John Lennon, "*Let It Be. Let It Be. Seeking Words of Wisdom, Let It Be.*" I smile. I play the song in my head. I am content to let it be, to let her figure it out.

I guess that's the ultimate secret of parenting. We have to let them discover for themselves how clueless they are, as our parents so gallantly did for us. They set us free to stumble or soar; to do the best that we could; and hopefully, to become someone along the way. We have to let our children live independent of us; to fumble through in their own way; through the joyous and the mindless moments of their lives. It is the synthesis of the moments that evolves the symphony; the past and the future rising in crescendo and crashing down in hushed wonder, melting into the next note and the next. Just as I knew that the last thing I wanted to be was "just a mother" when I was her age, I now know that motherhood is the greatest symphony of all. I smile as I drive away from the school parking lot, just me and my thoughts, an ordinary mom without a life.

Our hope for our kids is that somehow they have incorporated our values and our dreams into the core of their souls. The estuary can ebb and flow, but the essence of our life blood will always run through them, sometimes at the surface, other times deep in the murk of the muddy bottom, but always there. Our human cells have been passed forever into their thinking, their reflections, and their decisions of self. The journey of their life will add splendid rays of light or dark shades of color, a myriad of shapes or not. The prism of the mind has to find trust in the murky estuary of the soul to navigate the unknown, to discover how vast and wondrous a human life can become. The texture and the nuances are as infinite as the stars in the sky, but the roots of discovery will remain connected to the world that was ours to pass on to them.

I remember the analogy of life and death passed on to me by an older, southern gentleman; a kind and thoughtful ER doctor, who I worked with in Niceville for several years. He was about to retire. He loved practicing medicine, the human side of being a top notch clinician. He had little tolerance for the bean counters, the HMO business types, who had become more and more entrenched in the delivery of health care; dictating to doctors how to practice their craft. For example, abdominal pain presents in the ER in as many ways as our human frailty allows. He was disgusted that the corporate, administrative end of the health care system had set up protocols that removed the skill of the doctor as clinician from the diagnostic piece. Basically, every patient that came through the ER doors with abdominal pain would receive the exact, same work up. His view was that they did not need him for that. A computer was sufficient to execute the orders of the protocol. So, the abdominal aneurysm was given the same work up as a case of constipation. He felt that his experience and his judgment; the piece of examining the patient, laying hands on them, listening to their story, putting the pieces together—the practice of his craft was diminished and somewhat over taken by the budget spreadsheets driving the HMO directives. This would be the same frustration that I would see with experienced teachers in the public schools.

This kind and gentle doctor loved his life and his mission of helping others. He was never one to judge. He had a wonderful sense of humor. He knew that it was time to let go of his life work, to tip his hat to the next generation of healers. I think he was about 67 years old. He eloquently and yet begrudgingly hashed back and forth through his thoughts and his insights on letting go, linking voluntary retirement with the mortality aspect of our days on this place called earth. He said letting go was a little like death in old age. His years in the ER had given him great understanding and compassion for our natural and hesitant resistance to the inevitability of death. He talked gently and rather reverently about dieing and old age. He described it as like being at a really, fun party. You know the night is late, you've had enough to drink and to eat, and you've danced long enough. It's time to leave, but you are hanging on because you want to stay for one more dance, one more drink, one more conversation, one more laugh, just one more...You have to go, your wife is tugging at your sleeve. You know it's time to leave, but you yearn to stay for just a little bit longer. He said it wasn't sad, more of an appreciative and intense yearning; unless you never got to attend the party in the first place. Then the thing you yearn for is the life that you let slip away, the dances that you declined.

That is what I want to pass on to my child—an appreciation for the passion of living life in the music of her moments. I want her to have many wonderful experiences and intimate conversations in the evolving party of her tomorrows. I want her to have a purpose to her days, an infinite curiosity, and a deep yearning for the possibilities of her dances. I hope to have a few more dances myself. I want to blink my eyes thirty or even forty years from now, and know that my dance card is full. I want to know that I championed through the gift of my life as best as I knew how in the places of my moments. I was able to deal with my father's suffering and death through the insight of my doctor friend. I knew that my father's dance card was full. He rested through his last waltz, but he never missed an opportunity to absorb every nuance and every note in the dance of his life.

For my own personal dance, I have tried a lot of different steps. I have probably mastered none of them, but I like to think that my sense of balance and my fluidity of movement have been refined and deepened by my negotiation through the different jigs of my journey. I know that when we follow a single dance, we may become masters of that particular choreography. However, we have to be cautious of not drowning in our own perfection. The more perfect we become, the more we hesitate to take a risk, to test the waters. We're afraid of what's on the other side. We don't want to appear stupid. But the shore beckons. The far off lights twinkle and blink. What if? The music switches. The beat, the tempo is unfamiliar. We remain seated. The song is intriguing. We don't know the melody, but we tap our feet. We start to get up. We trip a little. We hesitate. What if?

I remember when I was one of the perfect people, sure of my righteousness. I was one of the honorable human beings, able to judge those less honorable than me. I was working at the Royal Jubilee in Victoria. I was very worldly and educated. I was tolerant and moral. A group of techs were on break, sitting at a long table in the cafeteria. We were all pretty young, probably early to mid 20's, except Louise. She was a granola; closer to 40 or perhaps even 50; eccentric and content in her hippy ways, which were out of sync in the hospital environment. I really liked her. We all did. She was just very different. We appreciated the flavor of her person. She always wore white knee socks to work, and she never shaved her legs. They were very hairy; long, dark hairs that screamed around the whiteness of her socks. I remember that because she never gave a hoot about surface things. She loved nature to the extreme, always eating her lunch outside on the grass, often preferring to sit off by herself. She would take off on weekends with her big, shaggy dog and her old Volkswagen van to the remote beaches and forests of Vancouver Island, and to the smaller islands that dot the coastline along there. She was very much her own person. She was kind to me. She took me with her a few times on her weekend trips. I saw the splendor of the Pacific North West through her tutelage and her quirky friendship. She knew every back road and every remote beach.

Anyway, she was one of the people sitting in our group in the cafeteria. I think she was probably the only person from British Columbia sitting with us that day. There was an American guy who worked in our department. He had come to Victoria to visit, liked it, and had stayed to work for a spell. I guess he had some type of work permit. Another tech was from New Zealand. She was married to a Canadian. Another tech sitting there was from India, a Hindu, who had British citizenship. The final tech was from South Africa. We had our own United Nations thing going on in that department; just a routine X-Ray Department; shift work, one patient after another—just a regular working day, a fifteen minute break in the afternoon, scheduled. We would go in two shifts. The techs would round each other up, walk to the cafeteria together, not leaving anyone out. We had a range of conversations; a group of working stiffs. It was nice.

Anyway, it was sometime in the spring or summer of 1981. Apartheid was a big thing in the news. The tech from South Africa was about my age. She was white. Our group conversation drifted to her thoughts. It was more like an inquisition, but in a very subtle and "take the high road" Canadian kind of way. The under currents were there. From our combined sense of indignant, self-righteousness, we drilled her for an explanation. We then proceeded to gently but meticulously scold her for the story of her life, as she shared it with us. She was not defensive, nor did she condone apartheid. She more or less spoke of her family, her life experience. She was close to her father. She was trying to figure it out as she spoke; the injustice and the reality. She appeared open, honest, and humble. She was a very quiet, soft type. She calmly listened to us coming at her in reactive, indignant, and mass protestation. She took it all in, quietly, graciously, and shamefully. I can now look back on that, and I realize that the shame was on us. She had no more control of being born the daughter of a white rancher in South Africa than I had of being born the daughter of hard working parents in the North Atlantic. We collectively passed a very harsh judgment of her life from the story of our individual lives.

I have learned through the experiences of my dance that we are born into a million and one different life circumstances, across history and across places. Each of us has to make our way through the labyrinth of our story. Our truth is relative. It is a function of what we are taught, how we live, and how we adapt to the twists and the turns along the way. It is very easy to judge others from afar. It seems such common sense, so obvious to us. If only those who don't know better would listen to us and follow our teachings; our model of how the dance of life should be played out. I have learned that it is through looking back that we can integrate the steps that we missed along the way. We were so naturally and perfectly gliding through the choreography of our practiced and known dance that we didn't pay attention to the beat of a more complex but glorious rendition of the possibility of some future dance.

These are my thoughts, as I try to scream from deep in my soul at the world events that seem to be spinning out of control. On a macro level, they mirror the individual struggles of our human condition. How do we learn from one another without destroying each other in the process?

Why did we ask our South African friend for her input, when we had already decided the right and the wrong of it? Did we trust our personal truth enough to even begin to process the reality of the circumstance of her life, a life that she was born into by the grace of God? I have learned enough to know that it is when we sit back in our comfortable world and think that we are better; that we are right; that this is the very time that we need to refocus the prism of our thoughts. We can gently adjust our lens until we merge the humanity of our souls into the foreground of our view. The background then becomes more blurry, less clear. We're not so sure. We are challenged to bring it back into focus; to explore further… slowly, carefully, and purposely. We are squinting into the sun. We want to define the image, to see it more critically. The ability to control the splendor of our prism through the murky estuary of our spiritual core is the defining greatness of our human journey; if only we dare to challenge our focus; to trust ourselves to extend the possibility of our horizon.

I don't know where my future will take me. Whatever it will be, I am open to it. I will steer my rudder, but the currents may drift me into unknown waters. I hope so. I like the twists and the turns that have been in my past. I look forward to the mystery of my future. I know that I am currently going through a transition phase. The physical processes of reaching half a century and the cognitive piece have meshed into a single, confusing whirlpool. The salt water and the fresh water are swirling. I am waiting for it all to settle down; for a calm sea to find its way back into my being. Women are definitely glued together with hormones and chemical components that juggle for equilibrium in the cruise of our life. I will pass through it as women have done from time immortal. I will chart my course eventually, or I will drink more heavily. Either way, I will make it through. Worse case scenario—I won't remember if I really mess it up. I am joking here; or, at least I hope I am. I am old enough to advocate alcohol and exercise in moderation. They complement each other nicely to sharpen the mind and to balance out the soul. I am a true Irish Catholic. I'm all about perspective and balance.

I know that I still listen attentively to the symphony of the birds in the morning, and to the hushed stillness of an early evening. I know that I still love the crash of the ocean, and the smell of fresh baked bread. I know that I still marvel at the peak of a snow—capped mountain, and the pregnant fullness of a lush, tropical rain forest. I know that I feel very alive and young when I hear the music of my youth mixing with the pulse of the younger artists blaring from my daughter's I-POD. We have similar tastes in music. I smile at this tidbit. I love to walk purposely through the streets of a safe and bustling city. I breathe in the humanity of the streets, the energy of people walking to and fro. I am happy that I think about these things; that I continue to engage my ambitions and my small joys in the perplexity of my future.

I know that I still love the brush of the wind on my face when I ride my bike fast down a steep and curvy hill. My husband and I were riding our bikes just a few days ago, picking up speed as we careened down a wonderful incline. A little boy, around five maybe, is yelling at us from the end of his driveway. I can't hear him as I speed by, on the other side of the street. I wave, but I don't slow down. I am in my element. My husband is behind me. He slows down and gives the screaming child the time of day, unlike me. The little guy is yelling very indignantly now, as he is aware that I did not pay any attention to him, "You're supposed to be wearing your helmets!" He screams it again, louder and more fiercely. "You're Supposed To Be Wearing Your Helmets!!!!!!" "Yes", my husband gently tells him, "You're right. We should be wearing our helmets."

We laugh at the child's tirade. We silently acknowledge that we no longer want to wear our helmets. At least not on quiet, well paved, neighborhood streets; where the drivers take wide berths in the pride of their safe, suburban living. We actually pay a lot for this privileged lifestyle that we have bestowed upon ourselves. We will continue to ride our bikes without helmets because we can. We have earned back the freedom of our childhood through the decades that have passed. We laugh at the self-righteous reprimand from the little boy. He is right. We are enjoying the small rebellion of our glorious day. We like the power of the moment. The sun is warm on our backs. The wind is invigorating. The brisk ride makes us feel younger than our years. We give the little guy his due. We ignore him, nevertheless.

I know that it will be the blink of an eye, and my future will be my past. That is why the present remains so important, so revered by me. Hence, I understand my frustration when my present is out of sync, and at the same time I relish in my awareness that the ebb and the flow is all part of the passage. I relish in my awareness that I still have a curiosity for the unknown adventures yet to be discovered; the intersection of future choices and destiny. It is the curiosity, the tenacity to keep seeking my fit, to deeply explore the mystery of my future that keeps my mind engaged in the puzzle of my present. I anticipate the outcome, but I hesitate to rush too fast. I want to walk slowly and boldly through the trails; stopping to pause in the delicate wonders, the wonderful shade tree, the wild rose, the eagle soaring effortlessly above, and the soft ground beneath my feet. I relish that I am alive in my present so that my passing will be a celebration of a life that I have tried to live the best that I know how. I relish that I have the courage to challenge my complacency. I relish that I know the difference of being alone or of being lonely. Sometimes I love the former, and I can cure the latter with the people of my life- my husband, my child, a phone call to my mother, my sister, my brothers, my nephews, my nieces, my dear, dear friends; the people of the places that I have been honored and deeply grateful to meet along my path.

The free world is fighting the madness of the present. The terrorists brag that they honor death, and that we honor life. For them, that is our weakness. I know that I have nothing stronger than my voice, the words of an ordinary person to stand up and challenge the absurdity of that claim. As my gentle and wise doctor friend so elegantly passed on to me, we nobly honor our mortality by dancing slowly and deliberately through the miracle of our life. Living and dying do not exist as separate entities. The latter is the result of the former. We celebrate awe in the crescendo of our symphony by seeking our passions; by challenging our hesitations; by defying the nonsense; by speaking our mind; by letting go of what we must; by intimately knowing the peace and the glory of our journey. It is only by honoring our living, that we can find meaning in our dying.

The leaf has to bud, to bloom, and to flutter bravely and daintily in the wind; a blink of an eye and summer idly merges into fall. The passage of the seasons deliberately strokes the leaf to metaphor through the muted reds and golds of a South Pacific sunset. Only then, can a single leaf drift gently and lazily to the ground. Children jump and play in the layers of the trees' blessings, the bold colors and the waxy textures enticing them to revel in the passage of the seasons; laughing loudly in the simple joy of a pile of leaves under their feet. Death does not exist without life. Individually, each of us, the ordinary people all over the world; we defy the madness of the terrorists by the goodness and the fullness of our daily living. The laughter of our children shows us the way.

Decent people all over the globe are caught up in a powerful tornado of hurricane force winds that are raging around each other. Individuals of good will can not break through, to find their way to the core of the eye, to quiet their fears, to still their hatred, to hear the silent screams from the soul of the storm. For the sake of the children, the adults have to navigate more diligently and more carefully to reach the eye, to engage our human commonalities, to understand our human fears, to acknowledge the relative truths of our histories, to quell the distrust and the anger. How do we break through? Who can lead the parties to take that first impossible step, a tentative tiptoe that the leaders of the opposing factions will dare to tread? A beginning may be to take the focus off of each other; to very delicately adjust the lens to highlight the children of the region. The players must trust themselves to engage in a raw, honest, and earnest dialogue; breaking it down to something as simple as removing children from the cross hairs, all children; Israeli children, Palestinian children, Iraqi children, Lebanese children, Iranian children, Syrian children, Jordanian children, Egyptian children, Yemeni children, the children of the Gulf States, and the children of Afghanistan. Can the wise leaders of the region negotiate for a truce that will dare to embrace everyone's child?

The most fundamental terrorist fighters will not rise to the occasion. We know that. The best among us can deal with the hard reality of our world. We have to remain cognizant that we do not have to mirror them to diminish them. The world's weapon is an honor of death through the glory of the possibility of a human life; young life being the most precious gift of all. Decent people from every corner of the globe desire the outcome of a good life for their offspring. Patriotic and noble soldiers are waiting for their leaders to find their way. They have left their children at home. Everywhere, the children are wary, but the innocent trust of their wonder bursts forth in the endless, laughing energy of their moments. The laughter of a child reminds us that the joy of living transcends the fear of living.

The hurricane force winds have blown everyone off course. Perhaps we can navigate through the waters of the perfect storm by pinging the sonic waves off of the outstretched hand of a single, small child; then another child; and another child. An Iraqi child is as important as an Israeli child is as important as a Palestinian child is as important as an Iranian child is as important as a child from Afghanistan is as important as an American child is as important as a British child is as important as an African child is as important as each and every child of the world.

If only, the laughter and the cries of the smallest among us can lead the way. If only, we dare to tread softly behind the imprint of the small, bleeding feet. I pray when I lay me down to sleep that the fathers and the brothers of the Mid-East dare to tread. The decent people of the world will follow. We are yearning to be shown the way. But, we will not find the foot steps through the shifting sands without your capable lead.